CATALOGUE OF SEALS
IN THE PUBLIC RECORD OFFICE

Monastic Seals
Volume I

CATALOGUE OF SEALS
in the
PUBLIC RECORD OFFICE

MONASTIC SEALS
Volume I

compiled by

ROGER H. ELLIS

with plates from photographs by J. D. Millen

LONDON
HER MAJESTY'S STATIONERY OFFICE

ISBN 0 11 440193 4

Contents

Introduction

This is the first of a series of volumes which will, when complete, catalogue all the impressions found in the Public Record Office of the seals used by and in monasteries. A monastery in this connexion is a religious house of monks, nuns or friars, following the Rule of one of the recognised Orders. Hospitals, where the master and brethren usually followed a Rule, are included; colleges, collegiate churches and other secular foundations are omitted.

The classes of the Public Records which have been examined for this volume are Ancient Deeds series AS (E 42), BS (E 329), DS (E 212), LS (DL 27), RS (E 213) and WS (E 43); Acknowledgements of Supremacy (E 25); Surrenders of the Monasteries (E 322); and Loose Seals (SC 13). In addition all the monastic seals already entered in the Card Catalogue at the Public Record Office, from whatever class of record, have been included. The result is a volume which identifies and describes 1434 impressions of seals used by or in religious houses in England, Wales and Scotland (but not in other countries). They derive from the period between the 12th century, when such seals came into general use, and the 16th century, when the houses using them were dissolved. Of these 429 are illustrated in the Plates.

Each entry in the Catalogue consists of:

(i) The name by which the religious house is generally known. In most cases this is a place-name, followed by the county, e.g. NEWSTEAD (Notts). Any alternative or subsidiary name will follow, e.g. WINCHESTER (Hants) (Hyde abbey, New Minster).

(ii) The Order (e.g. Benedictine, Cistercian) and the status (e.g. abbey, priory) of the house, followed by (F) if the house was a nunnery or (M and F) if it was for both male and female religious. Where no such special indication appears the house was for male religious only.

(iii) The identification of the seal (abbey seal, seal *ad causas*, etc.), with personal name when shown or indicated in the legend, e.g. prior's seal: John de Montmartin.

(iv) The serial number in this Catalogue, with the distinguishing prefix M for Monastic. This serial number is applicable not only to the impression described but to all impressions from the same matrix.

(v) An account of the seal's device. As the more complex seals catalogued are illustrated in the Plates, or in other works to which reference is made, an extended word-portrait of each has been judged unnecessary. The aim has been to indicate the general nature of the device (e.g. Under a gabled canopy, the Virgin, seated, holding the Child on her L knee) and thereafter to interpret rather than describe. As far as possible the figures are identified and named, inscriptions and legends within the device transcribed, allusions noted and explained, arms blazoned and attributed. Details are remarked and described if they are unusual, significant, or unclear in the Plate.

(vi) The legend; which is reproduced as nearly as modern typography will allow. Certain conventional symbols of abbreviation which modern founts do not include have been rendered as CON, US, PER, PRE, PRO, OR' AND AR'. A glossary of words commonly used in the legends, showing the abbreviated or contracted forms in which they appear in the seals here catalogued, will be found at the end of this introduction.

(vii) The seal's shape, and its dimensions in millimetres.

(viii) The colour, mode of attachment, quality of impression and present condition of the example catalogued.

(ix) Remarks on especially noteworthy features either of the matrix or of the particular impression or impressions catalogued.

(x) Notes for further impressions from the same

matrix, with Public Record Office references and (following in brackets) the dates of impression wherever these can be established or inferred (see (xiii) below).

(xi) Reference to descriptions or illustrations in certain other works, viz.

BM: *Catalogue of Seals in the Dept. of MSS., British Museum,* by W. de Gray Birch, vol. I, 1887.

Clay: 'The Seals of the Religious Houses of Yorkshire', by Charles Clay, *Archaeologia,* LXXVIII, 1928.

Laing: *Descriptive Catalogue of Impressions from Ancient Scottish Seals,* by Henry Laing, Edinburgh, 1850 and 1866.

Tonnochy: *Catalogue of British Seal-Dies in the British Museum,* by A. B. Tonnochy, London, 1952.

Pedrick: *Monastic Seals of the 13th century,* by Gale Pedrick, London, 1902 (the text is of little value but the plates, photographed from casts, are useful).

Two valuable sources to which specific reference has not been made but which students of monastic seals are advised to consult are *Catalogue of the Ecclesiastical Seals in the Treasury of the Dean and Chapter of Durham* by the Rev. W. Greenwell and C. H. Hunter Blair (1917–19), and the volumes of the Victoria County History.

(xii) The Public Record Office reference of the document whose seal is catalogued.

(xiii) The date of the impression catalogued. As far as possible every such impression is dated to a year. Usually this will be the date of the document, shown according to the modern calendar, e.g. St Crispin's Day 10 Edward III will appear as 1336. When the date is not stated in the document but can be inferred it is shown in brackets with or without a qualifying *circa,* e.g. (1317) or (c.1317). Where a date can be established within a period of years (for example, an abbot's known tenure of office) it is so shown, e.g. (1290–1312). A date broadly inferred from the style of either the document or the seal is shown as e.g. (13c). The letters n.d. mean that the document is undated and no date can be confidently inferred. Where the matrix is clearly of much earlier date than the occasion of its use this is noticed in the catalogue entry (see (ix) above).

The entries are arranged alphabetically by and within place-names (see (i) above). When a place has been known by various names cross-references are given from the less usual, e.g. WALDEN *see* SAFFRON WALDEN.

Key to Some Abbreviations Occurring in Legends

ABBATIS	ABBIS, ABB'IS, ABBT'IS	GRACIE	GRIE
ABBATISSE	ABBISSE	HOSPITALIS	HOSP'
AD CAUSAS	AD CAS	JERUSALEM	IER, IERL., IERLM
APOSTOLI	APL'I, AP'LI	JESUS	IHS, IHV
APOSTOLORUM	APL'ORUM, APOSTL'OR	JOHANNIS	IOH'IS
BEATE	BE', BTE	MAGISTRI	MAG'R, MAGRI
BEATORUM	BEATOR'	MARIE	MRIE
CAPITULI	CAP'LI	MATRIS	MRIS
CARTHUSIENSIS	CAR', CARTUS', CARTUSIESIS	MINORUM	MINOR'
CAUSAS	CAS	MONASTERII	MONESTII
CHRISTI	XPI	MONASTERIUM	MONAST'
CHRISTUM	XPM	MONIALIUM	MONIZ
CHRISTUS	XPVS	ORDINIS	ORD', ORDIS
COMMUNE	C'MUNE, C'MVNE, COE, COIE, COME, COMVNE	PREDICATORUM	P'DICATOR', PRED'
		PRESENS	P'SENS
CONVENTUALE	COVENTVAL'	PRIOR	P'OR
CONVENTUS	CONVET', COVE, COVENT', COVENTVS, COVET', COV'ET	PRIORIS	P'ORIS, PRI, PRIOR', PRIS
		PRIORATUS	P'ORATVS
DOMINI	DNI	PROTOMARTYRIS	P'TOMARTIRIS
DOMINUS	DNS	RECEPTORIS	RECEPTOR'
DOMUS	DOM	ROBERTI	ROB', ROB'TI
ECCLESIE	ECCE, ECCLE, ECCLIE, ECCL'IE, ECLE, ECLESIE, ECL'IE, ECLL'E	SANCTE	SCANTE, SCE
		SANCTI	SCI
		SANCTORUM	SCORVM
FRATRIS	FRIS, FR'IS	SIGILLUM	S', SI', SIG', SIGILL', SIGILLV'
FRATRUM	FRVM, FR'VM	TECUM	TECV
GRACIA	GRA	WILLELMI	WILL'I

Catalogue

ABBEYCWMHIR (Rad) Cistercian abbey
abbey seal
M001. Under an elaborate traceried canopy, the Virgin, crowned, enthroned, holding a sceptre in her L hand and the Child, with nimbus, on her R knee. On either side, smaller canopied niches containing standing figures: (L) an abbot holding a crozier and (R) (defaced). Below, a shield of arms: *quarterly, France modern and England, with a label of three points* impaling MORTIMER quartered with BURGH; and a scroll inscribed (illegible).
...ABBATI... (BL)
Pointed oval, c.65×c.42; red-brown, tongue. Deep impression, flattened, most of edge lost. Has three impressions of a counterseal, **M002.**
E 329/244 1533
counterseal
M002. The loop of a crozier?
No legend.
Oval, 14×10; red-brown, on tongue, as counterseal to **M001.** Complete, clear, three impressions.
E 329/244 1533

ABBEY DORE (Heref) Cistercian abbey
abbot's seal: (Stephen of Worcester)
M003. The abbot, standing, vested for mass, holding a chalice.
Legend lost.
Pointed oval, over 40×20; green, tongue. Central fragment of a deep impression.
E 329/210 1252
abbot's seal: (William)
M004. The abbot, standing on a corbel, holding a crozier and a book.
...IGILLVM:ABB/ATIS:DE:DOR... (Lom)
Pointed oval, 45×25; brown, tag. Deep clear impression, upper point lost. BM 3064.
DL 25/326 (temp. Edw. I)

ABBOTSBURY (Dors) Benedictine abbey
abbey seal
M005. The abbey church seen from N or S, showing a pitched roof, an aisle, a gabled transept with portal, and two smaller gabled projections; indication of a central tower. Below, a row of rounded arches.
Legend lost.

Round, c.40; red, tag. Large central fragment of a deep impression, heavily flattened. Described by VCH as from 11c. matrix. BM 2539.
E 322/1 1539

ABERCONWAY *see* CONWAY

ABERGAVENNY (Monm) Benedictine priory
priory seal
M006. In a canopied niche with tabernacle work at the sides, the Virgin, crowned, seated, holding the Child on her L knee. Below, under an arch, a figure, half-length, praying to L.
Legend defaced.
Pointed oval, c.43×c.25; light brown, tag. Nearly complete, indistinct impression, flattened.
E 25/10 1534

ABINGDON (Berks) Benedictine abbey
abbey seal
M007. The Virgin, in embroidered robes, seated on a bench-type throne, holding before her, upon her knees, the Child, his R hand raised in blessing.
...SIE S...MAR... (Lom)
Pointed oval, c.60×c.40; green, tag. Deep clear impression from a fine matrix. Has counterseal **M009.**
E 40/14256 Pl 56 1344
abbey seal (ad causas?)
M008. The Virgin, crowned, seated on a bench-type throne with cushion, her feet on a carved corbel, under a gabled canopy supported by two slender clustered shafts resting on the throne; with her R hand she gives her breast to the Child seated on her L knee, with nimbus.
S'.ECCLE.SCE MARIE ABENDON TAN...CAS (Lom)
Pointed oval, 70×44; brown, detached on red and yellow cords. Nearly complete, deep clear impression. Has counterseal, **M009.** Also on E 322/2 (1538);
E 210/6845 (1297).
E 33/26/1 Pl 28 1504
counterseal
M009. An antique gem: head of a bacchant (?) in profile to R, long curling hair, ringlets falling on shoulder.
No legend.

Oval, 40×33; brown, detached on red and yellow cords, as counterseal to **Mo08**. Complete, clear impression. Also on E 40/14256 (1344).

E 33/26/1   Pl 9   1504
abbot's seal: Robert (de Henreth)

Mo10. The abbot, standing on a carved corbel, vested for mass, holding a crozier and a book. On L, a short cross-staff; on R, a flaming star.

+SIGILLVM:ROBERTI:DEI...ABBATIS:ABBENDONIE (Lom)
Pointed oval, 65×38; uncoloured, tag. Nearly complete, deep but not sharp impression. BM 2543.

DL 27/31   1231
abbot's seal: Robert (de Gareford)

Mo11. Under a gothic canopy, the abbot, standing, blessing and holding a crozier. On either side, hung on the canopy's outer shaft, a shield of arms: (L) *an escarbuncle*; (R) ENGLAND.

...ILLVM.RO...BATIS.ABINDO...   (Lom)
Pointed oval, c.60×44; dark green, detached on tongue. Large central fragment of a deep clear impression.

SC 13/F33   (1328–33)
abbot's seal: Peter (de Hanneye)

Mo12. A shield of arms: *a cross flory between four martlets*; below, two palm branches.
Legend lost or defaced.
Round, 17; red, tongue. Deep impression, flattened, most of edge lost.

E 326/12612   1375
abbot's seal

Mo13. Under large and elaborate canopies amid tabernacle work, three niches containing: (centre) the Virgin, crowned, seated, holding the Child, with nimbus, on her L knee and a fleur-de-lys sceptre in her R hand; and standing figures of (L) a king, crowned, holding a fleur-de-lys sceptre and a staff, (R) a saint, with nimbus, holding a palm branch. Below, the abbot, mitred and holding a crozier, kneeling in prayer to L, between two shields of arms: (L) *on a fesse between three birds a man's head affronté between two covered cups*; (R) *a cross formy between four* (indistinct objects).

SIGILLVM.PENTECOST./ABBATIS.ABENDONIE   (BL)
Pointed oval, 80×50; red-brown, detached on pink tapes in tin skippet. Complete, fine impression.

SC 13/O3   Pl 33   (n.d.)

ACONBURY (Heref) Augustinian priory (F)
    priory seal

Mo14. The prioress standing on a corbel, holding a book in her L hand and a tall cross in her R hand.
SIG[ILL':] CONVENTVS:DE:CORN[BVR]IA:
Pointed oval, 48×28; red, tongue. Good impression, cracked, edge chipped. Also on E 42/322 (1412); E 326/2904 (1363); SC 13/R1a, 1b, 1c (n.d.).

Apparently from a 13c. matrix. BM 2547.

E 329/460   Pl 44   1447

ACRE *see* WEST ACRE

ALVINGHAM (Lincs) Gilbertine priory (M and F)
    seal ad causas

Mo15. On a corbel with branch-like decoration, the Virgin, crowned, seated on a bench-type throne, holding her breast with her R hand, the Child seated on her L knee.

...SANTE:MARIE:DE...GH...D CAVSA...   (Lom)
Pointed oval, c.45×c.35; light brown, tag. Deep impression, points lost, much flattened and cracked. Described in the sealing clause as *sigillum comune*, and by VCH as a 13c matrix. Also on E 101/568/49,no.8 (1304). BM 2556.

E 322/3   1538

AMESBURY (Wilts) Fontevraldine priory (M and F)
    prioress's seal: Isabella of Lancaster.

Mo16. In a traceried niche, the prioress, standing, holding a sceptre in her L hand. On L, a shield of arms: *quarterly, Old France and England* ...
Legend lost.
Pointed oval, c.60×c.30; red, tag. Central fragment. BM 2557.

DL 25/248   (1337–45)

ANGLESEY (Cambs) Augustinian priory
    priory seal

Mo17. The Virgin, seated, holding the Child on her L knee, each blessing with R hand; on either side of her head, an angel.

...NGELI:ANGLESIE:SVNT:SINGNA:TIP'Q:MARIE   (Lom)
Pointed oval, 50×32; green, tag. Nearly complete, deep clear impression. Also on E 40/6816 (n.d.), 14492 (1236), 14494 (n.d.), 14496 (1236).

E 40/14497   Pl 42   1236

ANKERWYKE (Bucks) Benedictine priory (F)
    priory seal

Mo18. A timber-framed rectangular building with hipped roof of thatch or Roman tiles, a tall finial at either end; in the centre, a round turret with conical roof.

+SIGILL' E...CLE.SCE.MARIE.MA[G DE ANK']WIC   (Lom)
Round, 45; uncoloured, varnished brown, detached on tongue. Nearly complete, deep clear impression. Also on E 42/323 (1270). BM 2559 and plate x. VCH notes an example on a deed dated 5 Ric. I (*Bucks*, vol. I, p. 357).

SC 13/R2   Pl 45   (12c)

ARBROATH (Forfar) Tironian abbey
abbot's seal

M019. In a central oblong panel, the martyrdom of St. Thomas, kneeling on R before the altar. Above, three adjacent niches containing the Virgin and Child (centre) between two kneeling angels. Below, under an arch with a quatrefoil in the tympanum, the abbot, holding a crozier, praying to R. On L and R in the field, an indistinct inscription.

...ABBATIS SCI THOME MARTYRIS DE AB'BRO... (Lom)
Pointed oval, c.50×32; bronze, detached on hemp cords. Deep but not sharp impression, upper point lost. Also obverse of SC 13/H33 (n.d.). Laing 978.
SC 13/D43 (13c)

ARBURY (Warw) Augustinian priory
priory seal

M020. The Virgin, seated on a bench-type throne with knobbed arm-rests, holding the Child on her L knee.
...CONVENT... (Lom)
Pointed oval, c.60×c.35; red, tag. Fragment (figure headless) of central and R part. Also on E 326/8728 (1416).
E 329/263 1445

ARTHINGTON (Yorks) Cluniac priory (F)
priory seal

M021. The Virgin, crowned, standing, turning to R, holding a fleur-de-lys in her R hand.
+SIGILLV.SCE MARIE D...N (Lom)
Round, 40; green, tag. Clear impression from an apparently 12c matrix, L edge lost. Clay, p. 12, pl. I. BM 2563.
DL 25/477 (c.1241)

ARUNDEL (Sussex) Holy Trinity, hospital
common seal

M022. In a canopied niche between tabernacle work, the Holy Trinity.
SIGILLV:DOM:ELEMOSINAR:SCE:TNITAT:ARVDELL (Lom)
Round, 40; red, tag. Complete, deep clear impression. BM 2565.
E 322/5 Pl 45 1546

ASHBY *see* CANONS ASHBY

ASHRIDGE (Herts) Bonhommes' college
common seal

M023. On a draped altar, the Lamb of God. Below, a lion rampant.
...COM...VIR... (Lom)
Pointed oval, 50×c.30; red, tag. Deep clear impression, cracked, most of edge lost. BM 2569.
E 25/3 1534

ATHELNEY (Som) Benedictine abbey
abbey seal

M024. The abbey church showing a central door, two towers (one central) each with a conical roof and knob finial, and transepts.
+SIGILLVM.SC...ELINC...E (Lom)
Round, 40; dark green, tag. Clear impression but much cracked and damaged. Above the impression is the print of an ornamental handle chased with acanthus foliage. BM 2570.
DL 27/87 Pl 10 (1155–64)
abbey seal

M025. In three adjoining niches with elaborate vaulted canopies, standing figures: (centre) Our Lord, with nimbus, blessing and holding an orb with a cross; (L) St Peter, with tiara, blessing and holding a tall patriarchal cross and keys; (R) St Paul, with nimbus, holding a sword erect in his R hand and a book. On either side, tabernacle work and a shield of arms: (L) *a horn between three crowns*; (R) *quarterly, 1 and 4 three crowns in pale, 2 and 3 a cross formy.*
SIGILLUM:COMUNE:ABBATIS:ET:[CONVENTUS:]MONAST-ERII DE ATHELNEY: (BL)
Round, 63; red-brown, tag. Almost complete, fine impression, slightly flattened. Also on E 25/5 (1534).
E 322/8 Pl 17 1539
abbot's seal: Benedict

M026. The abbot, vested for mass, standing on a corbel, holding a crozier and a book.
+SIGILLVM BENEDICTI.ABBATIS.ATHELINGIE (Lom)
Pointed oval, 65×37; dark green, tag. Complete, deep clear impression. BM 2572.
DL 27/87 Pl 42 (1155–64)

ATHERINGTON (Sussex) Benedictine alien grange
seal of the bailiwick

M027. A chalice between two fleurs-de-lys, and the hand of God issuing from a cloud above.
...RING... (Lom)
Pointed oval, c.40×c.25; dark green, tag. Deep clear impression, most of edge lost. This house has been variously described as a cell (Dugdale), a priory (Cottineau) and a grange (Knowles and Hadcock); this first publication of this seal may help to determine its status. The sealing clause reads ... *una cum sigillo comune baillie nostre de Atherington.*
E 329/40 Pl 43 1368

AXHOLME or **EPWORTH** (Lincs) Carthusian priory
priory seal

M028. In a broad niche under a double canopy with crocketed gables and pinnacles, the Visitation. On either side, a shield of arms: *a lion rampant*, (MOWBRAY, founder).

S:COE:DOM/US:V... (BL)

Pointed oval, c.50×c.35; dark green, tag. Deep clear impression, flattened, most of edge lost. Also on E 211/242 (1529). BM 2574.

E 322/9   Pl 42   1538

AYLESBURY (Bucks) Franciscan house
common seal

M029. On R, St Francis, standing, holding a long staff in his L hand, his R hand raised, preaching to the birds which perch in a tree before him. On L, under the branches, a friar, kneeling.

...COMUNITATIS.FRA...AYLESBURIE (BL)

Pointed oval, c.40×27; red-brown, tag. Deep uneven impression, flattened, upper and lower points lost. BM 2576.

E 322/10   1538

BALMERINO (Fife) Cistercian abbey
abbot's seal

M030. The abbot, standing on a corbel decorated with narrow arcading, holding a pastoral cross in his L hand, maniple on his wrist; on L, three stars and a fleur-de-lys.

S'ABBIS SCI EDWARDI IN SCOCIA (Lom)

Pointed oval, 50×28; mottled green, detached on hemp cords. Complete, deep clear impression. Laing 982. BM 15219.

SC 13/E44   Pl 8   (13c)

BANBURY (Oxon) St John the Baptist, hospital
common seal

M031. A double-barred cross fitchy.

+SIGILL...IS DE BANNEB' (Lom)

Pointed oval, 50×35; dark brown, tag. Nearly complete, uneven and indistinct impression. BM 2578.

E 329/197   (13c)

BARDNEY (Lincs) Benedictine abbey
abbey seal

M032. *Obv.* Standing figures: (L) St Paul, holding a sword and a book; (R) St Peter, holding keys and a book; each facing inwards. They stand under a double canopy of trefoiled arches below crocketed gables, supported by three slender columns each topped with a niche and pinnacle. The background is diapered with quatrefoils. Above the canopy, a crescent and a star. On either side, a scroll of leaves and roses. Below, under a rounded arch, the abbot, half-length, praying to L, holding a crozier, between initials R and G.

[S] CO/MVNE:ABBATIS:ET:COVENTVS/ MON:APL'ORVM:PETRI:ET:PAVLI (Lom)

Rev. St Oswald, crowned, seated under a gabled canopy on a bench-type throne with arcaded front and knobbed arm-rests, holding his L hand before him and in his R hand a flowered sceptre. The background is diapered with sexfoils. Below, under a rounded arch, a shield of arms: *a cross flory between four lions combattant* (the ABBEY).

ET:SANCTI:OSWALDI:GLORIOSI:REGIS:ET:MARTIRIS:DE:- BARDNEYA (Lom)

Pointed oval, 80×60; red, on green and red silk laces. Nearly complete, fine impression, slightly flattened. Also on E 25/7 (1534); E 322/13 (1538). BM 2582. The initials R and G on OBV are presumably those of Richard Gainsborough, abbot 1318–42.

E 329/423   Pl 17obv) and Pl 32 (rev) from E 322/13   1385

abbot's seal: John ...

M033. In a rich gothic housing, the abbot, standing, holding a crozier and a book. On either side, a shield of arms: (L) *a cross flory between four lions rampant* (the ABBEY); (R) *crusilly, a lion rampant*.

S' IOHAN...DE BARDENAY (BL)

Pointed oval, c.60×40; dark green, detached on tag. Deep impression, flattened, most of edge lost. BM 2586. John de Haynton was abbot 1385–1404, John Woxbrigg 1404–1413.

SC 13/F167   (c.1400)

abbot's seal: John H(aynton)

M034. A shield of arms: *a cross between four lions rampant* (the ABBEY).

S' IOHIS.H...ABB'IS...BARDNEY (BL)

Round, 25; red, tongue. Complete, fair impression.

E 135/10/20, no. 6   (c.1400)

abbot's seal: William Marton

M035. Under an ogee arch in a pinnacled gothic housing, the abbot, standing, holding a crozier and a book. On either side, a shield of arms: (L) *a cross between four lions rampant* (the ABBEY); (R) *a chevron between three crescents* (MARTON or MARTIN).

SIGILLU.WILLELMI.MARTON.ABBATIS.BARDENAY (BL)

Pointed oval, 70×45; red-brown, detached on silk cords in metal skippet. Complete, legend partly blurred, centre deep and clear. Also on SC 10/2518 (1536). BM 2587.

SC 13/O5   (1507–34)

BARHAM (Cambs) Crutched Friars' house
common seal

M036. A gothic housing containing figures above and below.

+AD LOM...BARGA... (Lom)

Pointed oval, c.55×35; red-brown, detached on tongue. Deep impression, badly cracked and defaced. BM 2592.

SC 13/R3   (1538)

BARKING (Essex) Benedictine abbey (F)
   abbey seal
M037. Under a triple canopy of cusped arches, three standing figures, perhaps St Ethelburga (centre) and two abbesses. Above, the Virgin and Child, seated between half-length figures of (L) St Peter and (R) St Paul. Below, under an arch, a half-length figure, praying to R.
   ...PEPERIT XPM CONVEN[TVM PROTEGAT ISTVM]   (Lom)
Pointed oval, c.70×c.50; uncoloured, tag. Deep but uneven impression, upper and lower edges lost, legend defaced. Also on DL 27/104, which has counterseal, **M038**. BM 2588.

E 322/14   1538
   counterseal
M038. The abbess, standing on a corbel, holding a cross and a book.
   GRACIA DEI SVM IT [QVOD SVM]   (Lom)
Pointed oval, 50×30; uncoloured, on tag, as counterseal to **M037**. Complete, deep indistinct impression, legend much defaced. BM 2589. Used by Alice, abbess in 1276.

DL 27/104   (c.1276)
   abbess's seal: Katharine Sutton
M039. In a cusped panel, the deep moulding enriched with quatrefoils, a shield of arms: *three chevrons* (hatched) (SUTTON). Above, the abbess, half-length, holding a crozier and a book.
Legend lost.
Round, c.34; red, tongue. Large central fragment of a deep clear impression.

E 43/106   Pl 27   1369
   seal ad causas
M040. The Virgin, seated, holding the Child on her L knee. Below, under an arch, the abbess, half-length, praying to L.
   [+S'.ABBATISSE ET CONVENT' D' BER] KI(NG AD CAS]
                                                           (Lom)
Pointed oval, c.50×c.30; red, tag. Central fragment. BM 2590, dated there as from a 13c matrix.

WARD 2/205/27   1520

BARLINCH (Som) Augustinian priory
   priory seal
M041. St Nicholas, standing, blessing and holding a crozier, the field diapered.
   ...IO...AI DE BERLIS...   (Lom)
Pointed oval, c.50×c.35; red, tag. Deep clear

impression from a probably 12c matrix, head, lower part and R edge lost. Mr R. C. Fowler was able to read the legend (in c.1925) as
   ...VNE.PORATV...CHOLAI : DE : BERLISZ.

E 326/8199   1410
   prior's seal
M042. In three adjoining canopied niches with crocketed gables, standing figures: (centre) St Nicholas; (L) a female figure; (R) a crowned female saint holding a palm branch. Below, under an arch, a half-length figure, praying to L.
   S'. PRIORAT...   (BL)
Pointed oval, c.40×c.25; red, tag. Deep clear impression, L side and most of edge lost.

E 326/8199   1410

BARNWELL (Cambs) Augustinian priory
   priory seal
M043. St Giles, standing, vested for mass, his L hand raised, holding a pastoral staff in his R hand. On either side, a curling sprig.
   ...SAN...II.D...BER   (Lom)
Pointed oval, c.60×45; bronze-green, tag. Deep clear impression, cracked, most of edge lost, figure headless. Also on E 322/15 (1538). BM 2606.

E 326/10410   1352

BASWICH (Staffs) Augustinian priory
   priory seal
M044. Under a pinnacled canopy with tabernacle work at the sides, St Thomas, seated, blessing and holding a pastoral cross. Under his feet, a masonry corbel.
   [SIGILL' COE]PRIORATUS. SCI.THOME. MARTIRIS. IUXTA.
   STAFFORD   (BL)
Pointed oval, 65×40; light red, tag. Deep clear impression of centre, edge uneven and damaged. Also on E 322/220 (1538). BM 4071.

E 329/373   Pl 3   1435
   counterseal?
M045. The martyrdom of St Thomas. Below, under an arch, the prior, half-length, praying to R.
Legend lost.
Pointed oval, c.35×25; brown, tag. Deep clear impression of a large central fragment. BM 4072, where the legend is given as
   TRINE DEVS P [RO] ME MOVEAT TE PASSIO THOME.

E 326/8503   (13c)

BATH (Som) Benedictine cathedral priory
   chapter seal
M046. On a diapered ground, under a triple canopy, St Peter (L) holding keys and St Paul holding a sword, both standing and holding between them a model of the

abbey church. The canopy has three trefoiled arches under crocketed gables and rests on two slender outer columns and two inner corbels. Below the ledge on which the saints stand, under three pointed arches, three monks, half-length, praying to L.

SIGILLVM.CAPITVLI.BATHONIENSIS.ECCLESIE (Lom)

Pointed oval, 95×60; bronze, tag. Complete except for upper point, deep clear but slightly uneven impression. Also on E 326/8860 (1366), 11023 (n.d.); fragments only. Pedrick, plate XVII, 34. BM 1441.

E 25/8/1   Pl 35   1534

BATTLE (Sussex) Benedictine abbey
  abbey seal
M047. The abbey church, shown with a tall central tower and four lesser towers all with conical roofs, windows in aisle and clerestory, and a high central portal with trefoiled arch and doors closed.

[SI]GILLVM.CONVENTVS.SANCTI.MARTINI.DE.BELL[O]
(Lom)

Round, 70; uncoloured, tag. Nearly complete, deep impression, partly indistinct. Has counterseal, **M050.** Also on E 210/2526 (with counterseal **M048**, 1392); E 329/185 (with counterseal **M049**, 1522). Closely resembles BM 2616, but the flags upon the towers shown there in plate X are not visible in this impression.

E 322/16   Pl 35   1538

  abbot's seal: John Crane
M048. In a canopied niche, the abbot, standing, vested for mass, holding a crozier and a book. On L, in a smaller niche, a female saint, standing, holding a palm-branch, her L hand raised. Below her, a shield of arms: *quarterly, Old France and England*. Below the shield, initial I. Beaded border.

.../RA.ABBATI... (Lom)

Pointed oval, c.60×c.35; red, on tag, as counterseal to **M047.** Large fragment of a fine impression from a fine matrix of apparently earlier date.

John Crane, who was abbot 1383–98, may have used a matrix made for one of his predecessors John de Thanet, John de Whatlington, John de Northburne and John de Pevense who were abbots successively 1297–1324.

E 210/2526   Pl 42   1392

  abbot's seal: Lawrence Champion
M049. In a canopied niche, an abbot, standing, mitred and vested for mass, holding a crozier and a book. On L, in a smaller niche, a saint, standing, holding a palm-branch in his R hand and an indistinct object in his L hand.

[SIGILL' LAVRENCI DEI GRA...] (BL)

Pointed oval, c.55×c.40; red, on tag, as counterseal to **M047.** Central fragment of a deep clear impression.

Closely resembles **M048.** A complete example is described and illustrated by C. L. Kingsford in *Archaeologia*, LXV (1914), pp. 266–7 and plate 35. The abbot's name is awkwardly engraved, suggesting an alteration to the matrix.

E 329/185   1522

  abbot's seal: John Hamond
M050. In a vaulted and canopied niche, the abbot, standing, mitred and vested for mass, holding a crozier and a book. Above, in a niche within the canopy, St Martin, on horseback, dividing his cloak with the beggar. On either side, in a canopied niche, standing figures: (L) a female saint, holding a palm branch in her R hand and an indistinct object in her L hand; (R) a bishop. Below them, two shields of arms: (L) *quarterly, France modern and England*; (R) *on a cross between four crowns impaled on swords, a mitre* (the ABBEY).

SIGIL IOHIS DEI GRA/ABBATIS DE BELLO (BL)

Pointed oval, 69×44; red, on tag, as counterseal to **M047.** Complete, deep clear impression with much sharp detail. Closely resembles **M048.**

E 322/16   Pl 35   1538

BAYSDALE (Yorks) Cistercian priory (F)
  priory seal
M051. The Virgin (?), seated on a carved chair ornamented with rounded arches, before a lectern on R.

...RIE...(?) (Lom)

Pointed oval, c.60×? ; red, tag. Central fragment of a clear impression.

E 210/5245   1323

BEAULIEU (Hants) Cistercian abbey
  abbey seal
M052. The Virgin, crowned, seated in a canopied and panelled niche, holding the Child, with nimbus, on her R knee. On either side, in a similar but smaller canopied niche, five monks, kneeling. Below, under a rounded arch, between (L) a fleur-de-lys and (R) a lion, a shield of arms: *a crown impaled on a crozier* (the ABBEY).

SIGILLUM:COMUNE:MON/ASTERII:BELLI [LOCI]REGIS
(BL)

Round, 63; red-brown, tag. Nearly complete, deep clear impression, parts flattened. BM 2621.

E 322/17   Pl 51   1538

  abbot's seal: Peter
M053. The abbot, standing on a carved corbel, vested for mass, holding a crozier and a book.

+...S (Lom)

Pointed oval, c.60×c.35; dark green, tongue. Central fragment of a fine impression, detail clear.

DL 27/123   Pl 35   1311

abbot's seal: Walter (Herring)

Mo54. In a niche with pinnacled canopy, the abbot, standing, vested for mass, holding a crozier and a book. On either side, a tall traceried panel bearing a shield of arms: (L) *quarterly*, *Old France and England*; (R) *a cross between four lions* (?).

[SI]GILLVM:FRIS:WALTERI...　　　　(BL)

Pointed oval, c.45×35; dull red, tongue. Deep impression, much flattened, most of edge lost.

E 213/81　　　　1386

BEAUVALE (Notts) Carthusian priory
priory seal

Mo55. Our Lord, with nimbus, seated in a canopied niche, his R hand raised in blessing, holding an orb with cross in his L hand. Below, under an arch, a monk, kneeling in prayer to R.

... OMVNE.DOMVS/BE...VALL' ORD' CAR'　　(Lom)

Pointed oval, 58×32; red-brown, tag. Nearly complete, deep impression, indistinct in parts. Also on E 135/10/21, nos. 6 (1400), 14 (1400); E 326/5237 (1463); E 326/7087 (1374); E 326/9781 (1538). BM 2623.

E 322/18　　　　1539

prior's seal

Mo56. In an oval panel, between lunettes of tracery, Our Lord, crucified. Below, under an arch, a monk, praying.

...TIMI.../TV MISERR'...　　　　(Lom)

Pointed oval, 25×20; red, tongue. Complete, deep impression, badly flattened.

E 213/51　　　　1371

prior's seal: Thomas Quyxley

Mo57. In a canopied niche, between panels of tracery, the Holy Trinity.

Legend lost or defaced.

Oval, c.28×c.25; dark green, tongue. Deep indistinct impression, most of edge lost.

E 213/335　　　　1413

BEELEIGH (Essex) Premonstratensian abbey
abbey seal

Mo58. The abbot, standing on a mount, vested for mass, holding a crozier in his L hand and a book in his R hand.

+SIGILL':ABB'IS:ET:CONVENTVS:DE:MAVDVNE　(Lom)

Pointed oval, 45×25; mottled green, tag. Nearly complete, deep impression, slightly rubbed. BM 3591.

DL 27/70　　　　1257

abbey seal

Mo59. St Nicholas, mitred and vested for mass, blessing and holding a crozier, seated on a throne between pinnacles. Below, under a gable and a trefoiled arch, the abbot, holding a crozier, kneeling in prayer to L.

S'/ABBATIS ET CONV/ENTVS DE MALDONA　(Lom)

Pointed oval, 50×30; light brown, detached on tag. Complete, deep clear impression. Has counterseal, **Mo60.** Also on E 326/6918 (1529); E 329/160 (1535); SC 13/R5B, 6A, 6B (all n.d.). BM 3592.

SC 13/R5A　　　Pl 44 from E 329/160　　(c.1536)
counterseal

Mo60. Between (L) a palm branch and (R) a saltire, an initial I (Lom).

No legend.

Round, 15; light brown, detached on tag, as counterseal to **Mo59.** Complete, clear impression. An abbot's signet?

SC 13/R5A　　　　(c.1536)

prior's seal: John

Mo61. The Annunciation.

MATER DEI MEMENTO MEI　　　　(Lom)

Round, 23; uncoloured, tag. Nearly complete, clear impression.

E 329/85　　　　1279

BEESTON (Norf) Augustinian priory
priory seal

Mo62. The Virgin, half-length, holding the Child. Below, under a triple arch, a priest, kneeling before an altar and chalice. Above him, AVE MARIA.

+S...'IE DE BESTH...　　　　(Lom)

Pointed oval, 40×c.25; uncoloured, tag. Indistinct impression, edge damaged.

E 40/4918　　　　(c.1267)

BERDEN (Essex) Augustinian priory
priory seal

Mo63. Under a tall pinnacled canopy, between two niches with window-like tracery, St John the Evangelist, standing, with nimbus, holding the devil in a cup.

SIGILLVM COM[MUN]E DOMVS[SCI IOH]ANNIS
EVANGELISTAE DE BERDEN　　　　(BL)

Pointed oval, 55×35; red, tag. Nearly complete, clear impression, flattened. Has counterseal, **Mo64.**
BM 2632.

E 42/288　　　Pl 42　　　　1455
counterseal

Mo64. A dolphin.

No legend.

Round, 9; red, on tag, as counterseal to **Mo63.** Complete, clear impression. May be the signet of John Dane, prior.

E 42/288　　　　1455

BERKELEY (Glos) Holy Trinity, Longbridge, hospital
common seal

Mo65. Our Lord, with nimbus, seated on a bench-type throne, blessing and holding a book.

+S'HOSPITALI[S:SCE:TRINTATIS:IVXTA:]LANGEBRVG' (Lom)

Pointed oval, 57×34; bronze-green, tag. Deep clear impression, lower part lost. BM 3574.

E 42/203   Pl 47   1337

BERMONDSEY (Surrey) Cluniac priory, later abbey
   priory seal
Mo66. Our Lord, seated on a bench-type throne, blessing and holding a book.

SIGILLVM SCI SAL...   (Lom)

Round, c.50; bronze-green, on pink and yellow plaited laces. Deep impression, L edge lost.

E 42/396   (1184–6)
   priory seal
Mo67. Our Lord, between (L) and the sun and (R) the moon, seated on a bench-type throne, under a canopy with trefoiled arch and slender pillars, blessing and holding a book.

...ORIS S...RMONDESE   (Lom)

Pointed oval, 50×35; uncoloured, varnished, tag. Deep clear impression, edge damaged. Has counterseal, **Mo68**. Also on E 40/767(1232).

E 42/324   Pl 44   1274
   counterseal
Mo68. The Virgin and Child, seated on a throne with tall arms.

+MATER DEI·MEMENTO MEI   (Lom)

Round, 18; uncoloured, varnished brown, on tag, as counterseal to **Mo67**. Complete, clear impression. May be the seal of prior Henry de Monte Mauri.

E 42/324   Pl 15   1274
   priory seal
Mo69. The Transfiguration. Between (L) the sun and (R) the moon, Our Lord, with cruciform nimbus and four rays radiating from him, standing on a mount, his R hand raised in blessing, holding a book in his L hand; on L, Moses, horned, standing, holding a book; on R, Elias, standing, holding a book; in the foreground, three Apostles, sleeping.

+SIGILL':EC[CLIE]:SCI:SALVATORIS:DE:BERMONDESEYE (Lom)

Round, 60; bronze-green, tag. Nearly complete, deep clear impression. Has counterseal, **Mo70**. Also on E 326/7865 (1346). BM 2634.

E 329/328   Pl 28   1356
   counterseal
Mo70. Our Lord, half-length, with cruciform nimbus, blessing with his R hand and holding an orb with cross in his L hand.

+EGO:SVM:VIA:VERITAS:ET:VITA   (Lom)

Round, 30; bronze-green, on tag, as counterseal to

Mo69. Complete, deep impression, rubbed.

E 329/328   1356
   abbey seal
Mo71. *Obv.* The Transfiguration. Our Lord, with nimbus, irradiate, standing within an arch of clouds (nebuly), hands raised, between half-length figures, each with nimbus, of (L) Moses with sun above and (R) Elias with moon above; the field sown with stars. Below, the three Apostles, each with nimbus, seated on the ground in adoration; foliage in the field.

SIGILLUM COMUNE MONASTERII SANCTI SALVATORIS DE
BERMENDESEY   (BL)

   Rev. Our Lord, with cruciform nimbus, half draped, seated on a rainbow, blessing and holding an orb with cross, between two demi-angels each holding a shield of arms: (L) *quarterly, France modern and England*; (R) *England*. The field, sown with stars and (L) the sun and (R) the moon. Below, the abbot, mitred and holding a crozier, and four monks, all looking up; foliage in the field.

[P]ER VIRTUTEM SANCTE CRUCIS SALVA NOS XPE
SALVATOR   (BL)

Round, 75; orange, detached on cords. Nearly complete, fine impression.

SC 13/H82   (16c)
   prior's seal: John de Chartres
Mo72. The Flight into Egypt. On R, a servant with a stick and a sack over his shoulder leads the way; the Virgin and Child follow, riding L to R on an ass, a star above; St Joseph, holding a staff, follows on L. Above, a pointed arch enclosing a trefoiled arch with tracery between. Below, under the ass's hoofs, a building with arcades, tiled roof, and a central arch above a figure, half-length, praying to R.

*S' IO[HANNIS PRIORIS) DE B'MVNDESEYE   (Lom)

Pointed oval, c.50×30; uncoloured, varnished, tongue. Deep clear impression, R and lower parts lost.

E 42/397   Pl 42   1271

The seals of Bermondsey abbey catalogued here as **Mo66** to **Mo72** are described and illustrated by Rose Graham in *Surrey Archaeological Collections*, vol. XXXIX (1931). pp. 78–81 (reprinted from her *English Ecclesiastical Studies*, 1929).

BERWICK UPON TWEED (Northumb) Trinitarian house
   seal of the minister of the Order
Mo73. Our Lord, with nimbus, seated on a bench-type throne, hands uplifted, his feet on a rainbow (inscribed ?). On either side, a hand issuing from the border holding (R) the Cross and (L) the emblems of the Passion. Below, a friar, kneeling in prayer to L.

+SI MINISTRI.ORDINIS.SCE/TRINITATIS.DE.BERWIK
                                                     (Lom)

Pointed oval, 48×28; mottled green, detached on hemp cords. Complete, deep clear impression. BM 15223.
SC 13/D46   Pl 44   (14c)

BEVERLEY (Yorks) Dominican house
common seal
Mo74. In an elaborate late gothic housing, St Paul, with nimbus, standing, holding a sword and a book. Under his feet, a moulding with four quatrefoils. Below, in the exergue, a triple flower.
SIGILLV':PR...FRATR...ORDINIS P'DICATOR' BEV'LACI (BL)
Pointed oval, 50×30; red, tongue. Complete, deep clear impression. Clay, plate I, 3. BM 2638.
E 329/398   1524

BICESTER (Oxon) Augustinian priory
chapter seal
Mo75. A panel of scrolled ornament based on vine, ears of corn and fleurs-de-lys.
...VLI ECCLESIE DE BERNECESTR'   (Lom)
Pointed oval, 60×c.45; dark brown, detached on cords. Deep clear impression, most of R side lost. Has counterseal, **Mo77**. Also on DL 25/71 (1285). BM 2772.
SC 13/E46   (13c)
priory seal
Mo76. In two adjacent canopied niches with tabernacle work at the sides, standing figures: (L) the Virgin, crowned, holding the Child on her L side and a flowered sceptre in her R hand; (R) St Edburga, crowned, holding a cup and a book. Below, between sprigs, a shield of arms: *barry nebuly* (BASSET, founder)
S' CO...P[R]IORATUS...BURENCESTR'   (BL)
Pointed oval, 60×40; red, tag. Deep clear impression, much lost from R side. BM 2773.
E 25/21   1534
prior's seal
Mo77. The prior, standing, holding a book before him.
+SIGILL':PRIORIS D' BVRN...   (Lom)
Pointed oval 48×30; dark brown, detached on cords, as counterseal to **Mo75**. Fine impression, upper L part lost.
SC 13/E46   Pl 41   (13c)

BIDDLESDEN (Bucks) Cistercian abbey
abbey seal
Mo78. The Virgin, standing, holding the Child, between two saints.
Legend lost.
Small central fragment, red, tag.
E 322/22   1538

BILSINGTON (Kent) Augustinian priory
priory seal
Mo79. In a broad canopied niche with panelling at the sides, against a diapered ground, the Coronation of the Virgin; an angel leaning down, placing the crown on the Virgin's head. Below, under an arcade on corbels, the founder, holding up a model of the church, and a group of canons, kneeling.
SIGILLVM COMVNE ECCLIE/BE MARIE DE BILSINGSTONE
                                                      (Lom)
Pointed oval, 70×43; light brown, tag. Complete, fine impression. Also on E 322/20 (1538). BM 2639.
E 25/11   Pl 10   1534

BINDON (Dors) Cistercian abbey
abbey seal
Mo80. In a gothic housing, two crowned figures, standing, holding up a crown with a tall central cross. On either side, a shield of arms (defaced). Below, under an arch, the abbot, holding a crozier, praying to L.
Legend lost on R, defaced on L.   (Lom)
Pointed oval, c.50×35; red-brown, detached on tag. Large central fragment of a deep indistinct impression. Has counterseal, **Mo81**. Also on E 322/21 (1539).
SC 13/R7   (n.d.)
abbot's seal: William Comere
Mo81. Initials WC (Lom), with an ornament between. No legend.
Shield-shaped, 17×12; red-brown, detached, on tag, as counterseal to **Mo80**. Complete, deep uneven impression.
SC 13/R7   (n.d.)

BINHAM (Norf) Benedictine priory
priory seal
Mo82. The Annunciation. The Virgin, with nimbus, seated R on a bench-type throne with cushion, her head turned to L, holding an open book and a lily in her L hand, her R hand clasping the front of her robe; the dove descending on her R and the archangel Gabriel approaching from L, his R hand and forefinger extended.
SIGILLVM E[CC]L'E SCE MARIE DE BINEHAM   (Rom)
Oval, 65×51; uncoloured, tag. Deep clear impression, faces flattened, edge chipped. BM 2642.
E 42/399   Pl 17   (1189–93)

BIRKENHEAD (Ches) Benedictine priory
prior's seal: R prior
Mo83. A standing figure.
Legend lost.
Pointed oval, c.40×c.20; uncoloured, tag. Fragment.
E 210/11250   (n.d.)

BISHAM (Berks) Benedictine abbey
abbey seal
Mo84. In a canopied niche of Renaissance style, the Holy Trinity, seated on a gothic throne. Below, a shield of arms: *quarterly, France modern and England.*
S.COE/NOVI.MONASTERII.REG./HEN...OCTAVI.DE.BISH (Rom)
Pointed oval, 80×48; red, tag. Nearly complete, deep clear impression, slightly flattened. BM 2645.
E 322/39   Pl 3   1538

BLACKMORE (Essex) Augustinian priory
priory seal
Mo85. Under a trefoiled arch on two slender shafts with foliated capitals, St Lawrence, standing, vested for mass, holding a palm branch.
+SIGILL':CONVENT.ECCL...KEMORE (Lom)
Pointed oval, c.70×c.45; uncoloured, tag. Deep impression, rubbed, much of edge lost. Has counterseal, **Mo86.**
DL 27/65   Pl 28   (1242)
prior's seal: William
Mo86. Under a rounded arch with cusping, a half-length bearded figure, facing to R, both hands raised. Above, between two turrets with conical roofs, an angel leaning down from heaven, holding a crown from which a scroll or ribbons (?) fall into and past the hands of the figure below.
+SIGILL'.WILL...DE BLAKEMORA (Lom)
Pointed oval, c.50×30; uncoloured, on tag, as counterseal to **Mo85.** Good impression, lower point and edge lost.
DL 27/65   Pl 9   (1242)

BLYTHBURGH (Suff) Augustinian priory
priory seal
Mo87. The Virgin, crowned, seated on a throne with knobbed finials on either side, holding the Child, with nimbus, before her and a long sceptre with a flowered tip in her R hand.
SIGIL...DE BLITBVRHC (Lom)
Pointed oval, 65×45; red-brown, tongue. Complete, deep clear impression at centre, legend blurred. Apparently the same seal as BM 2675, where it is attributed to Blithbury nunnery, Staffordshire.
E 25/13   Pl 10   1534

BODMIN (Corn) Augustinian priory
priory seal
Mo88. In an elaborate gothic housing, standing figures: (L) the Virgin, crowned, holding the Child on her R arm and a sceptre in her L hand; (R) St Petroc, blessing and holding a crozier. On a concave moulding below

their feet, their names S MARIA and S PETRV. In base, a shield of arms: *three fishes naiant in pale.*
SIGILLU:COIE CONVENTUS BE MARIE/ET SANCTI PETROCI DE BODMYN (BL)
Pointed oval, 60×40; red, tag. Nearly complete, deep sharp impression, uneven and much flattened. Also on E 322/23 (1539). BM 2677 gives a variant reading of the legend.
E 25/14   Pl 10   1534

BOLTON (Yorks) Augustinian priory
prior's seal: John de Landa
Mo89. Under a canopy, the Virgin, half-length, holding the Child on her L side. Above, Our Lord, half-length, showing his wounds, between two demi-angels, holding (L) the nails and (R) the crown of thorns. Below, under an arch, the prior, half-length, praying to R.
ESTO MEMOR SERVI VIRGO MARIA TVI (Lom)
Pointed oval, 37×23; uncoloured, varnished brown, tag. Complete, good impression, flattened. Clay, p. 12, plate I.
DL 27/332   1310

BORDESLEY (Worcs) Cistercian abbey
abbey seal
Mo90. Under a double canopy of trefoiled arches under crocketed gables, the Coronation of the Virgin. Below, under a trefoiled arch, the abbot, half-length, holding a crozier, praying to L.
...ILL.ECLE.B...MARIE.DE.BORD... (Lom)
Pointed oval, c.60×38; red-brown, tag. Deep uneven impression, flattened, upper and lower points and edge lost. BM 2680.
E 322/26   Pl 10   1538
abbot's seal
Mo91. The abbot, standing, vested for mass, holding a crozier and a book. On either side: (L) the sun; (R) the moon.
+SIGILL'.ABBATI[S] DE BORDESLEYA (Lom)
Pointed oval, 45×27; dark green, tag. Deep impression, rubbed, points lost. Also on E 326/8971 (1302); E 329/178 (1250 ?). BM 2683.
E 329/100   (13c)
abbot's seal: William (de Heyford ?)
Mo92. The abbot, standing, vested for mass, holding a crozier and a book.
[+SI]GILL...BORDESLEY (Lom)
Pointed oval, 40×25; bronze-green, tag. Deep impression, head distorted, edge damaged. The O and R of the legend are conjoined.
E 329/148   (1277–1309)
abbot's seal: Walter
Mo93. The abbot, vested for mass, blessing and

holding a crozier, standing on a corbel carved with a crouching beast. On either side, a face in a quatrefoil between four fleurs-de-lys, one above and three below.
...TERI... (Lom)
Pointed oval, c.60×38; uncoloured, tag. Deep but not sharp impression, most of edge lost. Has counterseal, **M094**.
E 327/268 (13c)

counterseal
M094. The Coronation of the Virgin, with a crescent above. Below, under an arch, the abbot, half-length, mitred, praying to R.
VIRGO...TRONVS SIS HIC ITE'VM... (Lom)
Pointed oval, c.45×25; uncoloured, on tag, as counterseal to **M093**. Deep impression of centre, legend uneven.
E 327/268 (13c)

abbot's seal: Richard Feckenham
M095. Between two words too faint to be read, the monogram of Maria under a crown.
No legend.
Oval, 10×9; red, tag. Complete, deep uneven impression.
E 327/588 1431

BOURNE (Lincs) Augustinian abbey
abbey seal
M096. St Peter, with nimbus, enthroned, his R hand raised in blessing, holding in his L hand a key over his shoulder. The throne faces to L, showing turned legs and stretchers; St Peter sits frontal with legs extended to L.
...IGILLV...CCLESIE.BEATI.PETRI.AP'LI.DE.BRVN (Lom)
Round, 55; red, tag. Nearly complete, deep clear impression.
E 25/19 Pl 5 1534

abbot's seal
M097. Under a double gothic canopy, two standing figures.
SIG... (BL)
Pointed oval, c.50×c.30; red, tongue. Indistinct impression, most of edge lost.
E 135/10/20, no. 2 (c.1400)

BOW (Midd) Benedictine priory (F)
priory seal
M098. Under a canopy resting on corbels, an abbot (St Leonard ?), standing, blessing and holding a crozier.
...M : SANCT[I:L]EONARDI... (Lom)
Pointed oval, 60×40; dark green, tag. Deep clear impression, upper edges lost.
E 42/471 (13c)

prioress's seal:
M099. The prioress (?), standing before the Virgin and Child enthroned on L.
Legend lost.
Pointed oval, c.25×c.15; red, tongue. Fragment of an indistinct impression. BM 4116.
E 329/200 1506

BOXGROVE (Sussex) Benedictine priory
priory seal
M100. The Virgin, seated, holding the Child on her R knee.
Legend indistinct.
Pointed oval, c.50×c.30; red, tag. Large fragment of a very indistinct impression from a 12c matrix. BM 2690.
E 326/11757 1532

BOXLEY (Kent) Cistercian abbey
abbey seal
M101. *Obv.* Under a canopy, the Virgin, seated on a throne with arcaded front, holding the Child on her L knee, her R hand raised. On either side, on the piers supporting the canopy, a quatrefoil aperture enclosing a head, full-face. Below, under a trefoiled arch, a monk, praying to R. On either side, a leafy branch.
(outer legend) ...MARIE.DE.BO... (Lom)
(inner legend) ...CORDI.VIRGO.B...
Rev. Under adjoining canopies, two standing figures); (R) an abbot, holding a crozier; (L) a headless figure. On either side, a twining branch.
(Outer legend) ...VDA...HIC / T...DEA... (Lom)
(inner legend) ...DOM.PPICIA.FACITO...
Round, 50; red-brown, detached on tag. Large fragment of a very deep clear impression from a 13c (?) matrix. BM 2691.
SC 13/R8 Pl 27 (1535)

BRADENSTOKE (Wilts) Augustinian priory
priory seal
M102. The Virgin, crowned, seated on a bench-type throne with coffered panels, holding the Child at her L knee. Above, rising from the throne on slender pillars, a trefoiled arch supporting a church-like canopy and pinnacles bearing flags and cross. On the outer sides of the canopy's pillars, two censing angels. On either side of the Virgin's head, (L) a crescent moon and (R) a sun. In the carved corbel beneath the Virgin's feet, a quatrefoil opening containing a monk's head.
SIGILL':ECCL'IE:BEAT[E.MARIE.D]E.BRADENSTOKA (Lom)
Pointed oval, 75×50; mottled green, tag. Nearly complete, deep clear impression, lower point lost. Has counterseal, **M105**. Also on E 322/27 (1539). Pedrick, plate XVI, 31. BM 2697.

E 329/137   Pl 20   (13c)
prior's seal: Simeon
M103. A standing figure.
...EMAR...   (Lom)
Pointed oval, c.40×c.25; uncoloured, varnished, tag.
Fragment of a good impression. Has counterseal,
M104.
E 42/326   (c.1233)
counterseal
M104. A bust under an arch ?
...RIORIS.DE.B...   (Lom)
Pointed oval, c.30×c.20; uncoloured, varnished, on
tag, as counterseal to **M103**. Fragment of an indistinct
impression.
E 42/326   (c.1233)
prior's seal: Geoffrey
M105. Under a trefoiled canopy, the Virgin and Child,
both half-length. Below, under a trefoiled arch, the
prior, kneeling in prayer to L.
S' PRIORIS DE / BRADENESTOK'   (Lom)
Pointed oval, 35×23; green, on tag, as counterseal to
M102. Complete, clear impression. BM 2698.
E 329/137   (13c)

BRADLEY *see* MAIDEN BRADLEY

BREAMORE (Hants) Augustinian priory
priory seal
M106. St Michael, in embroidered robes, wings
outspread, facing half R, standing on the dragon,
holding a long sword nearly level in his R hand and a
tall shield with boss upright in his L hand.
...LL...ELE   (Rom)
Pointed oval, c.60×40; orange-pink, tag. Deep clear
impression but most of edge lost. Has counterseal,
M109.
E 42/403   Pl 11   1277
priory seal
M107. St Michael slaying the dragon.
S' COMMV...ECCE.CONV...AELIS.DE BROM/...   (Lom)
Pointed oval, 60×45; red, tag. Deep distinct
impression, flattened, part of edge lost. From a matrix
closely resembling but not identical with that of **M106**.
E 329/70   Pl 47   1497
priory seal
M108. St Michael, robed, wings outspread, standing
on the dragon and thrusting a long spear into its mouth.
On his L arm, a shield charged with a cross formy.
Scrolls and pellets in the field on either side.
*S' COM[MV]...[ECCE.CO]NVENTVALIS/SCI/
MIC[HAELIS.DE.B[ROM/MORE]   (Lom)
Pointed oval, 65×40; coral-red, tongue. Deep clear
impression from a 13c matrix, slightly rubbed, edge

damaged on either side. BM 2734.
E 42/402   Pl 42   1531
prior's seal: Thomas
M109. St Michael, robed, wings outspread, standing
on the dragon and thrusting a long spear into its mouth;
holding in his L hand a shield charged with a cross, a
star and a crescent moon.
S' THOME PRIORIS DE BROMMORE   (Lom)
Pointed oval, 38×28; orange-pink, on tag, as
counterseal to **M106**. Complete, deep clear impression.
E 42/403   Pl 8   1277

BRECON (Brec) Benedictine priory
priory seal
M110. In a vaulted and panelled niche with pinnacled
canopy above and tabernacle work at the sides, the
eagle of St John the Evangelist, wings outspread,
reguardant, standing on a demi-wheel. Below,
arcading.
...LLVM.CONVENTVALE.DOMVS...BRECONIE   (BL)
Pointed oval, 73×45; bronze, tongue. Deep clear
impression, flattened, much lost on L side and upper R.
BM 2705. For the significance of the wheel see
Ezekiel, x, 13–14.
E 25/15   Pl 12   1534

BRETTON *see* MONK BRETTON

BREWOOD (Staffs) Benedictine priory (F)
priory seal
M111. The Virgin, seated in a canopied niche, her feet
on a carved corbel, holding the Child, with cruciform
nimbus, on her L side and a lily sceptre in her R hand.
...GILLUM COMUNE NIGRAR'MONIALIUM DE BRE...   (BL)
Pointed oval, c.54×42; red-brown, tag. Deep
impression, flattened, upper point and edge lost.
BM 2707.
E 322/29   1538

BRIDGNORTH (Salop) Holy Trinity, hospital
common seal
M112. Under a panelled canopy, the Holy Trinity.
Below, under an arch, a clerk, praying.
...PITAL SCE...TAT... NO   (BL)
Pointed oval, c.50×c.25; red, tag. Fragment, indistinct
impression.
C 146/5188   1457

BRIDGWATER (Som) St John the Baptist, hospital
common seal
M113. Under a triple canopy, on a four-arched
crenellated bridge with water flowing beneath, against a

diapered background, standing figures: (centre) the Virgin, holding the Child on her L side; (L) St John the Baptist, holding the Holy Lamb and Cross on a disk; (R) St Paul, holding a sword and a book.
S'.[COM]VNE.HOSPITALIS.SANCTI.[IOHANNIS.BAP...] ALTE... (Lom)
Pointed oval, c.68×45; red, tongue. Deep uneven impression, flattened, points and L edge lost. Also on E 25/16 (1534). BM 2709.
E 322/30   Pl 15   1539

BRINKBURN (Northumb) Augustinian priory
   prior's seal: William
M114. The prior, standing, vested for mass, blessing.
...D' BRINCBVRN... (Lom)
Pointed oval, c.35×c.23; uncoloured, tag. Indistinct impression, headless.
E 42/400   1254

BRISTOL (Glos) St Augustine's, Augustinian abbey
   abbey seal
M115. The abbey church. The facade contains two doorways each containing a figure, standing, mitred, blessing and holding a pastoral cross in his L hand. Beside each doorway, a rounded arch with tracery. Above, a pitched roof with cross finials, and a tall central tower with two arcaded storeys and a low conical spire, on either side of which is a pierced star. Below, two arches: under (L), a bishop or abbot, kneeling in prayer to R.
SIGILLVM.COM...STOLI... (Lom)
Pointed oval, c.73×c.43; red, tag. Deep uneven impression, flattened, much of edge lost. BM 2719.
E 25/17   Pl 4   1534
   abbot's seal: John
M116. The abbot, standing, vested for mass, holding a crozier and a book.
SIGILL' IOHIS ABBATIS SCI AVG:... (Lom)
Pointed oval, 50×30; dark green, tag. Deep clear impression, upper L edge lost. BM 2720.
E 327/46   Pl 25   (13c)

BRISTOL (Glos) St John the Baptist, Redcliff, Augustinian hospital
   common seal
M117. In a cusped oval, St John the Baptist, standing. Below, under an arch, a patriarchal cross.
...COMUNE HOSPITAL' SANCTI IOHA...BAPTISTA BRISTOLLIE (BL)
Pointed oval, 60×35; red, tag. Complete, deep uneven impression, centre much flattened. BM 2723.
E 322/31   1543

BRISTOL (Glos) St Mark's (Gaunt's), Augustinian hospital
   common seal
M118. Under a double canopy with crocketed gables and tabernacle work at the sides, two figures: (R) seated; (L) standing (the Annunciation ?). Below, between two shields (blank), a figure, kneeling in prayer to R.
...SCI.MARCI... (Lom)
Pointed oval, 55×32; red, tag. Nearly complete, deep impression almost effaced by flattening.
E 25/18   1534

BROOMHALL (Berks) Benedictine priory (F)
   priory seal
M119. St Margaret, crowned, standing on the dragon and thrusting a long spear into its mouth. On either side, a head facing inwards.
...CO...L (Lom)
Pointed oval, c.50×30; uncoloured, tongue. Rough impression, most of edge lost. Also on E 135/21/4 (1291).
E 42/401   Pl 26   1392

BRUERN (Oxon) Cistercian abbey
   abbey seal
M120. The abbot, standing, holding a book in his L hand.
+SIGILL...A (Lom)
Pointed oval, c.40×c.20; brown, tag. Small upper fragment. BM 2740.
E 326/11639   1213

BRUTON (Som) Augustinian priory, later abbey
   priory/abbey seal
M121. Under a church-like canopy resting on corbels, the Virgin, crowned, seated on a bench-type throne, holding the Child, with nimbus, on her L knee. On either side, a deeply-sunk pointed oval containing a man's head facing inwards; above them, (L) a star and (R) a crescent. Below the throne, under a trefoiled arch flanked by pinnacles, the prior and three monks, kneeling in prayer to L.
SIGILLVM:ECCLESIE:BE/ATE:MARIE:BRIUTONIE (Lom)
Pointed oval, 80×55; mottled green, detached on tag. Complete, fine impression. Has counterseal, **M122**. Also on E 25/22 (1531); E 322/33 (1529). BM 2743.
SC 13/F152   Pl 44   (n.d.)
   seal ad causas
M122. Under a trefoiled arch and a church-like canopy, the Virgin, seated on a bench-type throne, holding the Child on her L knee.
S' ECCLIE.BRV/TON.AD CAVSAS (Lom)

Pointed oval, 35×22; mottled green, detached on tag, as counterseal to **M121**. Complete, deep impression partly indistinct.

SC 13/F152   (n.d.)

prior's seal: Stephen

M123. The Virgin, crowned, seated on a throne, leaning to R, holding the Child, with nimbus, on her L knee. The throne has arcading below the seat, and has back and arms with a curved and crested upper rail and turned finials. Above, (L) a sun or wheel, (R) a crescent and star. Above the Virgin's head, tracery and a large quatrefoil panel with inscribed edge (illegible) containing a hand holding a pastoral staff between (L) a crescent and (R) a star. The Virgin's feet rest on a string-course with an (illegible) inscription; below, a clerk, half-length, praying to R.

...STEPHANI PRIO/...WTONIE   (Lom)

Pointed oval, c.50×30; green, tag. Very deep clear impression with much sharp detail, upper point lost and edge damaged. Has counterseal, **M124**. BM 2745.

DL 27/15   Pl 26   (13c)

prior's seal: Stephen

M124. Under a five-lobed arch resting on two traceried pinnacles, the Virgin, half-length, looking to R, holding the Child on her L knee. Below, under a trefoiled arch, the prior, half-length, praying to L.

+SIGILL' STEPH'I:PRIORIS D' BRIWTONE   (Lom)

Pointed oval, 35×24; green, on tag, as counterseal to **M123**. Complete, deep clear impression, slightly rubbed. BM 2744.

DL 27/15   (13c)

BUCKENHAM (Norf) Augustinian priory
priory seal

M125. Under a triple canopy with crocketed gables and pinnacles tipped with fleurs-de-lys: (centre) St James, standing, wearing pilgrim's hat, blessing with his R hand; (R) a monk, praying to L, beneath a shield (defaced); (L) (lost).

[S'P]RIOR.ET.CO...AP'LI.CANO...   (Lom)

Round, 50; red, tag. Deep clear impression, cracked and much lost. BM 2748.

E 25/20/1   1534

BUCKFAST (Devon) Cistercian abbey
abbey seal

M126. In a canopied niche with crockets and pinnacles, the Virgin, crowned, standing, holding the Child on her L side. On either side, a wavy branch of fruit and foliage; background hatched. Outside the canopy's shafts, indications of masonry.

S' CONVENTV/S : BVC/FESTRIE   (lom)

Round, 33; red, tag. Complete, deep clear impression, flattened. BM 2746.

E 322/34   1539

BUCKLAND (Som) Knights Hospitallers' priory, later Augustinian priory and hospital (F)
prioress's seal: Alice Reskemere

M127. In a cusped circle, hung from a tree, a shield of arms: *three wolves passant*.

...E PRIORISSE   (BL)

Round, c.30; dark brown, tongue. Deep impression, flattened, most of edge lost.

E 213/2   1429

prioress's seal (?)

M128. Between HEL and BRO (BL), a whelk shell. No legend.

Octagonal, 11; black, tongue. Complete, deep uneven impression.

E 213/3   1430

prioress's seal

M129. A patriarchal cross.

...PRIORISSE   (BL)

Round, 23; red, tag. Nearly complete, but distorted and flattened.

E 322/36   1539

BULLINGTON (Lincs) Gilbertine priory (M and F)
priory seal

M130. The Virgin, enthroned, holding the Child before her.

SIGILLVM [CAPIT]VLI PRIORIS ET CONVENTVS DE BV...GTON   (Lom)

Pointed oval, c.68×42; uncoloured, tag. Complete, uneven impression, partly defaced, cracked. From a 14c matrix. Has counterseal, **M131**. BM 2766.

E 322/24   1538

seal ad causas

M131. The Virgin, crowned and with nimbus, seated in a canopied niche, holding the Child on her L knee. Below, under a pointed arch, the prior, kneeling in prayer to R.

S' PRIOR'ET CONVENTVS DE BOLINGTON AD CAVSAS   (Lom)

Pointed oval, 55×30; uncoloured, on tag, as counterseal to **M130**. Complete, deep impression, cracked, parts flattened. BM 2769.

E 322/24   1538

prior's seal: Gilbert

M132. The bust of a tonsured man, looking to L. Legend lost.

Pointed oval (size uncertain); brown, tongue. Fragment only.

E 101/568/55, no. 3   1305

BURNHAM (Bucks) Augustinian abbey (F)
abbey seal

M133. Under a double canopy of trefoiled arches with

crocketed gables and pinnacles, the Coronation of the Virgin. Below, between initials S and N, a shield of arms: *on a chief three lozenges*.
SIGILLVM : CONVENT...ALIVM : DE . BVRNHAM   (Lom)
Pointed oval, 60×43; red-brown, tag. Deep indistinct impression, centre cracked and flattened and points lost. BM 2776.
E 322/37   1539

BURSCOUGH (Lancs) Augustinian priory
priory seal
M134. The priory church seen from S, showing chancel, nave with clerestory, central lantern with conical roof and knob, and western tower with conical roof and round staircase turret. A causeway leads to a portal in the nave. Above, a six-pointed star.
+...NICHO.../ DE B...TVDE   (Lom)
Round, 44; red, tongue. Deep clear impression, edge chipped. BM 2777.
DL 27/110   Pl 11   1381

BURTON LAZARS (Leics) Hospital and principal house of the Order of St Lazarus of Jerusalem in England
common seal
M135. A priest, half-length, vested for mass, both hands raised, holding a sceptre (?) in his R hand.
...ZARI...   (Lom)
Round, c.50; mottled green, tag. Large fragment (headless) of a deep clear impression.
E 327/50   (c.1200)
common seal
M136. In a sexfoil within a circle, the moulding enriched with dogtooth ornament and the field hatched, a priest, full face, half-length, vested for mass, holding a book in his L hand and a short trident in his R hand; above either shoulder, a cross. On either side, a shield of arms: (L) *a lion rampant*; (R) *a cross on a squared field*. In base, the letters B Z.
*S' COMVNE:ORDINIS:MILICIE:HOSPITALIS;SCI;LAZARI.DE BORTONE   (Lom)
Round, 60; red, tag. Complete, fine impression. Also on DL 27/121 (1351). BM 2789.
E 329/334   Pl 48   1515

BURTON UPON TRENT (Staffs) Benedictine abbey
abbey seal
M137. The Virgin, crowned, frontal, enthroned on a church with round-arched windows, shingle roof and four towers with conical roofs.
...M SAN...   (Lom)
Pointed oval, c.75×c.55; red, detached, on tongue.

Very deep impression, centre flattened, L side and most of edge lost. BM 2778.
SC 13/F159   Pl 5   (n.d.)

BURY ST EDMUNDS (Suff) Benedictine abbey
abbey seal
M138. *Obv.* The abbey church, with pinnacled roof, round-arched windows and arcades, and pepper-pot towers. In the upper part, two deeply-sunk circular compartments each containing a crowned head. In the lower part, three niches under gabled canopies, in each a crowned king, holding a sceptre in his R hand and his L hand raised before him.
SIGILLV [M CONVENTVS*ECCLES...MVNDI*REGIS*ET* MARTIR'S]   (Lom)
   Rev. The seal is divided into compartments by a cross of St Andrew carved with three cusps on each limb. In base, the martyrdom of St Edmund; in the upper space, between two angels, God the Father, holding a crown; on the upper limbs of the cross, two angels bearing up the soul of the martyr in a cloth.
[TELIS CONFODITVR EADMVNDVS ET ENSE FERITVR BESTIA QVEM MVNIT DEVS HVNC CELESTIB' VNIT] (Lom)
Round, 98; red, tag. Fragments of a fine impression. The description given above is based partly on this impression and that attached to E 322/88, partly on the British Museum catalogue. BM 2797.
E 42/254   1260
abbey seal
M139. Both obverse and reverse closely resemble M138, but differences of detail (apparent in the Plates) show that M138 is from another and later matrix. The legend is very indistinct but appears to be the same.
E 322/38   1539
privy seal
M140. *Obv.* Under a triple canopy on corbels, St Edmund, crowned, seated on a bench-type throne, between two mitred bishops or abbots vested for mass, each holding a crozier and extending a hand towards the king. Over the central trefoiled arch of the canopy, a cruciform church with central tower and spire. Below, between two embattled towers with windows, rising from an embattled well, a deeply-sunk trefoil with beaded moulding and a bead in each lobe.
AGMINE:STIPATVS:SEDE[T]ED:REX:PONTIFICA[TVS]
                                                        (Lom)
   Rev. The Martyrdom of St Edmund the King. The saint, crowned, standing, bound to a tree, pierced with many arrows; on either side, archers with bent bows. Below, under a trefoiled arch, the saint, kneeling, is beheaded by a man with a sword; on R, the wolf, guarding the severed head; in base, a deeply-sunk trefoil.

[SIGN]VM:SECRETVM:CAP'LI...AEDMVNDI:REGIS:ET:
MARTIRI[S]   (Lom)
Pointed oval, 80×50; red, tag. Nearly complete, deep
clear impression, parts rubbed. Illustrated in VCH
Suffolk, vol. II; Pedrick, plate XXI. BM 2801.
E 329/413   Pl 39   1533
   abbot's seal: Simon de Luton
M141. The abbot, standing on a carved corbel, vested
for mass, holding a crozier. On either side, a deeply-
sunk oval containing the head of a clerk; below each, an
arrow with a crown above.
   ...RACI/...SAN   (Lom)
Pointed oval, c.70×c.40; red, tag. Deep clear
impression, edge broken, figure headless. Has
counterseal, **M142.** BM 2804 and plate VII.
E 42/254   1260
   abbot's seal
M142. The beheading of St Edmund, with the wolf
guarding the head. Above, under a trefoiled arch and
canopy, the Virgin and Child.
[VIRGO DEVM] FERT DVX CAPVD AVFERT Q[D LVP'HIC
FERT]   (Lom)
Pointed oval, c.50×c.30; red, on tag, as counterseal to
M141. Deep clear impression, upper point lost.
BM 2804 and plate XII.
E 42/254   Pl 5   1260
   abbot's seal
M143. The abbot, standing on a corbel, vested for
mass, blessing with his R hand. Below, the wolf,
guarding St Edmund's head. On L, part of a shaft
supporting a canopy (lost) and an anchor.
   ...ABBAT...   (Lom)
Pointed oval, c.55×35; dark green, tag. Fragment of a
deep clear impression.
E 42/328   1331
   abbot's seal: William Babington
M144. In a grove of oak trees, the wolf, lying on the
ground with St Edmund's crowned head between its
paws; a scroll, lettered HER HER HER.
*SECRETV...BABYNGTON AB...BVRY   (BL)
Round, 38; dark red, tongue. Deep clear impression, L
and R edges lost.
E 43/509   Pl 11   1456
   abbot's seal: John Melford
M145. In a rich gothic housing with three canopied
niches, the Assumption of the Virgin between two
standing female figures, crowned, each holding a
sceptre and palm branch. Below, under an arch, the
abbot, mitred and holding crozier, kneeling in prayer to
R; on either side, a shield of arms: (L) *three crowns* (the
ABBEY); (R) *quarterly, France modern and England*.
SIGILLU IOHIS MELFORD ABBAT'/MO/N...TARII SCI
EDMUDI DE BURY   (BL)
Pointed oval, 82×56; red-brown, detached, in metal

skippet. Complete, deep uneven impression, some fine
detail. BM 2805.
SC 13/O59   Pl 44   (1514–39)

BUSHMEAD (Beds) Augustinian priory
   priory seal
M146. *Obv.* Under a canopy with slender side-shafts,
the Virgin, seated on a bench-type throne, holding the
Child on her L knee. On either side, a bishop,
half-length, facing inwards, mitred and holding a
crozier; below each, under an arch, a tonsured head
facing inwards.
   ...NA...   (Lom)
      Rev. The Dormition of the Virgin. Her body lies
prone on a draped bed. Above, the Virgin, enthroned, is
carried up into heaven by two angels who hold the
throne in a sheet slung between them. On either side, a
crowd of mourners.
   ...CCLIE.E...SCE...   (Lom)
Round, c.40; red, tag. Large central fragment of a fine
impression. BM 2646.
E 25/12   Pl 30   1534
   prior's seal: William
M147. In a canopied niche, the Virgin, seated, facing
half R, holding the Child on her knees; before her, on
R, a clerk, kneeling; flowers in the field.
AVE MARIA GRA PLENA DNS   (Lom)
Oval, 26×20; red, tag. Complete, deep impression with
sharp detail. BM 2648.
DL 27/225   1392

BUTLEY (Suff) Augustinian priory
   priory seal
M148. Under a gothic canopy, the Virgin, crowned,
enthroned, holding the Child on her L knee.
Legend lost.
Pointed oval, c.70×c.45; red, tag. Central fragment of a
deep impression, much flattened. BM 2816.
E 322/40   1538

BYLAND (Yorks) Cistercian abbey
   abbey seal
M149. Under a tall gothic canopy resting on two
slender columns, the abbot, standing, vested for mass,
holding a crozier and a book. On either side, a gabled
niche containing three monks facing inwards. Above, in
a gabled niche within the canopy, the Virgin, crowned,
seated, holding the Child on her L knee.
S' SCE MA...ATIS...   (Lom)
Pointed oval, 65×40; red, detached, on tongue. Deep
impression, L side lost, legend blurred. Clay, p. 13,
plate I, 9 and 10.
SC 13/F115   (n.d.)

CALAIS (Pas de Calais, France) Hospital
common seal
M150. The Virgin, standing, holding the Child on her L side, both with nimbus.
S.GASTEIUS.VAN.KALES (BL)
Pointed oval, 45×28; red, tag. Deep clear impression, flattened, points lost.
E 25/23/2 1535

CALDWELL (Beds) Augustinian priory
priory seal
M151. Under a triple canopy with crocketed gables and pinnacles, standing figures: (centre) the Virgin, crowned, holding the Child on her L side; (L) St John the Evangelist, holding a palm; (R) St John the Baptist, clad in skins, holding the Holy Lamb on a disk. Below, under an arch between tracery, the head and shoulders of a monk, praying to L.
SIGILLVM:COMVN...ORATVS.DE.CALDEWELLE (Lom)
Pointed oval, 65×40; red, tag. Complete except for points, deep clear impression, slightly flattened. Also on SC 13/D164 (fragment, n.d.). BM 2823.
E 25/26/2 Pl 19 1534

CAMBRIDGE (Cambs) Dominican house
common seal
M152. On a carved corbel, the Crucifixion, with the Virgin and St John. Above, on L, a star.
+S'.C...ICATOR...E (Lom)
Pointed oval, 47×c.30; dark green, tongue. Fragments of a fine impression.
E 43/114 1326
prior's seal: Richard Burton
M153. Under a canopy of a trefoiled arch resting on slender side-shafts, Our Lord, crowned and with nimbus, seated on a bench-type throne with arcaded front, his R hand raised in blessing. Below, under a rounded arch inscribed on the moulding ...NITATIS, a friar, half-length, praying.
S'.PRIORIS.FRVM.P/RED' CANTEBRVG (Lom)
Pointed oval, 33×22; brown, tongue. Nearly complete, deep uneven impression. Also on E 43/116 (1329).
E 43/115 1330

CAMBRIDGE (Cambs) Franciscan house
seal of the warden (custos)
M154. A splayed eagle, with nimbus, beak upraised, standing on a scroll lettered IOHAN'. In base, a friar, half-length, praying to L.
...NTIS:SVB:PEDE:PVRI (Lom)
Pointed oval, 31×19; red, tongue. Complete, deep impression, clear except for parts of legend.
E 43/117 Pl 31 1329

CAMBUSKENNETH (Stirling) Augustinian abbey
abbot's seal: John
M155. Under an elaborate canopy resting on four slender pillars, the Virgin, crowned, holding the Child on her L side, both half-length. Below, under a smaller canopy, the bust of the abbot, holding a crozier, facing L.
S' IOHANNIS AB...E KAMBISKINEL (Lom)
Pointed oval, 40×27; dark green, detached, on tag. Nearly complete, fine impression. Laing 991.
BM 15,230.
SC 13/B46 Pl 29 (n.d.)
abbot's seal: Patrick Dunbar
M156. Under a gabled and crocketed canopy with corner lanterns, the Virgin, seated, holding the Child on her L knee. Below, under a trefoiled arch, a canon, kneeling in prayer to R.
S' PATR' ABBATIS DE CABVSKYNETH (Lom)
Pointed oval, 43×25; mottled green, detached, on cords. Complete, deep clear impression. Laing 992.
BM 15,232.
SC 13/E47 (13c)
abbot's seal: Robert
M157. In a late gothic housing, the Virgin, standing, holding the Child on her R side. Below, under a mitre, a shield of arms (defaced).
S' ROB.../I.A...CA...KYN (Rom)
Pointed oval, 60×40; red, detached, on tag. Complete, very uneven and indistinct impression.
SC 13/F121 (n.d.)
office of abbot
M158. Under a gothic canopy with conical roof, the Virgin, crowned, standing, holding the Child on her R side, foliage around her. Below, on a crozier, a shield of arms: *on a fesse between three mullets, three roundels*.
S' OFFICII...ABB'IS.D'.CAMBVSKYNET (BL)
Pointed oval, 60×35; red, detached, on tag. Complete, deep uneven impression. Also on SC 13/F34 (n.d). Laing 993. BM 15233. Birch and Laing read the third word in the legend as OFFICIALITATIS, which from this impression is unlikely.
SC 13/F35 Pl 29 (n.d.)

CAMMERINGHAM (Lincs) Premonstratensian priory
prior's seal: Ralph
M159. An eagle, facing R.
Legend defaced.
Pointed oval, (uncertain); dark brown, tongue. Fragment only.
E 101/568/51, no. 4 1303

CAMPSEY ASH (Suff) Augustinian priory (F)
priory seal
M160. Under an elaborate canopy of three arches with

pinnacles, crockets, and tracery panels on either side, the Virgin, crowned, seated on a bench-type throne, looking to L and holding the Child who stands on her L knee.

...IORESSE.ET.CONVE...E.DE.CAMPISSEY   (Lom)
Pointed oval, c.60×40; dark brown, tag. A fine impression, lower part lost. BM 2830.
DL 27/18   Pl 24   1352

CANONS ASHBY (Northants) Augustinian priory
priory seal
M161. The Virgin, with nimbus, frontal, seated, holding the Child before her on her lap and a fleur-de-lys sceptre in her L hand.

+SIGILLVM SANCTE MARIE DE ESSEBI   (Lom)
Pointed oval, 57×38; brown, tag. Complete, deep and very clear impression. BM 2566.
DL 25/329   Pl 34   1334
priory seal
M162. The Virgin, crowned, seated on a bench-type throne with arcading on the front panel and a tall turned finial at either end, holding the Child on her L knee, the field diapered lozenge. In base, DE' above S.A.

...E ESSEBI CANONICORVM   (Lom)
Pointed oval, 55×35; red, tag. Deep clear impression, cracked, parts of R side lost. BM 2567.
E 25/2   Pl 21   1534
prior's seal: Geoffrey
M163. The prior, standing, his R hand before him, holding a tall cross in his L hand. On R, sprigs of foliage; on L, a small figure of an archer (?).

SIGILL': GALFRIDI:PRIORIS:DE:E...(Lom)
Pointed oval, 45×25; orange, tag. Nearly complete, deep but not sharp impression.
E 329/188   (13c)
prior's seal: Adam de Buckingham ?
M164. The Virgin, standing, holding the Child on her L arm; on R, a canon, kneeling in prayer.

...RIS:DE:AS...CORVM:A...   (Lom)
Pointed oval, c.40×c.32; brown, tongue. Clear impression, much of edge lost. Also on E 135/21/43 (1326). BM 2568.
E 326/8925   1327

CANONSLEIGH (Devon) Augustinian abbey (F)
abbey seal
M165. Under an arch within a gabled canopy, the Virgin, crowned, seated on a bench-type throne, holding the Child on her L knee, her R hand on her breast; under her feet, a carved corbel. To either side of the throne, kneeling figures: (L) a monk holding up a feather or ear of corn? (R) a nun.

S' CONVENTVS A/BBAT[IE.D]E.LEY/A CANONICARV (Lom)
Pointed oval, 63×38; red, tag. Complete except for points, deep clear impression, slightly uneven and flattened. BM 3436.
E 322/123   Pl 29   1539

CANTERBURY (Kent) Christ Church, Benedictine cathedral priory
priory seal
M166. *Obv.* The cathedral church, seen from W. A steep roof with diaper pattern, and a clerestory of pointed arches. Three towers, one central, two attached to transepts, all with three tiers of arcading. The central tower has a tall shingled spire, between corner pinnacles, topped with a fleur-de-lys. Each transept tower has a spire between pinnacles and two deeply-sunk openings, each containing a head; in the lower openings, (L) St Elphege and (R) St Dunstan. On the W front, double doors, closed, beneath a large triangular tympanum containing the head and shoulders of Our Lord between IC and XC and above EST.DOMVS.H'.XPI. On either side of the central tower, a censing angel leans down from clouds. Beyond the transept towers, the N and S fronts of the transepts are half seen. Below, in front, the city wall, crenellated, with two watch towers and inscription MVRI.METROPOL'.ISTI.

SIGILLVM:ECCLESIE:XPI[STI:CAN]TVARIE:PRIME:
SEDIS:BRITANN[IE]   (Lom)

Rev. The martyrdom of St Thomas, seen through the great portal of the cathedral. The portal consists of two pointed arches, with cusped inner mouldings, resting on a clustered central shaft and contained within a large rounded arch in whose tympanum is a mandorla containing the head and shoulders of Our Lord. The martyrdom scene, deeply sunk within the arches, shows (R) the archbishop, kneeling, and Grim, holding a cross; (L) two knights, in chain mail and surcoats, running in, holding swords and shields (one showing part of *a bear*, FITZURSE). Above the portal, in three rounded arches, two demi-angels lift the martyr's soul to heaven. Above, in a trefoil within the central gable, Our Lord, half-length, with nimbus and with a crown before him. The corner buttresses are carried up into pinnacles. On either side extend the transepts (?) each having a round-arched portal containing (L) two knights in armour, (R) three monks. On either side of the central gable, an angel leans down holding a crown.

+EST:HVIC:VITA:MORI:PRO:QVA:DVM:VIXIT:AMORI
MORS:ERAT:ET;MEMORI:PER:MORTEM:VIVIT:
HONORI   (Lom)
Round, 93; light red-brown, cords. Complete, deep clear impression of a very fine and elaborate

architectural design in the style of the earlier 13c. Also on E 33/2 (1504); E 30/1400 (1362); E 211/68 (1515); E 329/401 (1477); SC 13/A163 (a loose impression possibly dateable to 1233). BM 1373–8, described as Third Seal; *see* especially the particulars given under 1373 and 1374. *See* also V.C.H. *Kent*, vol. II, pp. 120–121 for a description of this seal (by R.C. Fowler, from BM 1373) and illustration.

E 25/25   Pl 17   1534

prior's seal: (Roger of St Elphege)
M167. A small defaced fragment; red, tag.

E 135/6/1   1243

prior's seal: John (de Woodnesbergh)
M168. In a canopied niche, the Virgin, crowned, and with nimbus, seated, holding the Child who stands on her L knee. On either side, a canopied niche containing emblems of the four Evangelists: (L) St John and St Mark; (R) St Luke and St Matthew. Below, under an arch, the prior, kneeling in prayer to L.
...RRIN:/...   (Lom)
Oval, 28×25; red, tongue. Deep impression, flattened, most of edge lost.

E 213/424   Pl 31   1411

CANTERBURY (Kent) St Augustine's, Benedictine abbey

abbey seal
M169. *Obv.* In the central lower compartment, the baptism of King Ethelbert: the king, frontal, crowned, up to his chest in a carved font; on L, St Augustine, standing, mitred, blessing the king, his pastoral staff behind him. On R, a priest, standing, asperging the king; above, the Dove, descending. In the central upper compartment, within a double-canopied housing, seated figures: (L) St Peter, holding a book and keys; (R) St Paul, holding a book and a sword. Above, Two shields of arms: *two keys in saltire*. On either side, a transept, with diapered roof and gable-end and two tiers of arcading, containing (L) two monks and (R) a king and a monk, all kneeling in prayer and looking inwards to the baptism; above, on either side, a censing angel, leaning down from heaven.
SIGILL'.MONASTERII.BEATOR'.PETRI.ET.PAVLI. SCIQ'.AVGVSTINI.ANGLOR.AP'LI.CANTVAR   (Lom)
Rev. In the centre, under a canopy with cusped arch and ogee gable, St Augustine, enthroned, blessing and holding a pastoral cross; in the field, the inscription AV/G'/TI/NI. On St Augustine's breast, a round reliquary, resembling a seal, containing three crowned heads surrounded by an unclear legend; below his feet, a string course inscribed P. AVGVSTIN'.ANGL'.APL'S and quatrefoils below. Above, under arched canopies, small figures of two archbishops, named on the plinths as S'ME[LLITVS] and S'LA[VRENTIVS]; between them,

two shields of arms: *a cross*. On either side of St Augustine, a standing figure of (L) a bishop and (R) a queen, named on the plinths as S' BIRINVS and BERTA; above, under arched canopies, two archbishops, enthroned, named on the plinths as S'TEODOR and S'IVSTVS. Below, in the exergue, a horned mask between (L) a lion and (R) a wyvern.
ANGLIA:Q':DOMINO:FIDEI:SOCIATVR:AMORE HOC:AUGUSTINO:DEBETVR:PATRIS:ONORE   (Lom)
Round, 95; brick-red, detached, on red and white plaited silk laces in silver skippet. Complete, fine impression of a fine and elaborate architectural design, slightly flattened. Also on E 42/235 (1393); E 322/49 (1539). BM 2845, 2846. A fine and complete impression, attached to a charter of Thomas Hunden, abbot 1405–1426, was sold at Sotheby's 26.6.1967 (lot 733).

SC 13/I90   Pl 41   (n.d.)

CANTERBURY (Kent) St Gregory's, Augustinian priory

priory seal
M170. *Obv.* Under a trefoiled arch on slender columns, archbishop Lanfranc (the founder), seated, mitred, blessing and holding a pastoral cross. On either side, under a half-arch, a seated figure: (L) the head only; (R) St Edburga, with nimbus, on a bench-type throne, holding a crozier and a book, beside her the vertical inscription S'EDBVRGA.
SIGILLVM.CONVENTVS.ECCLESIE.S...NTVARIE   (Lom)
Rev. An all-over design of four-petalled flowers each enclosed in two concentric beaded circles, with a smaller flower in the space between each group of four (contiguous) circles.
No legend.
Round, 75; bronze-green, tag. Deep clear impression, one quarter lost (lower L side of Obv). BM 2855.

E 25/26/1   Pl 51   1535

CANTERBURY *see also* THANNINGTON

CANWELL (Staffs) Benedictine priory
prior's seal ?
M171. The prior, standing, blessing and holding a crozier(?).
Legend lost.
Pointed oval, c.70×?; red, tongue. Small central fragment.

E 327/30   1407

CARISBROOKE (IOW, Hants) Benedictine priory
prior's seal: Andrew
M172. The Virgin, half-length, turning to R, holding

the Child on her L side. On R, a long-stemmed trefoil. Below, under a pointed arch between gabled and traceried piers, a figure, half-length, praying to R.

SIGILLVM.ANDREE.PRIOR...ROC (Lom)
Pointed oval, 43×25; mottled green, tongue. Deep clear impression, L edge lost. BM 2876.
E 329/166 1271

CARMARTHEN (Carm) Augustinian priory
priory seal
M173. In a canopied niche with tabernacle work at the sides, a standing figure.
S CA...TUS.CA...(?) (BL)
Pointed oval, c.50×35; red, tongue. Impression almost entirely effaced by flattening, points lost.
E 25/23/1 1534

CARTMEL (Lancs) Augustinian priory
priory seal
M174. The Virgin, seated on a bench-type throne, holding the Child on her R knee.
[...IGIL...NVEN...E:MAR]IE:DE[KERMEL] (Lom)
Pointed oval, c.75×c.50; uncoloured, varnished brown, tag. Central fragment of a very deep clear impression of a fine seal. Has counterseal, M175. BM 2882.
DL 25/290   Pl 29 (13c)
counterseal
M175. St Michael, standing on the dragon, holding a shield and spear.
...M SE...TI... (Lom)
Pointed oval, c.50×c.35; uncoloured, varnished, on tag, as counterseal to M174. Large central fragment of a very deep clear impression. BM 2882.
DL 25/290 (13c)
prior's seal: William
M176. The Virgin, crowned, standing, holding a lily and book.
+SIGILL'W...S DE KERMEL (Lom)
Pointed oval, c.35×23; uncoloured, tag. Deep impression, rubbed, lower edge lost. BM 2883.
DL 27/133 1214
prior's seal: Absalon
M177. The Holy Lamb with banner.
+SIGILL'FRIS ABSALON' PRIORIS DE KMEL (Lom)
Pointed oval, 30×20; red, tag. Complete, clear impression.
DL 25/282 [1285/8]

CATESBY (Northants) Cistercian priory (F)
seal ad causas
M178. Under a panelled canopy, the Virgin, enthroned, holding the Child on her L knee. Below,

under a trefoiled arch, a figure, half-length, praying to L.
...SBI AD CAVS... (Lom)
Pointed oval, 50×30; red, tag. Badly flattened, most of edge lost. Also on E 41/203 (1458). BM 2889.
E 326/11436 1434
priory seal (used as)
M179. In a beaded circle, a hare.
+P...SMIV(?) (Lom)
Round, 18; light brown, tag. Deep clear impression, part of edge lost. This is apparently the personal seal of a layman, although used by Orabilla the prioress and described as the common seal in the sealing clause.
E 327/206 1354
prioress's seal: Isabel or Elizabeth Benett
M180. Under a canopy with panelled sides, the prioress, standing, holding a staff in her L hand.
SIG DOMINE (?) ELISABETHE BENETTE PRIORIS... (BL)
Pointed oval, 45×30; red, tag. Nearly complete, badly flattened. The name in the legend is badly cut in a later style of lettering.
E 40/5021 1469

CATLEY (Lincs) Gilbertine priory (M and F)
priory seal
M181. The Virgin, crowned, seated, holding the Child on her L knee. Below, under an arch, the prior, half-length, praying to R.
S'.PRIORATVS/.DE CATTELE (Lom)
Pointed oval, 35×21; red-brown, tag. Complete, deep impression, cracked. BM 2981.
E 322/51 1538

CERNE ABBAS (Dors) Benedictine abbey
abbey seal
M182. The facade of the abbey church: two lateral towers with spires flank the W end of the nave, with portal below (doors open), windows above of lancets and plate-tracery, and gable with leafy crockets on L of which a bird perches. Below, under masonry arches, two figures, half-length, upholding the edifice, of (L) St Augustine and (R) Aylmer, earl of Cornwall, the founder; on L, a cinquefoil.
Legend lost.
Pointed oval, c.75×c.55; red, tag. Very deep clear impression, all edge lost. Also on E 322/52 (1539); E 326/6354 (1515); SC 13/R11 (n.d.). Pedrick, plate XLI, 82. BM 2892.
E 326/12255   Pl 29 1534
abbot's seal: Thomas Corton
M183. In three adjoining niches with rich late gothic canopies, standing figures: (centre) the Virgin, crowned and with nimbus, holding the Child on her R side and a

fleur-de-lys sceptre in her L hand: (L) St Katharine, crowned, holding her wheel; (R) St Margaret, crowned, with dragon and lance. Below, under an arch, the abbot, frontal, holding a crozier, kneeling in prayer, between two shields of arms: (L) *a lion rampant and a bordure charged with roundels* (earl of CORNWALL, founder); (R) *a cross engrailed between four lilies slipped* (the ABBEY).

...DE CEERNE (BL)

Pointed oval, 70×43; red, tongue. Deep impression with detail, partly flattened, edge lost or defaced. BM 2893

E 326/11764 (1525–9)

CHACOMBE (Northants) Augustinian priory
priory seal

M184. St Peter, standing, holding keys ...

...ILL.APOSTO... (Lom)

Pointed oval [70×40]; red, tag. Fragment. The matrix of this seal, formerly in the Tyssen collection, is described by C. S. Perceval in *Proceedings of the Society of Antiquaries of London*, 2nd series, Vol. IX, p. 37. BM 2896 is a cast from this matrix and shows standing figures of St Peter, holding keys, and St Paul, holding a sword; above, a hand of blessing; below, under a rounded arch, the prior, praying to L; legend +SIGILL'.APOSTOLORV.PETRI.ET.PAVLI.DE.CHAVCVMBA (Lom)

E 25/29 1534

prior's seal: Henry de Kegworth

M185. Under a double canopy with pinnacles and crockets, standing figures: (L) St Paul holding a sword; (R) St Peter holding keys. Below, under a rounded arch, the prior, kneeling in prayer to L.

S'HEN...ORIS DE CHAVCOMBE (Lom)

Pointed oval, 38×22; red, tag. Nearly complete, clear impression. BM 2897.

E 329/177 1353

prior's seal

M186. Under an arch, the prior kneeling in prayer to R. In base, on L, a shield of arms (?)

...DE... (BL)

Pointed oval, c.50×c.30; red, tongue. Small lower fragment.

C 146/1110 1432

CHATTERIS (Camb) Benedictine abbey (F)
abbey seal

M187. The Virgin, crowned, seated on a throne with animal-headed arms, holding a sceptre with flowered end in her R hand and a book in her L hand.

+SIGILLVM SANCTE [M] ARIE (Lom)

Pointed oval, 65×48; red, tag. Nearly complete, deep impression from a fine 12c matrix, flattened, edge

defaced. BM 2895.

E 322/53 Pl 56 1538

CHEPSTOW (Monm) Benedictine priory
priory seal

M188. In a canopied niche with tall pinnacles and with tabernacle work at the sides, the Virgin, crowned, seated on a panelled throne, holding the Child on her R knee. Below, a shield of arms: *a gate or portcullis with pendent chains.*

S'CO...SCE.MARIE... (BL)

Pointed oval, 65×35; red, tongue. Nearly complete, deep impression, uneven and blurred. BM 2898.

E 25/30/1 1534

CHERTSEY (Surrey) Benedictine abbey
abbey seal

M189. St Peter, holding a key and book, seated in a niche under a pinnacled canopy. On either side, a traceried panel. Below, under an arch, a monk, praying to L.

...PE/TR... (Lom)

Pointed oval, 45×c.30; red, tongue. Large central fragment, headless, of a fine impression, cracked.

E 213/72 1372

abbey seal

M190. The abbey church seen from N, on a plinth of two steps. The aisleless nave, with sloping roof, has two upper windows and a central gabled porch; the E and W gables have cross finials; from the centre of the roof rises a tall tower of three storeys with conical roof. W of the nave projects a porch or narthex with an upper window; at E end is an apse with upper window and cross finial. Below, in the exergue, a scroll of foliage.

+[SIGILLVM.SANCTI.PETRI.CEROTIZ] AECLE
(Rom, but the last C is angular)

Oval, c.65×60; brown-red, tag. Deep clear impression from a 12c matrix, most of edge lost. Also on E 322/54 (1539); SC 13/F149 (n.d.). BM 2899.

E 212/64 Pl 51 1526

CHESHUNT (Herts) Benedictine priory (F)
priory seal

M191. The Virgin, seated, holding a fleur-de-lys in either hand, the Child on her lap before her. Legend lost.

Pointed oval, c.65×c.30; green, tag. Large central fragment. Also on C 146/2433 (1312), small fragment which supplies ...VENTVS... (Lom) of the legend. Temp. Denise, prioress.

E 326/11596 (n.d.)

prioress's seal: Margaret Charroy

M192. Small fragment, red, tongue.

E 135/2/41, no. 36 1533

CHESTER (Ches) St Mary's, Benedictine priory (F)
priory seal
M193. The Virgin, seated on a bench-type throne with turned legs, her feet on a corbel, holding the Child on her L knee and a flowered sceptre in her R hand.
...NIAL...CESTR... (Lom)
Pointed oval, c.70×50; dark green, tag. Deep clear impression, most of edge lost. BM 2917.
E 327/273   Pl 32   (temp. Edw. I)

CHESTER (Ches) St Werburgh's, Benedictine abbey
abbey seal
M194. *Obv.* The W front of the abbey church. Under a central arch, St Werburgh, seated on a bench-type throne, holding a crozier and a book. In a niche on either side, a monk, facing inwards; above him, in a deep quatrefoil opening, a head. In a trefoiled opening in the central gable, a head. Below, in the exergue, under a trefoiled arch, a head.
...ILLVM:CONVENTVS:E[C]CLESIE:SANCTE:WERBVRGE...
(Lom)

Rev. The facade of a church, less rich than on Obv. Under a central arch, St Oswald, crowned, seated, holding a sceptre and an orb with cross. In a niche on either side, standing figures: (L) St Peter; (R) St Paul.
...R:PRO...IGILLVM (Lom)
Round, 70; uncoloured, tag. Nearly complete, deep clear impression, cracked, Rev flattened and chipped. Pedrick, plate XIX. BM 2913.
E 42/388   Pl 33 (Obv)   1538

CHICKSANDS (Beds) Gilbertine priory (M and F)
seal ad causas
M195. Under a canopy with crenellated centre, the Annunciation. The angel, kneeling on L, appears to hold a cross. Below, under an arch, a canon, praying to R.
S' CONVEN...MARIE...CHIKESAND.AD CAUSAS (BL)
Pointed oval, c.53×c.37; red, tag. Deep uneven impression, flattened and defaced, part of R edge lost. BM 2954.
E 322/56   1538

CHIPLEY (Suff) Augustinian priory
prior's seal
M196. The Virgin and Child, both half-length. Below, under a trefoiled arch, a monk, kneeling in prayer to R.
+S' P[RIO]RIS DE [CH]IPPELEIA (Lom)
Pointed oval, 33×20; dark green, tongue. Clear impression, edge chipped. BM 2958.
E 42/338   1271

CHIRBURY (Salop) Augustinian priory
priory seal
M197. The W front of the priory church, with round-arched portal and windows and central and flanking towers.
...LVM SA... (Lom)
Pointed oval, 70×50; uncoloured, tag. Deep impression flattened, upper point lost, legend defaced. Has counterseal, **M198**.
E 326/8687   (13c)
prior's seal: Walter ?
M198. The prior, standing on a corbel, vested for mass.
SIGIL' WA... (Lom)
Pointed oval, 50×30; uncoloured, on tag, as counterseal to **M197**. Deep but very indistinct impression, upper L edge lost.
E 326/8687   (13c)

CHRISTCHURCH (Hants) Augustinian priory
priory seal
M199. The priory church, showing a gabled facade with arched window above porch; on either side, a transept with arched window, diapered (shingled ?) roof, and terminal tower with arched window, conical roof and knob finial; above, a large central tower with arcading, ribbed conical roof, knob and cross.
SIG[ILLV.ECCL]E SCE TRINITATIS DE TOINHAM   (Lom)
Round, 63; mottled green, tag. Nearly complete, deep clear impression, in a linen bag with parchment label. Also on E 326/5185 (1282) and 9158 (1324); E 328/121 (1323); E 329/355 (1323). BM 4220.
DL 27/25   Pl 10   (12c)
priory seal
M200. Very closely resembles **M199**.
SIGILLVM:XPI:ECCLESIE:DE:TWOVNH[AM]   (Lom)
Round, 60; green, tag. Nearly complete, deep clear impression. Also on E 326/9413 (1283); E 327/121 (1323). BM 4221.
E 326/9158   1324
prior's seal: Edmund
M201. In a canopied niche with trefoiled arch and crocketted gable, Our Lord, seated, blessing and holding a book. In base, under an arch, the prior, praying.
S':FRIS:EDMVNDI:PRIORIS/XPI ECCL'IE DE TWYNHAM
(Lom)
Pointed oval, 56×25; dark green, on red and yellow plaited silk laces. Complete, deep clear impression. Also on E 326/5321 (1324); SC 13/R12 (n.d.). BM 4224.
E 329/355   1323

CIRENCESTER (Glos) Augustinian abbey
abbey seal
M202. On a carved corbel, under a tower-like canopy with tabernacle work at the sides, the Coronation of the Virgin.

...CLESIE...ARIE.CIR...TRIE (Lom)
Pointed oval, 80×55; red, tag. Deep uneven impression, much cracked and damaged, from a fine matrix. BM 2959.
E 25/31 1534
privy seal
M203. The Virgin, crowned, half-length, holding the Child; below, a shield of arms: *on a chevron three ram's heads caboshed*.

S' SECRETVM CIRENCESTRIE (BL)
Round, 18; red, tongue. Complete, clear impression.
E 43/107 1446
abbot's seal: John Leckhampton
M204. In three adjoining canopied niches: (centre) the Virgin, crowned, seated, holding the Child on her L knee, a plain shield below; (L) St Katharine, crowned, standing, holding her wheel; (R) St Margaret, standing, holding a spear. Below, under an arch, a canon, half-length, praying to R.

SIM PROCVL A PENA PROCVL AVE GRA PLENA (BL)
Round, 29; red, tongue. Complete, deep clear impression, flattened.
C 148/67 1410
abbot's seal: John Sobbury
M205. The Virgin, crowned, half-length, holding the Child on her L side; above her, a shield of arms: *on a chevron, three hearts*.

SIGILLU IOHIS SOBBURY ABB'TIS CIRENCESTRIE (BL)
Round, 25; red-brown, detached, in tin skippet. Complete, deep clear impression. Also on E 329/268 (1476).
SC 13/069 (1461–c.1478)

CLATTERCOTE (Oxon) St Leonard's, Gilbertine hospital
priory seal
M206. St Leonard, standing, vested for mass, holding a crozier and a book.

+[SIGILL' SCI LEONARDI DE] CLATRECOT (Lom)
Pointed oval, 50; uncoloured, tag. Complete, indistinct impression.
E 42/265 (c.1200)

CLEEVE (Som) Cistercian abbey
abbey seal
M207. Under a three-gabled canopy with tabernacle work at the sides, the Virgin, crowned, standing, holding the Child on her L arm.

SIGILLVM...MMV...BATHIE:DE:CLY... (Lom)

Pointed oval, 55×40; red-brown, tag. Deep clear impression of an elegant seal, points lost, edge chipped.
WARD 2/176/1 Pl 56 1534

CLERKENWELL Augustinian priory (F)
priory seal
M208. The Virgin, with nimbus, frontal, seated on a bench-type throne, hands extended, holding a lily in her L hand; before her, on her lap, the Child, with cruciform nimbus, frontal, holding a sceptre tipped with a cross in his R hand.

+SIG...RIE...[FON]TE CLERICOR' (Lom)
Pointed oval, c.80×c.60; bronze, tag. Deep clear impression, cracked and parts lost. Also on E 42/88 (c.1200). Illus. (woodcut) in W. J. Pinks, *History of Clerkenwell*, 1881, p. 31. BM 2962.
DL 27/64 Pl 32 (1214–55)
official seal (of prioress ?)
M209. Under a small canopy with spiral columns, the Virgin, crowned, standing, holding the Child on her R arm.

...OFFICII... (BL)
Pointed oval, c.42×c.25; red, tongue. Clear impression, points and most of edge lost. BM 2964.
E 329/93 Pl 38 1530
prioress's seal: Rose Reigate
M210. Used by the prioress, but apparently the same matrix as **M211**.

...LERKENWELL (BL)
Pointed oval, c.40×c.25; red, tongue. Two impressions, indistinct and broken.
E 213/431 1521
seal of the receiver of revenues
M211. Under a canopy, the Virgin, crowned, seated, holding the Child on her L knee. Below, under a rounded arch, a figure, half-length, praying to R.

[S' RECEPTOR' REDDIT' DE CLERENWEL] (Lom)
Pointed oval, 40×25; red, tongue. Complete, indistinct impression. Illustrated and described in W. J. Pinks, *History of Clerkenwell*, 1881, p. 31.
E 329/161 1514

CLERKENWELL St John's, Hospitallers' house
counterseal
M212. St John (?), his R hand raised.

+S FRATR... (Lom)
Pointed oval, c.40×c.32; brown, tag. Large fragment of an indistinct impression.
E 40/14312 (13c)
seal of indulgence
M213. In a pointed oval panel, the Holy Lamb, with banner and cross. Below, a large shield of arms: *a cross* (hatched). Round the panel's inner edge, a fringe.

+S' INDULGENCIE HOSPITALIS / IHERUSALEM IN ANGLIA (BL)

Pointed oval, 55×30; red, tag. Complete, clear impression, slightly flattened.

E 212/82   Pl 32   1534

prior's seal: Guarneri of Naples

M214. The prior, kneeling before (L) a patriarchal cross on a pedestal. In the field, SALVE CRUX SCA ARBOR DIGNA.

[S'.PRI]ORIS:FR[ATRVM : HOSPITAL'...A]NG[LIA]   (Lom)

Round, c.50; uncoloured, varnished brown, tag. Deep clear impression, most of edge lost. Has counterseal, **M215.** Also on DL 25/320 (1190). BM 4524.

E 40/6708   1189

counterseal

M215. The head of St John the Baptist, frontal.

S' GARN' PRIORIS HOSP IER IN ANGLI'   (Lom)

Round, 30; uncoloured, varnished brown, on tag, as counterseal to **M214.** Complete, clear impression. BM 4527.

E 40/6708   1189

prior's seal: used by William de Tottehale

M216. Within a circle of pellets, the bearded head of St John the Baptist, frontal, between (L) the sun and (R) the moon.

+S' PRIORIS:HOSPIAL':IERL' IN ANGL'   (Lom)

Round, 38; dark brown, tag. Complete, clear impression. Has counterseal, **M217.** Also on E 40/14312 (n.d.); E 42/49 (1323) used by Thomas Larcher, prior; E 212/95 (1371), two impressions, both in blue damask bags, one has a fine head, used by John Pavely: E 329/15 (n.d.), used by John Pavely. BM 4531.

E 329/55   Pl 42   1302

prior's counterseal: William de Tottehale

M217. A shield of arms, defaced.

*S'FRIS WILLI DE TOTHALE   (Lom)

Round, 25; dark brown, on tag, as counterseal to **M216.** Complete, legend clear, shield defaced.

E 329/55   1302

prior's seal: Philip de Gragnana

M218. A griffin, walking to R.

+S' PRECEPTOR...M   (Lom)

Round, c.32; bronze, tag. Deep clear impression, lower part lost. Has counterseal, **M219.**

E 41/193   1313

seal of visitor?

M219. In a panel of eight cusps, a shield of arms: *a lion rampant.*

...VARZEBVRG+   (Lom)

Round, 30; dark green, on tag, as counterseal to **M218.** Deep rather indistinct impression, lower part lost.

E 41/193   1313

prior's seal: John Supton

M220. In a triangular panel with curved sides and cusping, a shield of arms: *a fesse between three mullets.*

...S'DE...   (Lom)

Round, 23; red, tongue. Shield clear, edge lost.

E 213/360   1388

prior's seal: John Weston

M221. A shield of arms: *ermine, on a chief five roundels.* Legend lost.

Round, c.32; green, tag. Clear impression, edge lost.

E 327/593   1481–2

prior's seal: William Weston

M222. A shield of arms: *ermine, on a chief five roundels;* above, a helmet, with mantling and crest: *a crowned and bearded head.* The scrolled mantling fills the field.

WILLELMVS:WESTON:PRIOR:HOSPITALIS:S:IOHIS:IERLM:-IN:ANGLIA   (Rom)

Round, 50; red-brown, detached, in tin skippet. Complete, fine impression, cracked.

SC 13/O36   (n.d.)

conservator's seal

M223. A tall patriarchal cross between two canopies, beneath which stand on corbels, (L) St Peter, holding keys, and (R) St John the Baptist holding the Holy Lamb, their inner hands touching the cross.

SIGILLVM:CONSERVATORIS:IVRIUM:ET:PRIVILEGIOR:DOM:SCI: IOHIS:IERLM:IN:ANGLIA   (BL)

Pointed oval, 32×50; red, tag. Complete, fine impression, embedded in uncoloured wax. Also on E 21/3/35, 7 and 13 (1525); SC 13/H68 (n.d.).

E 21/3/15   1524–5

proctor general's seal: Leonard de Tibertis

M224. In an oval panel, a winged demi-lion, issuing from waves, holding a book. On either side, a shield of arms: (L) *three flowering mounts (?)*; (R) *quarterly, 1 and 4 barry, 2 and 3 a lion rampant.*

S'LEON/A...TOR   (Lom)

Round, 33; dark green, tag. Nearly complete, fine impression of centre, legend chipped and blurred. Has counterseal, **M225.**

E 41/193   1313

proctor general's privy seal: Leonard de Tibertis

M225. An oval gem in a round setting: Demeter, seated on a throne, holding two ears of corn in her R hand.

+SECRETVM...ARDI   (Lom)

Round, 25; dark green, on tag, as counterseal to **M224.** Fine impression of centre, legend fainter, lower L part lost.

E 41/193   1313

COCKERSAND (Lancs) Premonstratensian abbey
abbey seal

M226. Under a trefoiled arch, the Virgin, crowned, half-length, holding the Child on her L side. Below, under a pointed arch, the abbot, half-length, praying to R. Above, under a canopy, Our Lord, half-length, with nimbus, between two censing demi-angels.

S' BE MARIE ET AVGV/STI C...   (Lom)

Pointed oval, c.50×30; red, tag. Large R fragment of a deep impression, legend blurred. BM 2975.

E 322/58   1539

COGGESHALL (Essex) Cistercian abbey
abbey seal
M227. Under a vaulted canopy with crocketed gables, the Virgin, crowned, seated, holding the Child, with nimbus, on her R knee. On either side, under a lesser canopy, a group of six monks. Below, each under an arch, two shields of arms: (L) *quarterly, 1 and 4 France modern, 2 and 3 England*; (R) lost.

SIG...NAST...DE CO...   (BL)

Round, c.53; uncoloured, tag. Deep clear impression, most of edge lost. BM 2972.

E 322/57   Pl 38   1538
abbot's seal
M228. The abbot, standing on a carved corbel, vested for mass, holding a crozier and a book.

+SIGILL' ABBATIS:DE:COGGESHALE   (Lom)

Pointed oval, 41×24; mottled green, tag. Complete, deep clear impression. Also on LR 14/543 (temp. abbot Robert, c.1364–80).

E 42/407   Pl 32   (13c)
abbot's seal: William
M229. A cock.

GALLVS CANTET   (BL)

Round, 13; red, tag. Complete, clear impression.

C 146/10015   1456

COLCHESTER (Essex) Benedictine abbey
abbey seal
M230. *Obv.* Under a deep vaulted canopy, St John the Baptist, with nimbus, seated, pointing to the Lamb and Flag on a disk held in his L hand. On either side, under a smaller canopy, smaller standing figures: (L) St Peter, holding keys, (R) St Paul holding a sword; beyond them, tabernacle work. Below St John's feet, a shield of arms: *a cross within a bordure, overall an escarbuncle* (the ABBEY).

SIGILLVM COMUNE MONASTERII SANCTI IOHIS BAPTISTE COLCESTRIE   (BL)

Rev. Under a deep vaulted canopy, St. John the Evangelist, with nimbus, seated, holding a palm branch in his L hand and a chalice with serpent in his R hand. On either side, under a smaller canopy with an eagle above, a demi-angel, standing, holding a censer; beyond each of these, a penthouse of masonry with a loggia above from which an angel holds out a shield of arms: (L) *quarterly, Old France and England*, (R) (defaced). Below, under an arch, the abbot, holding a crozier, seated between two small figures in niches.

O:MATRIS...ALME:IOH'S CONSERVES:OMES:PCIE...ATQ...S   (BL)

Round, 70; red, tag. Very deep clear impression,

slightly uneven and cracked. BM 2981.

E 25/34   Pl 45   1534
seal ad causas
M231. St John the Baptist, with nimbus, hirsute, dressed in skins, holding a roundel with the Holy Lamb in his L hand and pointing to it with his R hand.

+S'ABB'IS:ET:COVENT:SCI:IOHIS:COLECESTRIE AD C'SAS   (Lom)

Pointed oval, 60×35; bronze-green, tag. Complete, deep clear impression, slightly uneven. Also on DL 26/28, 29, 30 (all 1537–8). BM 2982.

DL 27/307   Pl 38   1538
abbot's seal: Adam
M232. The abbot, standing, vested for mass.

...GILLVM:A:E:AB...COL...   (Lom)

Pointed oval, 50×30; uncoloured, tag. Deep indistinct impression, edge chipped.

E 40/14130   (c.1206)
abbot's seal: John de Wymondham
M233. The abbot, standing in a carved niche, vested for mass, holding a crozier and a book. On L, the Lamb and Flag of St John the Baptist; on R, the eagle of St John the Evangelist.

...IOHANNIS DE W...DAM ABBATIS COLCE...   (Lom)

Pointed oval, c.58×35; brown, tag. Fine impression, upper edge lost (abbot headless). BM 2984.

DL 25/192   Pl 35   1328
abbot's seal: (Roger Best ?)
M234. A robed figure?

Legend lost.

Pointed oval (?); bronze-green, tag. Fragment, indistinct.

E 40/3729   1413
abbot's seal: William de Audley
M235. In a roundel with cable border, St John the Baptist's head.

S MOY PEVR NOS...(?)   (BL)

Round, 10; red, tag. Complete, deep and partly clear impression.

E 327/741   1446
abbot's seal: Thomas Marshall
M236. In two canopied niches within a gothic housing, standing figures: (L) St John the Baptist; (R) St John the Evangelist, pointing to the cup held in his L hand. Below, in a panel, the abbot, half-length, mitred and holding a crozier, between two shields of arms: (L) *quarterly, France modern and England*; (R) *a cross within a bordure, overall an escarbuncle* (the ABBEY).

S':THOME./ABBATIS.SCI:IOHIS:COLECESTR'   (BL)

Pointed oval, 63×38; red-brown, detached, in metal skippet.

Complete, deep uneven impression. Also on E 327/626 (1536).

SC 13/O34   (n.d.)

COLCHESTER (Essex) Augustinian priory
priory seal
M237. Our Lord, seated on a bench-type throne, blessing and holding a book on his L knee. On L, a bishop; on R, an abbot or prior, each vested and holding a crozier and a book. Below, under a trefoiled arch, a steepled building with moon and star above.
+SIGILL:ECCLESIE SA[NCTI B]OTVLFI DE COLECESTR'
(Lom)
Pointed oval, 65×40; brown, tag. Nearly complete, deep clear impression, faces flattened. Pedrick, plate VII, 14. BM 2985.
E 42/408   1298

COLNE see *EARLS COLNE*

COMBE (Warw) Cistercian abbey
abbey seal
M238. Beneath a double-gabled canopy resting on slender shafts, against a hatched field, standing figures: (L) the Virgin, crowned, holding the Child on her L side; (R) an abbot, holding a crozier and a book. Below, between two lions, a shield of arms: *three leopards and a label of three points.*
*SIGILL'.COMVNE.CAPITVLI MONACHOR' DE CVMBA
(Lom)
Pointed oval, 80×55; dark green tag. Complete, deep clear impression, some sharp detail. Also on E 40/4306 (1483). Pedrick, plate XX, 40. BM 2989.
E 322/59   Pl 32   1539
abbot's seal
M239. The abbot, vested for mass, holding a crozier and a book.
+SIGILL' ABBATIS...BA   (Lom)
Pointed oval, C.35×25; uncoloured tag. Deep but not sharp impression, L side lost. Also on E 210/9602 (n.d.). BM 2990.
DL 27/31   1231
abbot's counterseal
M240. A vested hand issuing from R, holding a crozier; the field diapered.
*CONTRASIGILLVM.ABBATIS.DE.CVMBA   (Lom)
Pointed oval, 40×23; dark green, tag. Complete, fine impression. BM 2992.
E 329/102   Pl 56   1311
abbot's seal: Alexander
M241. In a beaded circle, the Annunciation. No legend.
Round, 12; red, tongue. Complete, deep clear impression.
E 40/8848   1466

COMBERMERE (Ches) Cistercian abbey
abbey seal
M242. In a cusped circle, the abbot, standing, holding a crozier and a book, between six heads couped at the neck and two fleur-de-lys; on L, a pierced mullet. The legend, defaced, is punctuated with leaves.
Round, 40; red, tag. Deep indistinct impression, top edge lost. BM 2995.
E 322/60   1538
abbot's seal: R...
M243. The abbot, standing, holding a crozier and a book; on L, a crescent.
*...IGILL:R...EMAR   (Lom)
Pointed oval, c.30×20; green, tag. Large fragment of a clear impression.
C 146/5852   (c.1304)

COMBWELL (Kent) Augustinian priory
abbey seal
M244. *Obv.* The priory church, with a pediment containing two small lancets and three roundels enclosing heads. Under a trefoiled arch, Our Lord sits at table between two disciples; below, St Mary Magdalene washes his feet, with the box of ointment and the devils cast out of her. On the table's edge is inscribed MARIA:FIDES:TVA:TE:SALVAM:FECIT. In the field above, a crescent and star.
*SIGILL':ECCLESIE:SANCTE:MARIE:MAGDALENE:DE: CVMBWELL   (Lom)
    Rev. Under an arch on two clustered columns, the Noil Me Tangere scene. Our Lord, with nimbus, standing on R, holding a staff; St Mary Magdalene prostrates herself before him; a spreading tree fills the field. On either side, a roundel containing a head.
FACTVM:ANNO:GRAC...M°:C:XXX:TERCIO:MENSE: NOVEMBRI   (Lom)
Round, 70; red, tag. Complete except for some chipping at edge, very fine impression. Pedrick, plate II. BM 3000.
The first part of the date in the legend on *Rev.* (M°:C:XXX) appears to have been cut by another and less skilful hand, and neither this date, 1133, nor the alternative, 1233, offered by Birch accords easily with the style of the matrix.
E 25/39/1   Pl 52   1534

CONWAY (Aberconway) (Caern) Cistercian abbey
abbey seal
M245. Under a small canopy, the Virgin, crowned, standing, facing R, holding the Child, with nimbus, on her L side; before her, on R, the abbot, kneeling, holding a crozier. Background patterned with diaper and sprigs of globular fruit.

S'COMMVNE ABBATIS ET [CO]NVENTVS DE ABERCONWY (Lom)

Pointed oval, 60×30; bronze-green, tag. Nearly complete, fine impression, a little rubbed.
E 42/321   Pl 56   1350

COOK HILL (Worcs) Cistercian priory (F)
   priory seal (used as)
M246. A lady, standing, hands outstretched.
SIGILL' SANCTE...   (Lom)
Pointed oval, 50×35; red-brown, detached, on tag. Deep indistinct impression, L side lost. BM 2974.
SC13/R13   (n.d.)

CORNWORTHY (Devon) Augustinian priory (F)
   priory seal
M247. A tower, with narrow arched portal and windows above.
...L COM...   (Lom)
Pointed oval, c.40×c.25; red-brown, detached, on tag. Large central fragment of an indistinct impression. BM 3003.
SC 13/R14   (n.d.)

COTHAM see NUN COTHAM

COUPAR ANGUS (Perth) Cistercian abbey
   abbot's counterseal
M248. A dexter hand, with sleeved forearm, issuing from R, holding a crozier; on either side, a fleur-de-lys.
+CONTRASIGILLVM ABB'IS DE CVPRO   (Lom)
Pointed oval, 36×24; dark green, detached, on tag. Complete, fine impression. Laing 999. BM 15,255.
SC 13/A128   Pl 38   (n.d.)

COVENTRY (Warw) Benedictine cathedral priory
   priory seal
M249. The Virgin, crowned, seated on a throne with curved arms, holding the Child on her R side.
+SIGILLVM SANTE [MA] RIE DE COVENTRE   (Lom)
Pointed oval, 75×50; dark green, silk laces. Nearly complete, deep but not distinct impression. Has counterseal, **M253**.
Also on C 82/32 (1537); E 210/1276 (n.d.); E 322/61 (1539) which has counterseal, **M 250**; E 326/6917 (1538); 8926 (1425); 8930 (1368); E 329/119 (1445, a good example), 417 (1536); SC 13/F137 (n.d.).
DL 27/109   Pl 27   1285
   counterseal
M250. Noah's ark on the waters, the dove on its roof.
SIGNVM CLEMENCIE DEI   (Lom)

Pointed oval, 30×20; uncoloured, on tag, as counterseal to **M249**.
Complete, deep but uneven impression. BM 1656.
E 322/61   1539
   prior's seal
M251. The prior, standing.
+S...IORIS COVENTN   (Lom)
Pointed oval, c.40×c.20; green, tag. Central fragment.
E 210/1276   (1216–35)
   prior's seal
M252. The prior, standing, blessing and holding a book before him in his L hand.
...IG...NTRIE   (Lom)
Pointed oval, 45×35; uncoloured, tag. Deep indistinct impression, most of edge lost.
DL 27/31   1231
   prior's seal: Thomas
M253. An antique gem: a figure, wearing a helmet, standing facing R.
+S'THE PRIOR'.ECCE.COVEN   (Lom)
Oval, 32×25; dark green, on silk laces, as counterseal to **M249**.
Complete, indistinct impression.
Dl 27/109   1285
   prior's seal: Richard Crosby
M254. In a vaulted niche beneath a pinnacled canopy, with elaborate tabernacle work at the sides, the Virgin, crowned, seated, holding the Child on her R knee.
Legend lost.
Round, C.35; dark green, tag. Large fragment of a fine impression.
E 326/8128   1415
   prior's seal: Thomas Wisford
M255. Under a double canopy, the Virgin, crowned, seated, holding the Child on her L knee.
...ESI...ATU...E MARIE COVETR   (BL)
Pointed oval, c.70×c.30; red, tag. Much damaged at edge.
Also on SC 10/2521 (1531).
SC 10/2520   1531
   treasurer's seal
M256. A splayed eagle.
+SIGILLVM OFFICII THESAVRARII COVEN   (Lom)
Oval, 30×25; red, tongue. Complete, indistinct impression.
E 329/168   1503

COVENTRY (Warw) Carmelite house
   common seal
M257. Under a canopy, standing figures. Below, on R, a shield of arms (?)
Legend lost.
Pointed oval (?); red, tag. Fragment, indistinct.
E 322/65   1538

COVENTRY (Warw) Carthusian priory
prior's seal
M258. Between a crescent and a star, the prior, standing, blessing and holding a book.
...IG...VENTRIE
Pointed oval, c.50×c.30; uncoloured, tag. Clear impression, lower part and much of edge lost.
DL 27/31   1231
prior's seal: Thomas
M260. Under a canopy with a fan-like vault, St Anne, teaching the Virgin to read, both standing.
No legend.
Oval, 22×20; bronze-green, tongue. Uneven impression, flattened. Also on E 322/63 (1538).
E 42/410   1529

COVENTRY (Warw) Franciscan house
common seal
M261. Under a canopy, two standing figures.
Legend lost.
Pointed oval, c.55×c.35; red, tag. Fragment, indistinct.
E 322/62   1538

COVENTRY (Warw) St John the Baptist, Benedictine priory and hospital
common seal
M262. In a niche with pinnacled canopy and a traceried panel on either side, St John the Baptist, standing, holding the Lamb of God in his L hand and pointing to it.
S'HOSPITAL.../...COVENTRE   (Lom)
Pointed oval, c.55×33; scarlet, tag. Deep impression, partly flattened, lower edge lost. BM 3010.
E 322/64   1544

COVERHAM (Yorks) Premonstratensian abbey
abbey seal
M263. Under a gabled canopy resting on slender columns, the abbot, standing on a corbel, holding a crozier and a book, the field diapered; on either side, under (L) a crescent and (R) a star, a canon facing inwards.
S'COE CAPITULI DE COVERHAM+   (Lom)
Pointed oval, 42×29; dark red, tag. Complete, fine impression.
Clay, p.14, plate I. Pedrick, plate XXIII, 45. BM 3011.
E 326/9422   Pl 27   1405
seal ad causas
M264. Under a gabled canopy, the Virgin, crowned, seated, holding the Child on her L knee; on either side, under a smaller canopy, (L) a canon and (R) the abbot, both kneeling in prayer.
S'ABBAT E...D...SAS   (Lom)

Pointed oval, 45×30; red, tag. Large upper fragment of a deep clear impression.
E 135/6/82   1479–80

COXFORD (Norf) Augustinian priory
priory seal
M265. The Virgin, crowned, seated, holding the Child, with nimbus, on her L knee, and a fleur-de-lys sceptre in R hand; on either side a kneeling figure; in the field (L) a crescent and (R) a star. Below, under a trefoiled arch, the prior, hooded, kneeling in prayer to R; in the field, stars and (L) a crescent.
S'PRIORIS:ET CONVEN...BEATE MARIE DE COKISFORD
     (Lom)
Pointed oval, 75×45; red, tongue. Nearly complete, deep impression, cracked and flattened. BM 2977.
E 25/33   Pl 33   1534

CRABHOUSE (Norf) Augustinian priory (F)
priory seal
M266. A splayed eagle.
S'SAN[CTI] IOHAN[NIS] EVANGELISTE   (lom)
Pointed oval, 55×40; red-brown, detached on tag. Nearly complete, deep indistinct impression from a 12c style matrix. BM 3012.
SC 13/R16   Pl 27   (n.d.)

CROWLAND (Croyland) (Lincs) Benedictine abbey
priory seal
M267. In a pointed oval with beaded moulding on corbels, under a church-like canopy, standing figures of (L) St Bartholomew, holding his flayed skin (?), and (R) St Guthlac, holding his scourge with three loaded thongs, facing one another over a bird on a bush.
SIGILL' COMMVNE ABB[ATIS ET CO]NVENTVS CROYLANDIE   (Lom)
Pointed oval, c.65×40; bronze-green, tag. Deep clear impression, points lost. Also on E 25/38 (1534).
Pedrick, plate V, 10. BM 3021.
E 328/15   Pl 35   1413
abbot's seal: John Welles
M268. In a vaulted niche within a gothic housing, St Guthlac, standing, with nimbus, holding a crozier and a book, between two shields of arms: (L) *three knives*; (R) (an indistinct charge) *within a bordure crusilly*.
SIGILLV IOHANIS WELLE/ABBATIS DE CROYLADIE   (BL)
Pointed oval, 65×40; red-brown, detached, in metal skippet.
Complete, deep impression, cracked and flattened.
SC 13/O67   (c.1512)

CROXDEN (Staffs) Cistercian abbey
abbey seal
M269. Under a canopy with ogee arch and crocketed

gable, the Virgin, crowned, seated, holding the Child on her L knee. On L, a shield of arms: *fretty* (the founder, Bertram de VERDUN). Below, under an ogee arch, the abbot, standing, frontal, holding a crozier and a book. The field diapered.

S'ABBATIS ET COVETVS VALLIS SCE MARIE DE CROKESDEN (Lom)

Pointed oval, 43×26; red, tag. Deep clear impression, slightly flattened, upper point lost. BM 3014.

E 322/66   Pl 38   1538

CROXTON (Croxton Kerrial) (Leics)
Premonstratensian abbey
abbey seal
M270. The Virgin, with nimbus, seated on a bench-type throne, holding the Child, with nimbus, on her L knee. The throne and the Virgin's feet rest on the back of an eagle, standing with head turned back upon a scroll lettered IOH/ES.

...IGILL':COVET'SCI:IOHIS...DE VALLE:DE:CROXT... (Lom)
Pointed oval, c.55×40; red, tag. Deep clear impression, the figures flattened. Pedrick, plate XLVIII, 96. BM 3015.

E 322/67   Pl 56   1538
abbot's seal: William
M271. A draped figure.
Legend lost.
Pointed oval (?); green, tag. Fragment.
E 101/568/57, no. 7   1305

CROYLAND see CROWLAND

CULROSS (Fife) Cistercian abbey
counterseal
M272. A dexter hand issuing from L, holding a crozier; on R, a star above a crescent.

*CONTRASIGILL' DE CULENROSS   (Lom)
Round, 23; mottled green and yellow, detached, on hemp cords.
Complete, fine impression. Laing 998. BM 15249.
SC 13/B47   Pl 56   (n.d.)

DALE ABBEY (Stanley Park) (Derb)
Premonstratensian abbey
abbey seal
M273. Above a rounded arch and between two pinnacles each pierced and topped with a cross, the Virgin, half-length, turning to L, holding the Child. Below, under a trefoiled arch, the abbot, half-length, holding a crozier in both hands.

[*S'EC]CLESIE SANCT[E MAR]IE DE PARCO STANLEE
(Lom)

Pointed oval, 45×30; red, tongue. Deep clear impression, edge damaged. Also on SC 13/R 17A, R 17B, R 17C (all n.d.).
BM 4083–84.
E 329/333   Pl 29   1514

DARLEY (Derb) Augustinian abbey
abbey seal
M274. The Virgin, with nimbus, seated on a bench-type throne, holding the Child on her L knee.

...ILLVM SANC...RIE DE DERLE   (Lom)
Pointed oval, c.55×38; brown, tag. Deep impression, much flattened, upper and lower points lost. Also on SC 13/R18 (n.d.).
E 322/72   1539
abbot's seal
M275. Under a canopy supported by panelled piers resting on masonry, the Virgin, crowned, seated, holding the Child on her L side and her L breast with her R hand; her feet rest on a small dragon lying on its back on a carved corbel. On either side, a censing angel, wings outspread.

...L'ABBATIS...E MARIE DE DE...   (Lom)
Pointed oval, c.55×40; red, detached, on tag. Deep clear impression from a fine 14c matrix, points lost.
SC 13/R19   Pl 16   (n.d.)

DARTFORD (Kent) Dominican priory (F)
priory seal
M276. Under a panelled canopy, St Margaret, crowned, standing on a dragon and piercing its head with a long spear, holding a book in her L hand. Below, under an arch, Edward III as founder, kneeling and holding a model of the church. On either side, a shield of arms hung on a tree: *quarterly, France modern and England*. In base, a panel containing a head.

SIGILLU COE SORORU ORDINIS PREDICATORU DE DERTFORDIA   (BL)
Pointed oval, 70×45; red, on blue and white cords in metal skippet. Complete, heavily flattened. Also on E 40/5280 (1371). BM 3033.
E 25/39/2   1534
seal ad causas
M277. Under a double canopy with crocketed gables and pinnacles, the Coronation of the Virgin. On either side, a canopied niche containing: (L) St Margaret; (R) St George, holding a spear and standing on the dragon. Below, under a rounded arch, Edward III as founder kneeling and holding a model of the church.

...CAUSARU PRIORISSE & CO/VENT...   (BL)
Pointed oval, c.60×c.37; red, tongue. Three impressions, broken and flattened. Also on E 213/61 (1412). BM 3032.
E 213/339   Pl 24   1422–8

DAVENTRY (Northants) Cluniac priory
priory seal
M278. St Augustine, seated on a bench-type throne, blessing and holding a pastoral staff.
SI... (Lom)
Pointed oval, c.65×45; red, tongue. Clear impression from a 12c matrix, edge nearly all lost.
E 135/10/21, no.7 1400
prior's seal
M279. The prior (?), standing, holding a crozier.
+SIG... (Lom)
Pointed oval, c.45×c.30; mottled green, tag. Upper fragment of a deep clear impression. Has counterseal, M280.
E 326/11438 (temp. Hen. III)
counterseal
M280. Between a double canopy with two crocketed gables, a tall pinnacle.
No legend.
Pointed oval, (?)×(?); mottled green, on tag, as counterseal to M279. Small upper fragment of a deep clear impression.
E 326/11438 (temp. Hen. III)

DEER (Aberdeen) Cistercian abbey
abbot's seal
M281. The abbot, standing, turning to L, holding a crozier and a book.
SIGILLVM ABB/ATIS DE DER (Lom)
Pointed oval, 50×30; mottled green, detached, on hemp cords. Complete, deep impression, rubbed.
Laing 1003. BM 15260.
SC 13/F22 (n.d.)

DELAPRE see NORTHAMPTON

DENNEY (Cambs) Franciscan abbey (F)
abbey seal
M282. Under a triple canopy with panelled sides, the Coronation of the Virgin, Our Lord holding a church in his L hand, the field diapered. In base, a shield of arms: *barry, an orle of martlets* (VALENCE) *dimidiating three pales vair, in chief a label of five points* (ST POL).
...COMVNITATIS:S[OR]ORVM:MINORVM:IN EL...+ (Lom)
Pointed oval, 70×40; red, tag. Deep clear impression, L edge broken.
E 40/14327 Pl 16 1362
abbess's seal
M283. Under a canopy, a figure, standing, holding a crozier and book. Below, a shield of arms: *VALENCE dimidiating ST POL*, as in M282.
...ASTERII M...N' EVI (Lom)

Pointed oval, c.45×c.30; red, tongue. Fragments of a clear impression, flattened.
E 213/340 1400

DERBY (Derb) De Pratis or King's Mead, Benedictine priory (F)
priory seal (used as)
M284. Between (L) a star and (R) a crescent moon, the Virgin, crowned, standing on a corbel, holding the Child on her L side.
*AVE MARIA GRA PLENA DNS TECV (Lom)
Pointed oval, 40×23; red-brown, tongue. Three impressions, all incomplete, one clear. BM 3048.
E 213/341 1451-5

DERBY (Derb) Dominican house
common seal
M285. The Annunciation. On L, the Virgin, wrapped in a cloak, on R, the archangel with pointed finger, both standing on a trefoiled arch, facing inwards to a pendent scroll inscribed DOMIN... Under the arch, a friar, half-length, praying to L.
S' CONVENTVS FRM PREDICATOR' DEREBEYE (Lom)
Pointed oval, 50×27; red-brown, tag. Complete, deep impression, flattened, part of legend blurred. BM 3049.
E 322/71 1539

DIEULACRES (Staffs) Cistercian abbey
abbey seal
M286. Under a canopy, the Virgin, crowned, standing, holding the Child on her L arm and a sceptre in her R hand. Below, under an arch, the abbot.
...DELACRES (BL)
Pointed oval, 48×35; red, tag. Edge partly lost, badly flattened. BM 3056.
E 326/9052 1528
abbot's seal
M287. The abbot, standing, holding a crozier and a book.
...S DE D...SSE (Lom)
Pointed oval, 43×c.30; brown, tongue. Large fragment.
DL 25/479 (1198-1204)

DONCASTER (Yorks) Franciscan house
common seal
M288. A figure, with nimbus, seated on a bench-type throne, holding a cross or sceptre.
...TIS FRM MIN... (BL)
Pointed oval, c.45×c.32; red-brown, tag. Nearly complete, very heavily flattened and defaced. BM 3059.
E 322/73 1538

DONNINGTON (Berks) Crutched Friars' house
prior's seal
M289. A cross, surrounded by indistinct objects
(emblems of the Passion ?). Below, under an arch, a
half-length figure.
S'P'IORIS.DOM...DONYNGTO   (BL)
Pointed oval, c.40×c.28; red, tag. Uneven impression,
flattened, damaged at foot. BM 3060.
E 322/75   1538

DORCHESTER (Oxon) Augustinian abbey
abbey seal
M290. St Peter, standing, vested for mass, holding keys
and a book.
+SIGILLVM.CONVENT.SANTI.PETRI.DORCES   (Lom)
Pointed oval, 60×42; red, tag. Complete, deep clear
impression. BM 3061.
E 25/41   Pl 16   1534

DORE see ABBEY DORE

DOVER (Kent) St Martin's, Benedictine priory
priory seal
M291. *Obv.* The Vision of St Martin. St Martin lies on
a draped bed with decorated head and foot, his head
raised on a square pillow beneath a small canopy with
crockets and pinnacles; above him, appears Our Lord,
half-length, from clouds, with cruciform nimbus, his R
hand raised in blessing, holding a book and half of St
Martin's cloak in his L hand, between two small
censing demi-angels. Above St Martin's, feet, a circular
disk with cinquefoil tracery, a hanging lamp and a small
trefoil; below the bed, a scrolled band of leaves and
flowers.
MARTINI VES[TE] SVM TECT[VS] PAVPERE TESTE (Lom)
     Rev. St Martin, on horseback, riding to L,
turning backwards and with a long sword dividing his
cloak, which is received by the beggar, bearded and
wearing trousers, standing under a canopy on R. On L
of St Martin, a crescent and star; on R, a flaming sun.
Below the horse, a large boss in a circle and water
flowing under a bridge.
SIGIL...SIE SCI MARTINI DE DOVORIA   (Lom)
Round, 80; red-brown, tag. Nearly complete, very deep
impression, edge chipped, legend blurred, parts
flattened. Also on E 25/42 (1534). Pedrick, plate IX.
BM 3066.
E 322/78   Pl 34   1535
prior's seal?
M292. In a quatrefoil panel with mermen(?) in the
spandrels, St Martin, with nimbus, on horseback,
riding to L, dividing his cloak with the beggar,
half-length, on R.

SIGILLVM...DOVORIE   (Lom)
Round, 40; brown, detached, on tag. Deep clear
impression, L and R lower edge lost.
SC 13/D144   (n.d.)

DOVER (Kent) St Mary's or Maison Dieu,
Augustinian hospital: common seal
M293. Under a cusped arch, the Virgin, enthroned,
holding the Child on her L knee. On L, a star above a
crescent; on R, a censing demi-angel. Below, under a
cusped arch with trefoils pierced in the spandrels, the
master, half-length, praying to L. On either side,
breaking the legend, a deeply-sunk quatrefoil aperture
containing a clerk's head.
+SIGILL'. COMV/NE.DOM.HOSPITAL'.BE/MARIE.DOVOR
                                            (Lom)
Pointed oval, 60×40; light brown, tag. Complete, very
deep clear impression, partly flattened. Also on E 25/
43 (1534).
BM 3071.
E 322/77   Pl 18   1544

DRAX (Yorks) Augustinian priory
priory seal
M294. St Nicholas, standing, vested, with pallium but
without mitre, blessing and holding a crozier.
+SIGILLVM SANCT...COLAI EPISCOPI   (Lom)
Pointed oval, 70×45; uncoloured, tag. Nearly
complete, deep but not sharp impression. Clay, p.15,
plate II, 1. BM 3073.
DL 27/29   Pl 16   (1199–1211)

DRYBURGH (Berwick) Premonstratensian abbey
commendator's seal: James Ogilby
M295. In a canopied niche in an elaborate housing of
very late gothic design, the Virgin, crowned, standing,
holding the Child on her R side. Below, on a crozier, a
shield of arms: *quarterly, 1 and 4 a lion passant* (OGILBY),
2 and 3 crescents (SETON). Foliage fills the field.
S.M.IACOBI.OGLVBI COMENDA/TARII.MONASTERII.
DE.DRIBURGH   (Rom)
Round, 55; red, detached, on tag. Complete, deep and
very clear impression, slightly uneven. Laing vol. II,
1129. BM 15272.
SC 13/F23   Pl 43   (16c)

DUNDRENNAN (Kirkcudbright) Cistercian abbey
abbey seal
M296. Under a two-tiered canopy in a niche with
tabernacle work at the sides, the abbot, standing,
holding a crozier and a book.
S'ILL COVENTUS SCE MARIE DU DRAYNIN   (BL)

Pointed oval, 55×35; red, set in yellow wax, detached, on tag. Complete, deep indistinct impression.
SC 13/D68   Pl 16   (14c)

DUNFERMLINE (Fife) Benedictine abbey
abbot's seal: Ralph
M297. In a gothic housing, in the upper of two compartments, the Holy Trinity, enthroned between (L) a star and (R) a crescent; in the lower, the abbot, mitred and holding a crozier, kneeling in prayer to R.
S'RADVLPHI ABBAT/I/S DE DVNFERMELIN   (Lom)
Pointed oval, 63×35; mottled green, detached, on hemp cords. Complete, deep clear impression, rubbed. Laing 1014. BM 15282.
SC 13/F24   (13c)

DUNKESWELL (Devon) Cistercian abbey
abbey seal
M298. In three niches under an elaborate triple canopy with pinnacles, tracery and crocketed gables, standing figures: (centre) the Virgin, between two saints(?) each holding a pastoral staff and book. Below, under an arch, the abbot, half-length, mitred and holding a crozier; on either side, a shield of arms, (L) (lost), (R) *two bends wavy*.
...UNE:/...WILL'   (BL)
Pointed oval, c.65×c.52; red, tag. Large central portion of a deep clear impression, cracked, flattened, most of edge lost. BM 3078.
E 322/76   1538

DUNMOW see LITTLE DUNMOW

DUNSTABLE (Beds) Augustinian priory
priory seal
M299. St Peter, with nimbus, seated on a bench-type throne, blessing and holding keys.
Legend lost.
Round, c.65; red, tag. Clear impression, edge lost. Also on C146/3018 (1389). BM 3083.
E 25/44/1   1534
seal ad causas
M300. Above a trefoiled arch, St Edmund the King, headless, kneeling to R, holding his own crowned and severed head, the field inscribed ...ND'/S'/FREE (Lom). Under the arch, a man, tonsured, kneeling to L, his hands raised in prayer.
S' P'OR' ET COVENT...VNSTAP.AD CAVSAS   (Lom)
Pointed oval, 50×20; brown, tongue. Deep clear impression, cracked, lower point lost. Has counterseal, M301.
E 212/135   Pl 29   1297
counterseal
M301. St Peter, standing, holding keys and a book.

+SV...CELI...PETO PETRE REGE   (Lom)
Pointed oval, 35×23; brown, on tongue, as counterseal to M300. Deep impression, complete but cracked.
E 212/135   1297

DUNSTABLE (Beds) Dominican house
common seal
M302. Under a canopy, a saint, standing; on either side, three friars' heads.
S'CONVENTVS FRVM...REDICATOR DVNESTA...E   (Lom)
Pointed oval, 45×30; red, tag. Nearly complete, deep impression, flattened.
C 147/111   1458

DURFORD (Sussex) Premonstratensian abbey
abbey seal
M303. The abbot, standing, vested for mass, holding a crozier.
+SIG...ORD   (Lom)
Pointed oval, c.40×c.25; bronze-green, tongue. Deep clear impression, cracked, most of edge lost.
E 210/8479   1297
abbot's seal
M304. A figure, standing on a corbel; on R, a crescent.
S...ILL' ABB...S...   (Lom)
Pointed oval, c.35×c.25; bronze-green, tongue. Fragments of a deep sharp impression.
E 210/8479   1297

DURHAM (Durh) Benedictine cathedral priory
priory seal
M305. A slender cross formy, the arms fastened at the centre with diagonal cords.
+SIGILLVM CVDBERHTI PRAESVLIS SEI   (Rom)
Round, 48; dark green, tag. Complete, deep clear impression. Has counterseal, M306. Also on E 212/105 (1248). BM 2511.
E 329/445   Pl 16   1448
counterseal
M306. An antique gem; the head of Jupiter Serapis in high relief, facing half L.
+CAPVT.SANCTI.OSWALDI.REGIS   (Lom)
Round, 39; dark green, on tag, as counterseal to M305, complete, clear impression. Also on E 212/105 (1248). BM 2511.
E 329/445   Pl 16   1448
prior's seal: Richard
M307. Under a columned canopy, the prior, standing, vested for mass, holding a book in both hands; on either side, in a quatrefoil panel, an ox's head (?); field diapered with pierced cinquefoils.
SIGILLVM:RICARDI:PRIORIS:DVNELMENSIS.ECCLESIE
    (Lom)

Pointed oval, 75×35; light green, detached. Complete, deep clear impression.

SC 13/H30   Pl 29   (n.d.)

EARLS COLNE (Essex) Benedictine priory
priory seal
M308. Under a canopy with tabernacle work at the sides, the Virgin, crowned and with nimbus, seated, holding the Child, with nimbus, on her R side and a sceptre in her L hand.

...LV COMVNE PRIOR...NVENTVS DE...   (BL)
Pointed oval, c.35×28; red, tag. Fine impression, points and part of edge lost. BM 2988.

E 25/35   Pl 2   1534

EDINBURGH see HOLYROOD

EDINGTON (Wilts) Bonhommes' house
common seal
M309. In adjoining niches with panelling at sides and an elaborate pinnacled canopy above, standing figures: (L) St Peter, holding a key and a book; (R) St Paul, holding a sword and a book. Below, under an arch, a figure, half-length, facing L, mitred and holding a crozier. In a niche in the canopy, the Virgin, seated, holding the Child on her L knee.

S'COMMUNE RECTORIS/ET CONVENTUS DE EDYNDON   (BL)
Pointed oval, c.55×40; light brown, tag. Deep clear impression, upper and lower points lost. Also on E 329/374 (1521). BM 3102.

E 322/80   Pl 22   1539

ELLERTON (Yorks) Gilbertine priory
priory seal
M310. The Salutation: on R, the Virgin, facing the archangel on L.

...ANCTE MARIE DE EL...   (Lom)
Pointed oval, 50×35; red, tag. Deep clear impression, cracked, upper part lost. BM 3104.

E 322/81   1538

ELSTOW (Beds) Benedictine abbey (F)
abbey seal
M311. Under a double canopy with crocketed gable, pinnacles and tabernacle work at the sides. (L) the Virgin, crowned, seated, holding the Child on her L knee, and (R) St Helen, crowned, standing, holding a tall cross in her R hand. Below, under a trefoiled arch, between two nuns, half-length, the abbess, kneeling to L, holding a crozier.

S'C/OMMV...VLI SCE...ARIE ELEYNESTO/WE   (Lom)

Pointed oval, 75×48; bronze-green, tag. Nearly complete, deep clear impression, slightly flattened. Pedrick, plate XXIII, 46. BM 3105.

E 322/83   Pl 2   1539

ELY (Cambs) Benedictine cathedral priory
prior's seal: John (Boughton)
M312. Hung from a tree, held in the beaks of two supporting griffins, a shield of arms: *three crowns*. Legend lost.
Round, c.25; red, tongue. Large central fragment of a deep clear impression, flattened.

E 213/8   1373

EPWORTH see AXHOLME

EVESHAM (Worcs) Benedictine abbey
abbey seal
M313. *Obv.* the L part of a complex and eventful design. Below, within the part of the scroll inscribed ...N CLEPT EOVISHOM, can be seen Eove's sow with her suckling under a tree. On L, a tree. Above, on a plinth resting on a carved corbel, one of the royal patrons, crowned, kneeling, holding a cross; behind him, his two attendants, kneeling.

...EOVESHAMENS...   (Lom)
Rev. The R part of the design. Bishop Egwin, the founder, with a tree behind him, kneels and holds up the abbey church; below, he kneels, with his chaplain behind him, to receive the charter, shown with a fleur-de-lys and a crocketed gable above it and inscribed DAMVS/REGIE/LIBER/TATI.

...WINI DANT REGES MV...   (Lom)
Round, 75; bronze-green, detached, on tag. Large fragment of a deep, very clear impression, from a fine 13c matrix. Pedrick, plate VIII. BM 3113, where a full description will be found.

SC 13/R20   Pl 28   (n.d.)

abbot's seal: Randolph
M314. On L, a figure, robed, seated on an arcaded throne with footstool, handing a tall crozier to a man, standing on R, vested for mass.
Legend lost.
Pointed oval, c.50×c.50; uncoloured, tag. Large central fragment of a deep impression with much detail, figures headless. Has counterseal, M316. The sealing clause refers to 'sigillorum nostrorum appositione'.

E 329/83   (1213–29)

abbot's seal: Randolph
M315. The abbot, standing, vested for mass, holding a tall staff and a book. On either side, in the field, a cross

formy, that on R within a circle.

...RANDVLFI DEI G...VESHAMENS... (Lom)

Pointed oval, c.70×c.50; uncoloured, tag. Deep impression, rubbed, points lost, abbot headless. Has counterseal, M316.

E 329/83 (1213–29)

abbot's counterseal: Randolph

M316. The abbot, standing, vested for mass, holding a crozier and a book.

SIGILL'RANDVL DEI GRA ABBIS EVESHAMENSIS ECCL'E (Lom)

Pointed oval, 50×30; uncoloured, on tag, as counterseal to M314 and M315. Two impressions, one complete with legend clear but figure rubbed.

E 329/83 (1213–29)

abbot's seal

M317. In a gothic housing, standing figures: (centre, under a vaulted canopy) the Virgin, crowned, holding the Child on her R side and a sceptre in her L hand; (L) a bishop, (R) the abbot, both holding a crozier. Below, under a rounded arch, the abbot, half-length, mitred and holding a crozier. On either side, a shield of arms: (L) *quarterly Old France and England*; (R) *a chain between three mitres* (?) (the ABBEY).

...DEI:GRACIA/ABBATIS.EVESHAME (BL)

Pointed oval, 80×48; red, detached, in metal skippet. Nearly complete, deep uneven impression, cracked and flattened, from a fine 15c style matrix.

SC 13/O13 (n.d.)

EXETER (Devon) St John the Baptist, Augustinian
hospital common seal

M318. The hospital shown as a hall-like building, with a latticed *bifora* window in the side and at L a gabled front with a round-arched portal, doors closed, and above, in the gable, a tall round-arched window between two circular windows. The sloping roof shows some ornamentation and has a prominent roof-ridge. On either gable, a cross finial, in centre of roof between scrolled fronds, a cross on a ball.

...A.ORIENTAL...A.EXO... (Lom)

Round, c.60; light brown, tag. Centre well impressed but heavily flattened, R edge lost, L edge blurred. Also on E 25/48/2.

BM 3129.

E 322/84   Pl 4 1539

EYNSHAM (Oxon) Benedictine abbey
abbey seal

M319. In a canopied niche in an elaborate gothic housing, the Virgin, crowned, seated, holding the Child on her L knee; above the canopy, Our Lord, with nimbus, enthroned, blessing. Below, under an arch, the abbot, holding a crozier, kneeling in prayer to L. On either side, in a niche with spired canopy, standing figures: (L) St Peter holding keys; (R) St Paul holding a sword.

SIGILLVM ECC...E MARIE ET APLOR PET'ET PAVLI EGNESHAM (Lom)

Pointed oval, 88×55; light brown, tag. Deep clear impression, slightly uneven, edge lost at top and R side. Also on E 25/50 (1534); E 326/11196 (1483).

BM 3142.

E 326/11125   Pl 2 1538

FAVERSHAM (Kent) Benedictine abbey
abbey seal

M320. *Obv.* In three adjoining canopied niches with panelled piers between, seated figures: (centre) Our Lord, (L) St Peter (lost), (R), St Paul holding a sword, each with cruciform nimbus. Each canopy has a crocketed gable between pinnacles, enclosing tracery and a trefoiled arch. The central niche is diapered. Above either side canopy, a sprig of hop. Below, arcading with tracery; in centre, two roundels each containing a crowned head, full-face.

S' COM...STERII : SCI : S... (Lom)

Rev. The abbey church, shown as a facade with three towers, each with shingled spire and corner pinnacles, the walls decorated with arcading and quatrefoils. Under a trefoiled arch below the central tower, Christ in Glory; beside him, under similar but smaller arches, standing figures of (L) Moses, horned, and (R) Elias (lost), together comprising the Transfiguration. On the side towers, in deeply sunk quatrefoils, emblematic heads of the four Evangelists. On the central spire, a weathercock; on either side, a censing demi-angel leaning down. Below, under a plinth, crouching figures of the damned.

+...ET : SOL :... . (Lom)

Round, 70; red, tag. Fine impression, slightly rubbed, more than half lost. Also on E 25/51/2 (fragment, 1534). Pedrick, plate XI. BM 3148.

E 322/86 1538

FELLEY (Notts) Augustinian priory
priory seal

M321. The Virgin, crowned, seated on a bench-type throne, holding the Child on her L knee and a fleur-de-lys sceptre in her R hand.

SIGILLVM... (Lom)

Pointed oval, 48×32; light brown, tag. Complete, indistinct impression. BM 3152.

E 135/2/60 1497

FERRIBY see NORTH FERRIBY

FINESHADE (Northants) Augustinian priory
priory seal
M322. Under a canopy of a trefoiled arch on two columns, the Virgin, seated, her feet on a corbel, holding the Child, with nimbus, on her L knee. On either side of her head, a star.
S'ECCLI[E:]BEATE : MARIE : DE : CA...O : YMIELIS　(Lom)
Pointed oval, 70×45; brown, tag. Nearly complete, clear impression, flattened.
Also on E 329/109 (1482). BM 3153.
E 25/51/1　　Pl 5　　　　　　　　　　1534

FLAMSTEAD (Herts) Benedictine priory (F)
prioress's seal
M323. The Virgin, seated, holding the Child on her L knee.
Below, under an arch, the prioress, kneeling.
...:IOH'E : PRIORES[S]E : SCI : E...　(Lom)
Pointed oval, c.40×c.25; green, tag. Clear impression, edge damaged.
E 210/1423　　　　　　　　　　1296

FLAXLEY (Glos) Cistercian abbey
abbot's seal: William de Rya
M324. Under a canopy, the abbot, standing, vested for mass, holding a crozier and a book. Springing from the base and from the capital of the canopy's R column, cinquefoils.
S'ABBATIS.DE.FLAXLE　(Lom)
Pointed oval, c.50×30; red, tag. Nearly complete, deep clear impression. Has counterseal, **M325**. Also on DL 25/257 (1315). BM 3155.
E 42/412　　Pl 49　　　　　　　　1316
abbot's counterseal
M325. A sleeved forearm and hand issuing from R and holding a crozier in pale, between (above) flowers and (below) (L) a fleur-de-lys and (R) a star above a crescent.
*CONTRASIGILL' ABBATIS DE FLAXLE　(Lom)
Pointed oval, 32×20; red, on tag, as counterseal to **M324**. Complete, fine impression. Also on DL 25/257 (1315).
E 42/412　　Pl 49　　　　　　　　1316
abbot's seal: Hugh
M326. The abbot, standing, vested for mass, holding a crozier and book; on L three stars, on R four stars.
+SIG...VM...S DE DENA　(Lom)
Pointed oval, c.40×20; brown, tag. Deep clear impression, parts of edge lost.
C 106/53　　　　　　　　　　1276

FOLKESTONE (Kent) Benedictine priory
priory seal
M327. In a round-headed niche with dog-tooth

moulding flanked by traceried panels with pinnacles, St Eanswith, crowned, standing, holding a sceptre in his L hand and a book in his R hand. Above, in a smaller canopied compartment, the Virgin, crowned, standing, holding the Child on her R arm and a sceptre in her L hand. Below, under the plinth, a half-length figure, frontal.
SIGILLV:COMUNE:PRIORATUS:DE;FOLKESTON　(BL)
Pointed oval, 55×35; light brown, tag. Complete except for upper point, clear impression, slightly flattened.
Also on E 25/53(1534).
BM 3163.
E 322/87　　　　　　　　　　1535

FORD (Dors, formerly in Devon) Cistercian abbey
abbey seal
M328. Design almost entirely effaced except for (perhaps) the standing figure of an abbot or bishop, mitred and holding a crozier, in the lower part.
...ARIE...　(Lom)
Pointed oval, c.60×c.45; red, tag. Apparently a 14c seal, defaced by inexpert application and much flattened.
E 322/88　　　　　　　　　　1538

FORDHAM (Cambs) Gilbertine priory
common seal
M329. A stylised lion, curled up under a tree.
S'.THOMAE DE...MEDE　(Lom)
Oval, 25×20; red, tag. Complete, indistinct impression. BM 3165. Described as common seal in the sealing clause but apparently a 14c personal seal.
E 322/89　　　　　　　　　　1538

FOSSE (Lincs) Cistercian priory (F)
priory seal
M330. Under a pinnacled canopy with traceried panels at either side, the Virgin, crowned, seated, holding the Child, standing, on her R knee. Below, under an arch, St Nicholas, half-length, praying, mitred and holding a crozier.
...OMUS.BEATE.MARIE/& SCI.NICHOLAI.DE...　(BL)
Pointed oval, 55×35; red-brown, tag. Deep impression, rubbed, legend uneven, upper point lost. BM 3166.
E 322/90　　　　　　　　　　1539

FOUNTAINS (Yorks) Cistercian abbey
abbot's seal
M331. The abbot, standing, vested for mass, holding a crozier and a book.
+SIGILLVM:ABBA...ONTANIS　(Lom)
Pointed oval, 40×27; orange, tag. Deep clear

impression, lower point and part of edge lost. Clay, plate III, 4. BM 3170.

DL 27/133   Pl 2   1214
    abbot's seal: William Thirsk

M332. Under a triple canopy, the Virgin, seated, holding the Child on her R knee and a sceptre in her L hand, between standing figures: (L) St John the Baptist; (R) St John the Evangelist. Below, under an arch set in masonry, the abbot, kneeling between two shields of arms: *three horseshoes* (the ABBEY).

...ABBAT...   (BL)

Pointed oval, c.75×c.45; red, tag. Clear impression, most of edge lost. Clay, plate III, 8.

E 326/3803   1529

FRITHELSTOCK (Devon) Augustinian priory
    priory seal

M333. A small church with three arched windows. Above the pitched roof is a tall central spire and four slender flanking towers with conical roofs and fleur-de-lys finials.

+S'.CONVENTVS DE FRITHELEWESTOK   (Lom)

Pointed oval, 45×30; red, tag. Nearly complete, clear impression, cracked, rubbed. BM 3176.

E 25/54   Pl 49   1534

FURNESS (Lancs) Cistercian abbey
    abbey seal

M334. Under a triple arcade springing from leopard's head corbels, the Virgin, crowned, standing, holding the Child on her L side and an apple(?) in her R hand. On either side, hung on an oak bough, a shield of arms: (L) *three leopards* (ENGLAND), (R) *three leopards and a label of three points* (LANCASTER), each supported by a kneeling monk. The field is diapered and filled with sprigs, flowers and trefoils. Below, in the exergue, a wyvern.

[+S'.COMMVNE.DOMVS.SANT]E.MARIE.DE. [FVRNESIO]
                                                     (Lom)

Round, 45; dark green, tag. Fine impression, slightly flattened, most of edge lost. Also on E 322/91 (1537). BM 3177.

DL 27/117   Pl 49   1344
    abbot's seal

M335. The abbot, standing, vested for mass, holding a crozier in his R hand.

+SIGILLVM ABB[ATIS.DE]FVRNEISIO   (Lom)

Pointed oval, c.35×25; uncoloured, tag. Clear impression, lower point and edge lost. Also on DL 25/280 (1243), 283 (n.d.).

DL 25/278   1230
    abbot's seal

M336. In a cusped oval, a dexter hand holding a crozier.

Legend lost.

Oval, c.25×(?); green, tag. Small fragment.

E 41/457   1363

GARENDON (Leics) Cistercian abbey
    abbot's seal

M337. A sleeved forearm and hand, issuing from R, holding a crozier.

SIGILL' ABB[ATIS DE]IERE'DONA   (Lom)

Pointed oval, 40×25; uncoloured, tag. Indistinct impression, R edge and lower part lost. BM 3181.

E 329/180   (1226–72)
    abbot's seal

M338. Under a canopy resting on slender pillars, the Virgin, standing, holding the Child on her L side. Below, under a pointed arch, the abbot, half-length, praying to L. On either side, lunettes of diaper ornament.

...VETV...E...EROVDON   (Lom)

Pointed oval, c.60×c.40; dark green, detached. Fine impression, upper part and most of edge lost.

SC 13/D143   Pl 31   (14c)

GINGES see THOBY

GLASTONBURY (Som) Benedictine abbey
    abbey seal

M339. *Obv.* In three adjoining canopied niches, standing figures: (centre) the Virgin, crowned, holding the Child on her L side and the holy thorn tree in her R hand; (L) St Katharine, crowned, holding her wheel in her L hand and a sword with its point resting on the ground in her R hand; (R) St Margaret, crowned, standing on the dragon which bites the foot of the long cross held in her R hand. Below them, on a plinth, S'KATERINA * S'MARIA * S'MARGARETA. In the field on either side, a fleur-de-lys. Below, in the exergue, between two perching birds, a small church or gatehouse, all set in rich tracery and panelling.

TESTIS.ADEST.ISTI.SCRI[PTO.GENETRIX.PI]A.XPI. GLASTONIE   (Lom)

    Rev. In three adjoining niches resembling those on *Obv*, standing figures, each vested and mitred: (centre) St Dunstan, blessing and holding a pastoral cross, (L) St Patrick, (R) St Benignus, each blessing and holding a crozier. Below them, on a plinth, s' PATRICIVS:S'DVNSTANVS:S'BENIGNVS. In the field on either side, a rosette. Below, in the exergue, three panels set in tracery and panelling showing: (centre) St Dunstan, wielding a hammer and pulling the Devil's nose with pincers; (L) an unidentified scene; (R) three fish, swimming.

CONFIRMANT.H[AS.RES.IN.SCRI]PTI.PONTIFICES.TRES
                                                     (Lom)

Round, 90; red, tag. Complete, except for small losses from legends at foot and from upper edge of *Obv*, very fine impression. The legends are punctuated with flowers, leaves and fleurs-de-lys. Pedrick, plate XV. BM 3189.

E 25/57/1   Pl 1   1534

GLOUCESTER (Glos) Benedictine abbey
abbey seal

M340. St Peter, bare-headed, wearing a cloak fastened with a clasp on his breast, seated on a bench-type throne with cushion and knobbed arms, holding a crozier.

+SIGILLV SCI.PETRI...CESTRA   (Lom)

Pointed oval, 65×45; uncoloured, tongue. Nearly complete, deep but not sharp impression from a matrix of 12c style. Has counterseal, **M342.** Also on DL 25/255 (1338), 256 (1339). BM 3192.

DL 27/107   Pl 19   1338

abbey seal

M341. In a canopied niche with tabernacle work at the sides, St Peter, with tiara of fleurs-de-lys, seated, holding a patriarchal cross in his R hand and keys in his L hand. Below, between sprigs, a shield of arms: *two keys in saltire, overall a sword in pale hilt downwards* (the ABBEY).

SIGILLUM.COMMUNE.MON...SANCTI.PETRI.GLOUCESTRIE   (BL)

Pointed oval, 75×50; bronze-green, tag. Nearly complete, deep clear impression, cracked, flattened. Has counterseal, **M343.** Also on E 329/462 (1471). BM 3195.

E 25/58/1   Pl 31   1534

abbot's privy seal: Adam de Stanton

M342. Under a canopy with tabernacle work at the sides, the abbot, standing on a carved corbel, vested for mass, holding a crozier and a book. In the field, vertical, his name STAVNTONE.

SECRETVM.ADE.ABBATIS.PETRI.GLAVCESTRIE   (Lom)

Pointed oval, 52×33; uncoloured, on tongue, as counterseal to **M340.** Complete, deep clear impression. Also on DL 25/255 (1333), 256 (1339). BM 3199.

DL 27/107   Pl 19   1338

counterseal or abbot's seal

M343. A shield of arms: *two keys in saltire, overall a sword in pale hilt downwards* (the ABBEY).

*S' WILL'I...   (Lom)

Round, 20; brown, on tag, as counterseal to **M341.** Complete, deep impression, legend blurred.

E 25/58/1   1534

GLOUCESTER (Glos) St Bartholomew's, Augustinian hospital

common seal

M344. Between (L) the moon and (R) the sun, the tall figure of St Bartholomew, holding a knife(?) in his R hand and a book in his L hand, standing behind the hospital shown as a rectangular masonry building with gabled porch and hipped roof with cross finials.

[SIGIL]L:HOSPITALI[S...]I DE GLOVCR...   (Lom)

Pointed oval, c.75×60; dark green, tag. Deep clear impression, lower edge lost. Also on E 42/300 (1318, which has counterseal **M346**), 414 (c.1318).

E 42/413   Pl 31   (1301–26)

common seal

M345. Under a Renaissance style canopy resting on fluted pilasters, St Bartholomew, standing.

...OSPITALIS... C...   (Rom)

Pointed oval, 60×35; red, tag. Large lower fragment of a deep clear impression.

E 25/58/2   1534

prior's seal: (John del Ok)

M346. St Bartholomew being flayed by two men with a knife and sword. Below, under a trefoiled arch, a figure, kneeling in prayer to R.

S' PRIORIS:SCI BARTHOL...GLO...   (Lom)

Pointed oval, 50×32; dark green, on tag, as counterseal to **M344.** Clear impression, edge partly lost or defaced. Also on E 43/414 (c.1318) BM 3205.

E 42/300   Pl 31   1318

GODSFIELD (Hants) Hospitallers' preceptory
master's seal

M347. A patriarchal cross.

SIGILL' DE H... TESIRE   (Lom)

Round, 30; green, tag. Clear impression, edge chipped.

E 326/11345   (13c)

GODSTOW (Oxon) Benedictine abbey
abbey seal

M348. On L, the Virgin, in an embroidered robe, seated on a throne, holding a palm branch. Before and facing her, on R, St John the Baptist, standing, holding in his L hand a pendent scroll inscribed ...GNVS DEI. The Virgin's L hand and St John's R hand uphold the Holy Lamb on a disk. Below and between them, St Ediva, the first abbess, wearing an embroidered robe with long sleeves, kneels and kisses the hem of the Virgin's robe; above, her name EDIVA.

SIGILLVM.SCE MARIE.ET.SCI...GODESTOENS ECCLIE   (Lom)

Pointed oval, 90×50; concave; green, tag. Complete, even but not deep impression. Also on E 42/341 (1303). BM 3209.

E 329/163   Pl 31   1284

abbess's seal: Katharine Bulkeley

M349. In a niche with two-tiered canopy and tabernacle work at the side, St John the Baptist, with nimbus, standing, holding the Holy Lamb on a disk and pointing to it with his L hand. Below, under a four-centred arch in masonry, St Ediva, crowned, holding a crozier, kneeling in prayer.

SIGILLU.CATERINE.../ABBATISSE.DE.GODSTOWE (BL)

Pointed oval, 60×37; red-brown, tag. Complete, deep sharp impression, parts rubbed, legend partly unclear. BM 3211.

E 322/93 1539

GOLDCLIFF (Monm) Benedictine priory
priory seal

M350. Under a double canopy with crocketed gables, standing figures: (L) the Virgin, holding the Child on her L side, and an apple in her R hand, with a crescent moon close to her feet; (R) St Mary Magdalene, with a star close to her feet. Background deeply hatched. Below, under an arch, a shield of arms: *three leopards* (ENGLAND).

...MAGDALENE DE GOLDCLI... (Lom)

Pointed oval, 67×41; red, tag. Fine impression at centre, edges blurred, cracked. Has counterseal, **M351**. Pedrick, plate X, 19. BM 3212.

E 42/342 Pl 24 1332

prior's seal: William Martel

M351. The Noli Me Tangere scene. Under a canopy resting on corbels, Our Lord stands on R, holding a tall cross and St Mary Magdalene kneels on L before him, a tree on either side. Below, under an arch, a clerk, half-length, praying to R.

S'FRIS.WILL'I.MAR/TE/L PRIS D' GOLDC[LIVIA] (Lom)

Pointed oval, 52×33; red, on tag, as counterseal to **M350**. Fine impression, upper half badly cracked and part lost. Also on E 42/418 (1332; complete but indistinct). BM 3213.

E 42/342 Pl 31 from E 42/418 1332

prior's seal: William St Aubyn

M352. The Noli Me Tangere scene. Under a double canopy with crocketed gables, St Mary Magdalene on L, holding a pot of ointment, kneeling before the risen Christ on R who holds a long-shafted cross in his L hand; between them, a tree. Below, under an arch, the prior, half-length, praying to R.

S'FRIS WILL'I DE [SCO ALBI/NO] PRIORIS DE GOLDCLIVIA (Lom)

Pointed oval, 55×34; dark green, tag. Complete, deep clear impression of central part, legend partly blurred. Has counterseal, **M353**. Also on E 42/415, 416, 343 (all 1340). BM 3214.

E 42/417 1340

prior's counterseal: William St Aubyn

M353. Under a canopy with crocketed gable resting on two slender columns, the Virgin, crowned, standing, holding the Child on her L side. Below, under an arch, the prior, half-length, praying to R. Diapered background.

SIGILLVM FRATRIS WILL'I DE SCO ALBINO (Lom)

Pointed oval, 40×24; dark green, on tag, as counterseal to **M352**. Complete, deep clear impression. Also on E 42/415, 416, 343 (all 1340). BM 3215.

E 42/417 1340

GORLESTON (Suff) Austin Friars' house
common seal

M354. In a niche framed by a channelled moulding with masks at the corners, a bishop, with nimbus, standing, holding a crozier and a book. Above, in a pediment, a winged cartouche (?); on either side, pendent sprays.

S' CONVENTVS ... RNEMVTHE.AO.D.15... (Rom)

Pointed oval, c.50×c.35; red, detached, on tag. Deep uneven impression, edge lost at foot and lower sides. An old note on the tag states that the seal is that of a conventual lease dated 14 March 21 Henry VIII. BM 3216.

SC 13/D64 (1529)

GRACE DIEU (Leics) Augustinian priory (F)
priory seal

M355. Under a trefoiled canopy on slender shafts, Our Lord, seated on a bench-type throne, blessing and holding a book. Below, under a trefoiled arch, the foundress, half-length, facing L, holding the charter with seal.

...GILL' CONV[ENTUS]...ALIV DE GRATIA... (Lom)

Pointed oval, c.45×33; red, tag. Deep impression, flattened, points lost. Pedrick, plate XII, 24. BM 3217.

E 322/69 Pl 31 1538

prioress's seal?

M356. A standing robed figure.
Legend lost.
Pointed oval?; dark green, tongue. Fragment.

E 135/21/5, no. 10 1264

GREAT GRIMSBY (Lincs) Franciscan house
common seal

M357. A seraph, standing; on L, a figure, robed, holding a staff.

...CONVET... (Lom)

Pointed oval, c.35×c.22; light brown, tag. Deep but indistinct impression, most of edge lost.

E 322/94 1538

GREAT MALVERN (Worcs) Benedictine priory
priory seal
M358. A seated figure?
Legend lost.
Central fragment of a deep impression, bronze-green, detached, on tag.
SC 13/R35   (n.d.)

GRIMSBY see WELLOW

GUISBOROUGH (Yorks) Augustinian priory
chapter seal
M359. *Obv.* In an elaborate gothic housing, under a church-like canopy and a trefoiled arch, the Virgin, seated on a bench-type throne, holding the Child, with nimbus, on her L knee; about her, a scroll lettered AVE MARIA GRACIA PL'. On either side, in a canopied niche with a censing demi-angel above, a monk, kneeling in adoration under a star.
S'CAP...VLI...   (Lom)
        Rev. In a similar housing, St Augustine, standing, mitred, blessing and holding a crozier; about him, a scroll lettered ORA P NOB BE AVGV. On either side, a monk, kneeling under a crescent.
...EC...NE   (Lom)
Round, c.65; bronze-green, detached, on tag. Fine impression, most of edge lost. Clay, plate III, 10 and 11. BM 3187.
SC 13/R23   Pl 30   (1538)

HALTEMPRICE (Yorks) Augustinian priory
priory seal
M360. In a gothic housing, kneeling figures.
Legend lost.
Small fragment, red, detached, on tag. Has counterseal, **M361**. Deep impression from the *Rev.* of the matrix dated 1322 in the British Museum (Tonnochy 841, plate XIX). Clay, p.20, plate IV. BM 3004–5 (as Cottingham).
SC 13/R24   1522
counterseal
M361. A shield of arms: *two bars, in chief three roundels*. No legend.
Round, 20; red, detached, on tag, as counterseal to **M360**.
Complete, clear.
SC 13/R24   1522
prior's seal
M362. An antique gem: a gryllus of three human heads in profile conjoined, with a tasselled cap.
[IVS]SA IOHIS AGO...[SIG]NAT IMA[GO]   (Lom)
Oval, 32×27; red, tag. Fine impression, part of edge lost. Clay, p.20, plate IV. BM 3248.
DL 25/330   1337

HAMPOLE (Yorks) Cistercian priory (F)
priory seal
M363. An eagle?
...VM COMMUNE...   (BL)
Pointed oval ?, c.50×c.30; red, detached, on tag. R fragment of a deep indistinct impression. Clay, p.21.
SC 13/R25   (1529)

HARBLEDOWN (Kent) Hospital
common seal
M364. St Nicholas as bishop, standing on a corbel, vested for mass, blessing and holding a crozier. Background diapered, with pierced mullets.
SIGILL'[INFIRMORIUM.HOSPTIALIS.SCI.NICH]OLAI.DE HERBALDOUNE   (BL)
Pointed oval, c.75×C.40; red, tongue. Large central fragment, blurred and flattened. Also on E 213/342 (1455). BM 3251 (cast from the matrix).
E 213/55   1412

HARROLD (Beds) Augustinian priory (F)
priory seal
M365. St Peter, standing, mitred and vested for mass, with pall, holding up keys in his R hand and a cross in his L hand.
...D'HARWOVLD.../DO...RARVM PETRE CHATENAS   (Lom)
Pointed oval, 60×37; red, detached, on tag. Complete, deep clear impression of figure, legend indistinct. BM 3252.
SC 13/R26   Pl 22   (n.d.)

HARTLAND (Devon) Augustinian abbey
abbey seal
M366. The head of St Nectan, facing L.
SIGILLVM NECTANVS   (Lom)
Round, 32; red, tag. Complete, deep clear impression. Also on E 135/2/35 (1534); E 322/101 (1534).
E 25/59   Pl 51   1539

HATFIELD BROAD OAK (Essex) Benedictine priory
chapter seal
M367. The Virgin, frontal, seated on a throne, holding the Child, with nimbus, on her R knee. The throne appears to have a back, with cresting, supported at the sides by small lions rampant.
...LL CAP'LL.DE...   (Lom)
Pointed oval, c.45×35; light brown, tag. Deep indistinct impression, rubbed, legend chipped and defaced, points lost. Also on SC 13/R27 (n.d.). BM 3255.
E 322/96   1534

HAUGHMOND (Salop) Augustinian abbey
abbey seal
M368. St John the Evangelist, in profile to L, seated on a throne, holding in his L hand a scroll on which he writes [IN PRINCIPIO]. On either side, a canon, standing, facing inwards, holding a book and a large key. Above St John's head, the hand of God; on L a star, on R a crescent. The throne, which has a decorated panel and a low back tipped with a fleur-de-lys, stands on the back of an eagle.
S'COMVNE.CAP/ITVLI.DE.HAGHEMON   (Lom)
Round, 52; red, tag. Complete except for chipped legend at foot, small crack in L centre, very deep clear impression. Pedrick, plate VI. 12. BM 3238.
E 322/95A   Pl 48   1539

HAVERFORDWEST (Pemb) Augustinian priory
priory seal
M369. Entirely defaced, except for a small part of the legend.
...VER...   (Lom)
Round, 36; red, tag. Complete, flattened.
E 25/61   1534

HEMPTON (Norf) Augustinian priory
priory seal
M370. In a niche under a vaulted canopy, St Stephen, standing between two tall tapers, holding three stones and a cloth in his R hand and a book in his L hand. Below, under an arch, a figure, kneeling in prayer to L.
SIGILLU.COMMU...D'.H...PTOUN   (BL)
Pointed oval, c.55×35; red, tongue. Deep clear impression, partly flattened, lower part lost. Also on SC 13/R28 (n.d.) BM 3266.
E 25/62/1   Pl 22   1534

HENWOOD (Warw) Benedictine priory (F)
priory seal
M371. St Margaret, standing on a dragon and piercing its head with a long cross; on L, a lily.
+SIGILLVM S'M[ARGA]RETE DE HINEWODE   (Lom)
Pointed oval, 55×40; green, tag. Nearly complete, deep clear impression. BM 3283.
E 326/11034   (13c)

HEREFORD (Heref) St Guthlac's, Benedictine priory
prior's seal
M372. An antique gem: a boy's head in profile to R, with a fillet round the hair.
...IS:':PRIORIS : HEREF...   (Lom)
Oval, 35×25; red, tongue. Clear impression, edge damaged. BM 3268.
E 329/151   1394

HERRINGFLEET (Suff) Augustinian priory
priory seal
M373. St Olave, crowned, seated on a decorated bench-type throne, holding a battle-axe in his R hand and an orb with tall cross in his L hand. On R, a flaming star.
+...MVN...LETE VP RIPA   (Lom)
Round, c.55; bronze, detached on tongue. Fine impression, lower and L and R edges lost. BM 3272.
E 25/97   Pl 22   1534

HEYNINGS (in Knaith, Lincs) Cistercian priory (F)
priory seal
M374. Under a large trefoiled arch resting on two slender columns, the Virgin, seated on a bench-type throne, her feet on a carved corbel, holding the Child, with nimbus, on her L knee. In the field: (L) two roses, a crescent and a star; (R) a rose and a crescent.
S'SANCTE.MARIE.ET.COVENTVS.DE.HEYNIGE   (Lom)
Pointed oval, c.55×36; red-brown, tag. Nearly complete, very deep but slightly uneven impression from a fine 14c style matrix. Pedrick, plate XIII, 25. BM 3278.
E 322/98   1539

HICKLING (Norf) Augustinian priory
priory seal
M375. Under a canopy of a trefoiled arch carrying an arcaded and gabled building, the Virgin, seated on a bench-type throne with diaper decoration, holding the Child on her L knee. On either side, three human heads in profile.
*SIGILL ECCE.SCE.MARIE.DE.HIKEL   (Lom)
Pointed oval, 50×32; dark green, tag. Complete, clear impression. Also on E329/106 (1380), 154 (1380); E 212/30 (1380); E 25/63 (1534).
E 329/89   1380

HINCKLEY (Leics) Benedictine priory
prior's seal: John Morelli
M376. Under a double canopy with pinnacles tipped with fleurs-de-lys, the Coronation of the Virgin. Below, under a rounded arch, the prior, kneeling in prayer to R.
S' PRIS IOHIS MOR/ELL PRI D' HIN/KL   (Lom)
Oval, 30×24; light brown, tag. Complete, deep impression, centre flattened, legend crudely engraved. Attached to the surrender of Haverholme priory, in place of the common seal referred to in the sealing clause. John Morelli, prior of Hinckley, died in 1367. BM 3282.
E 322/97   1538

HINTON CHARTERHOUSE (Som) Carthusian priory

priory seal

M377. The Virgin, seated, holding a sceptre in her L hand, and the Child, standing, on her R knee. Below, an arch; on either side, a panel of tracery.
Legend lost.
Pointed oval, c.35×c.30; dark green, tongue. Large central fragment of a deep clear impression.
E 213/425 (c.1437)

priory seal

M378. The Assumption. The Virgin, with a halo of three fleurs-de-lys, standing, ascending in glory; above her, the Dove, wings outspread; on either side, a saint, with nimbus, kneeling in prayer; below, three figures, kneeling, looking upwards and lifting their hands in adoration.
[SIGILL]UM DOM LOC[I DEI DE H]INTON ORDIS CARTUSIESIS (Rom)
Pointed oval, c.70×c.45; bronze-green, tag. Deep impression showing detail, but blurred, cracked and lacking edge at top and foot.
E 322/99 1539

prior's seal: William

M379. Under a double canopy, in a niche between tabernacle work, the Annunciation: the angel on L facing the Virgin on R; between them, a lily in a pot.
[AVE . MARIA . GRACI]A . PLENA . DNS . TECVM (BL)
Oval, 30×25; red, tongue. Deep impression, parts flattened, R side lost.
E 213/90 1434

HOLM CULTRAM (Cumb) Cistercian abbey

abbey seal

M380. In a canopied niche with diapered interior, the Virgin, crowned, standing, holding the Child on her L side. Under lower adjacent canopies, standing figures: (L) a king, crowned, holding a sceptre; (R) an abbot holding a crozier. Below the Virgin's feet, a shield of arms of ENGLAND (for Henry II, patron) supported by two quarter-length tonsured figures on whose heads rest the canopy's long slender columns; below, a lion, curled up.
S'CO...VATIS:ET:CONVENTVS:DE:HOLMCOLTRAM (Lom)
Pointed oval, 70×40; red, tag. Deep impression with detail, flattened, part of edge lost. Has counterseal, M383. Pedrick, plate X, 20. BM 3288.
E 322/103　Pl 47 1538

counterseal

M381. A vested forearm and hand issuing from R, holding a crozier; above, flowers.
+CON[TRA.SIGILLVM.DE.HO]LMO (Lom)
Pointed oval, c.30×20; dark green, tongue. Large

upper fragment of a deep impression. BM 3289.
E 213/6 1301

abbot's seal: Thomas

M382. Under a columned canopy, the abbot, standing, vested, holding a crozier and a book. On either side, foliage.
SIG...HOLMCOLTRAM (Lom)
Pointed oval, 40×25; red, tag. Deep clear impression, flattened, points and R edge lost. Laing 181. BM 3290.
DL 25/244 1330

abbot's seal: Robert Pim

M383. A crozier between initials RP.
...ROBTI PIM AB/BTIS D'HOLM (BL)
Round, 16; red-brown, on tag, as counterseal to M380. Complete, deep clear impression. Laing 182. BM 3291.
E 322/103 1538

HOLYROOD (in Edinburgh, Midlothian) Augustinian abbey

abbot's seal

M384. A hostiary in the form of a cross, with the head of Our Lord upon the host, filling the upper part of the field; below, on R, the abbot, holding a crozier and a book, kneeling before an altar, on L, on which is a chalice.
*S' ABBATIS SANCTE CRVCIS DE EDINGBORG (Lom)
Pointed oval, 45×28; mottled green, detached, complete, deep clear impression, slightly flattened. Also on SC 13/C54 (n.d.). Laing, 1041. BM 15293.
SC 13/D49　Pl 25 (n.d.)

HOLYSTONE (Northumb) Augustinian priory

priory seal

M385. The Virgin, seated, holding the Child on her L knee.
Legend lost.
Pointed oval, c.50×c.35; dark brown, tongue. Large central fragment of a deep impression.
E 213/76 1323

HOLYWOOD (Dumfries) Premonstratensian abbey

abbot's seal

M386. The abbot, standing on a carved corbel, holding a crozier in his L hand and a tree with a bird on it in his R hand. On L, a star; on R, a crescent.
*S' ABBATIS DE . SACRO NEMORE (Lom)
Pointed oval, 40×25; mottled green, detached, on hemp cords. Complete, deep clear impression. Laing 1044. BM 15,323.
SC 13/D50　Pl 24 (n.d.)

HORNBY (Lancs) Premonstratensian priory
priory seal
M387. A seal of gothic design: (possibly) two figures, under a canopy, standing on corbels; below, a half-length praying figure. On either side, a shield of arms (defaced).
Legend lost.
Round ?, c.40; red, tag. Central fragment, defaced, flattened.
E 322/104   1536

HORSHAM ST FAITH (Norf) Benedictine priory
priory seal
M388. In the upper part, in a niche under a trefoiled arch which supports a small church with transepts, the Virgin, crowned, enthroned, holding a fleur-de-lys sceptre; on either side, under a canopy with a spire below a censing demi-angel, a kneeling figure. In the lower part, an embattled gateway with large trefoiled arch under which St Faith, crowned, stands and raises up a prisoner; on either side, a bartisan containing (L) an armed knight, (R) a bowman with a cross-bow.
SIGILLVM:COMVNE:CAPITV...AM   (Lom)
Pointed oval, 80×50; red, tongue. Deep uneven impression, L edge lost. Also on E 40/13256 (1531). BM 3294.
E 25/94/2   Pl 47   1534

HORSLEY (Glos) Augustinian cell
prior's seal: William Cary
M389. In an oblong panel, the Virgin, seated on a bench-type throne, holding the Child; below, under an arch, a figure, half-length, praying to L. On either side, a lunette of tracery containing initials W and C.
SI:WILLELMI:CARI:PRIORIS DE HORSLE   (BL)
Round, 24; red, tag. Complete, deep but uneven impression. Also on E 326/11644 (1368). BM 3297.
E 42/421   Pl 55   1368

HOUNSLOW (Midd) Trinitarian house
common seal
M390. Under a canopy, Our Lord, seated on a throne with turned legs and diapered cover, his feet on a footstool, his R hand raised in blessing.
Legend lost.
Pointed oval, over 50×30; red, tag. Central fragment of a deep clear impression defaced by flattening.
E 42/422   1382
common seal
M391. Under a canopy of three gables, with tabernacle work at the sides, the Holy Trinity.
'S.SANC...TRINITE/DOMVS.DE...   (BL)

Round, 40; brown, tag. Clear impression, legend chipped and obscured.
C 148/116   Pl 22   1487

HULL see KINGSTON UPON HULL

HULME see ST BENET OF HULME

HULTON (Staffs) Cistercian abbey
abbey seal
M392. In a niche with pinnacled canopy and tabernacle work at the sides, the Virgin, crowned, holding the Child on her R knee and a long sceptre tipped with a fleur-de-lys in her L hand. Below, a shield of arms: *a fret* (AUDLEY, the founder).
SIGILLU.COMU...TE.MARIE.DE.HULTON   (BL)
Pointed oval, c.60×38; red, tag. Deep clear impression, slightly rubbed, points and lower edge lost. BM 3306.
E 322/106   Pl 11   1538

HUMBERSTON (Lincs) Benedictine abbey
abbey seal
M393. The Virgin, seated on a canopied throne of struts and bars resembling wickerwork, holding the Child on her L knee.
...LL' VEN...D' HVMBERSTA...   (Lom)
Pointed oval, c.55×26; red, tag. Deep clear impression, points lost. BM 3307.
E 25/65/1   Pl 22   1534

HUNTINGDON (Hunts) Augustinian priory
priory seal
M394. *Obv.* In a cusped roundel of 30 mm diameter, with trefoils deeply sunk in the spandrels, the Coronation of the Virgin. This roundel is upheld on either side by a seraph with one wing upraised. Above, the face of Our Lord between (L) initial A above a crescent and (R) O above a star. Below, the Resurrection: four of the dead arising, one from a coffin, as two angels blow their trumpets.
S'COMMVNE:[P...ET:CANONICORVM:SCE]MARIE:HVNTIN-GDONE   (Lom)
   Rev. The priory church with central spire, pitched roof and gables with cresting and finials. In the centre, under a trefoiled arch, St Augustine, enthroned as archbishop, blessing and holding a pastoral cross. On either side, in a niche with ogee arch, two canons, kneeling in prayer; above them, a deep roundel containing heads of (L) St Peter and (R) St Paul, with arcading above. Below, under arcading, four heads in profile to L, wearing shallow-crowned hats with brims.

To L and R of the spire, CLE and M V, in reference to Pope Clement V.

CANONICIS:LEGES:PR:AVGVS...DED:...H' PIA DONA TVIS (Lom)

Round, 60; red, tag. Fine impression, parts lost from lower half. The reference to Clement V (1305–14) perhaps dates the matrix. Also on E 322/107 (1538). BM 3308.

E 25/66   Pl 7   1534

HURLEY (Berks) Benedictine priory
prior's seal: Alexander de Newport
M395. A gem: the bust of a man, tonsured, in profile to R, his R hand raised.

...PENEITV...PACEM (Lom)

Oval, 25×20; red, tongue. Deep clear impression, edge lost at top and foot.

DL 27/138   Pl 6   1306

HYDE see WINCHESTER

INCHAFFRAY (Perth) Augustinian abbey
abbot's seal
M396. In two adjoining niches, standing figures: (R) a bishop, holding a crozier; (L) a saint, holding a palm branch. Above, under a crocketed gable, the Virgin, seated, holding the Child on her L knee. Below, the abbot, half-length, praying to R, holding a crozier.

S'ABBATIS DE I/NSVLA MISSARV (Lom)

Pointed oval, 40×27; light green, detached, on hemp cords. Complete, deep clear impression. Laing 1047. BM 15327.

SC 13/D51   Pl 34   (13c)

INCHCOLM (Fife) Augustinian abbey
abbot's seal
M397. On waves, a ship with mainmast, yard, furled sail and flying pennon; in it, (R) a bishop (St Columba ?), mitred and holding a crozier, and (L) the abbot, holding a crozier.

*S' ABBATIS.DE.INSVLA.SANCTI.COLVMB' (Lom)

Pointed oval, 40×25; mottled green, detached, on hemp cords. Complete, deep clear impression. Laing 1048. BM 15331.

SC 13/D53   Pl 19   (n.d.)

INGHAM (Norf) Trinitarian house
common seal
M398. In a niche with crocketed canopy, traceried field and tabernacle work at the sides, the Holy Trinity. Below, between traceried spandrels, a shield of arms: *a lion rampant* (STAPLETON, founder).

...SANCTE TRINITATIS CO... (BL)

Pointed oval, 60×c.40; red, tag. Deep uneven impression, R side lost, L edge broken. BM 3314.

E 25/67/1   1534

IPSWICH (Suff) Holy Trinity, Augustinian priory
priory seal
M399. In a quatrefoil with the emblems of the four Evangelists outside in the spandrels, Our Lord, seated on a bench-type throne, blessing and holding a book, between seven candlesticks (four to L, three to R) with a flaming star above each group.

...E:XPI.GIPEWI[CE]NSIS (Lom)

Round, 60; uncoloured, tag. Deep clear impression, R edge lost.

E 42/425   Pl 24   (c.1280)
counterseal
M400. The Holy Lamb with cross and flag.

+SE[CRE]T AGN[VS]IDEM...SERAT (Lom)

Round, 30; uncoloured, detached. Deep impression, R side lost.

E 42/426   (c.1200)

IPSWICH (Suff) St Peter and St Paul's, Augustinian priory
priory seal
M401. A cruciform church with tall central tower and spire and large clerestory windows, standing on waves. In roundels on either side of the tower, head of (L) St Peter and (R) St Paul.

SIGILLVM ECC...SWIC (Lom)

Round, c.54; dark green, tag. Deep clear impression, rubbed, most of edge lost. Has counterseal, **M403.** Also on E 40/3637 (n.d.); E 40/3861 (temp. Hen. III, which has counterseal **M402**); E 42/423 (1416). BM 3317.

E 42/424   Pl 19   1290
prior's seal
M402. A gem: a man's head, wearing close head-dress, facing R.

MITTENTIS CAPITI CREDIT SICVT EI (Lom)

Oval, 25×20; uncoloured, on tag, as counterseal to **M402**. Complete, fine impression, rubbed.

E 40/3861   Pl 19   (temp. Hen. III)
prior's seal: John
M403. A gem: a male figure, bearded, wearing hat and cloak, standing, facing L.

*IOHANNES.EST.NOMEN.EIVS (Lom)

Oval, 22×18; dark green, on tag, as counterseal to **M401**. Complete, very clear impression.

E 42/424   Pl 23   1290
prior's seal
M404. Under adjoining arches, St Peter and St Paul, standing; above, in a roundel, a head.

+SIGILL' PRIORIS APLOR...ES...CH PETRI D' GYPWICO (Lom)

Pointed oval, 48×33; green, tag. Clear impression, flattened, edge damaged.
E 40/3533   1295

IVYCHURCH (Wilts) Augustinian priory
priory seal
M405. Under a canopy, between panels of tracery, the Holy Trinity.
Legend lost or uncertain.
Pointed oval, c.35×23; brown, tongue. Large fragment of a deep impression, flattened.
E 213/343   1409
priory seal
M406. Under a pinnacled canopy with tabernacle work at the sides, the Virgin, irradiate, with nimbus, standing on a corbel carved with cinquefoils, holding the Child on her R side.
SIGILLUM C'MUNE MONASTERII.BEATE.MARIE. DE.EDER[OSE]   (BL)
Pointed oval, c.60×35; bronze-green, tag. Deep clear impression, points lost. BM 3329.
E 329/325   Pl 54   1423
prior's seal: Walter
M407. In an oblong panel with curved top, the Virgin, crowned, holding the Child on her R side.
...ARIA GRA...   (Lom)
Round, 20; dark brown, tongue. Complete, deep impression, partly indistinct.
E 213/344   1412
prior's signet: John Cheveley
M408. A shield of arms: *a cross*; held by an angel whose head, shoulders and wings appear above.
...ET CON': BEATE : MARIE   (Lom)
Round, 23; red, tongue. Complete, deep impression, heavily flattened; the legend's first half is unclear.
E 213/345   1432

IXWORTH (Suff) Augustinian priory
priory seal
M409. The Assumption of the Virgin in a mandorla of wavy clouds upheld by four angels in flight and a fifth, half-length, below her feet. Above, the Trinity, shown as three half-length crowned figures of equal size, surrounded by clouds and stars. On either side, a half-length figure: (L) a bishop, mitred and holding a crozier: (R) St John the Baptist, with nimbus, holding a long cross. Below, on the breasts of two angels, two shields of arms: (L) *barry of six, a bend* (MONCHENSY); (R) *lozengy* (BLUND).
SIGILLUM:COMUNE:COVE/SCE.MARIE.IKESWORTHE (BL)
Pointed oval, 70×42; red, tongue. Nearly complete, fine impression, slightly flattened. BM 3332.
E 25/68   Pl 16   1534

JEDBURGH (Roxburgh) Augustinian abbey
abbot's privy seal
M410. The abbot, standing, holding a crozier and a book; on L a crescent, on R a star.
SIGILL' SECRETI ABBATIS DE IEDEWRTHE   (Lom)
Pointed oval, 43×28; mottled green, detached, on red and white plaited laces. Complete, fine impression.
SC 13/E56   Pl 55   (n.d.)
seal of office of abbot
M411. In a niche with pinnacled canopy and tabernacle work at the sides, the Flight into Egypt; below, the abbot, kneeling in prayer to R, holding a crozier.
...OFFICII ABBATIS/...EDWOR   (Lom)
Pointed oval, 50×38; brown, detached, on tag. Uneven and blurred impression, parts of edge lost. Laing 1055. BM 15340.
SC 13/E55   (n.d.)

JERVAUX (Yorks) Cistercian abbey
counterseal
M412. A pastoral staff.
+CONT...LLIS   (Lom)
Pointed oval, c.25; red, on tag, as counterseal to an abbey seal now obliterated. Two clear impressions of upper half only. Also on E 326/6021 (1397). Clay, p.22, plate IV, 9.
E 326/11743   1397
abbot's seal: Richard Gower
M413. Under a vaulted canopy, the abbot, standing, facing half R, mitred and holding a crozier. On R, in a higher niche, a figure, robed, standing, holding a book, with a shield of arms below: *fretty, a chief* (FITZHUGH or ST. QUINTIN). Below, a larger shield of arms: *three bars, in chief three roundels* (GOWER).
Legend lost.
Pointed oval, c.55×c.35; red, tongue. Central fragment of a fine impression. Has a counterseal, M414. Also on E 326/8427 (1406). BM 3316.
E 329/138   Pl 24   1417
abbot's signet: Richard Gower
M414. A shield of arms: *three bars, in chief three roundels*. No legend.
Octagonal, 13; red, on tongue, as counterseal to M413.
Complete, clear.
E329/138   1417

KELSO (Roxburgh) Tironian abbey
abbot's seal
M415. Under a canopy resting on corbels, the Virgin, half-length, holding the Child, with nimbus, on her L side, between two censing angels. Below, under a scroll inscribed S.ABB'S DE.KELCHO, the abbot, mitred,

kneeling in prayer to R before an altar on which is a chalice; about him, three stars.

[VIR]GO TVVM NATVM LAC[TAN]S FAC ME SIB[I GRATVM]
(Lom)

Pointed oval, c.50×35; dark green, detached, on tag. Fine impression, points lost. Laing 1062. Also on SC 13/D67 (n.d.). BM 15353.

SC 13/C60   Pl 25   (n.d.)

KENILWORTH (Warw) Augustinian priory, later abbey

priory seal

M416. The Virgin, crowned and with nimbus, seated on the roof of the priory church, holding a sceptre in her L hand and a book in her R hand.

+...A   (Lom)

Round, c.65; dark green, tag. Deep uneven impression, most of edge lost. Has counterseal, M418. BM 3333.

E 327/684   Pl 9   (1235–9)

abbey seal

M417. In a canopied niche of Renaissance design, the Virgin, crowned and with nimbus, seated, holding the Child on her L knee and a sceptre in her R hand. On either side of the niche, a waving spray of foliage; below, a shield of arms: *quarterly, France modern and England.*

S'COE:MONASTERII:BTE:MARIE:DE:KENELLWORTH (Rom)

Pointed oval, 80×50; red, tag. Nearly complete, fine impression. Has counterseal, M418. BM 3338.

E 322/111   Pl 20   1539

counterseal

M418. A demi-angel, wings outspread, R hand raised.

+CERA PATENS CELAT QVE CARTVLA [SCIS]SA
REVELAT   (Lom)

Round, 35; dark green, on tag, as counterseal to M416 and M417. Nearly complete, deep clear impression, lgend chipped on L. About the impression is the imprint of the loop of the matrix. Also on E 322/111 (1539). Pedrick, plate XXXVII 73. BM 3333.

E 327/684   Pl 9   (1235–9)

prior's seal: Thomas

M419. The Annunciation.

AVE [MARIA GRATIA P] LEN [A...]   (Lom)

Oval, c.22×c.18; green, tongue. Large central fragment of a clear impression, flattened.

E 43/592   Pl 12   1339

prior's seal: Robert

M420. Under a double canopy, the prior, kneeling before St Helen, standing, holding the Cross; foliage above his head.

VIRGO SCA ELENA PRO...   (Lom)

Oval, 23×17; red, tongue. Complete, clear except for end of legend.

E 329/153   1423

abbot's seal: William Walle

M421. Under a pinnacled canopy with tabernacle work at the sides, the Virgin, crowned, seated, holding the Child on her L knee and a tall lily in her R hand. Below, under an arch, the abbot, kneeling in prayer.

S.WILLIAM /...LLE   (Rom)

Oval, 35×30; red-brown, tongue. Nearly complete, centre clear. Also on E 213/430 (1530). BM 3339.

E 329/209   Pl 7   1533

KERSEY (Suff) Augustinian priory

priory seal

M422. In the upper part, in a crescent of clouds, a bust of the Virgin, crowned. Below, under an arch, a man's head wearing a round cap. Between them, (L) a flaming sun and (R) a crescent.

+SIGILL' SCE.MARIE.ET.SCI.ANTONII.DE.KERSEIA (Lom)

Pointed oval, 60×36; mottled green, tag. Complete, deep clear impression. Has counterseal, M423. BM 3343.

E 42/427   Pl 22   (c.1240–50)

prior's seal: Henry

M423. A pig's head couped at the neck, and a bell hanging below (St Anthony's emblems).

S'HENR.PRIORIS D': S'ANTONII   (Lom)

Pointed oval, 30×20; mottled green, on tag, as counterseal to M422. Complete, deep clear impression. BM 3344.

E 42/427   (13c)

KEYNSHAM (Som) Augustinian abbey

abbey seal

M424. In three adjoining niches with elaborate vaulted and pinnacled canopies, standing figures: (centre) the Virgin, crowned and with nimbus, holding the Child, with nimbus, on her R side and a sceptre tipped with fleur-de-lys in her L hand; (L) St Peter, with nimbus, holding keys; (R) St Paul, with nimbus, holding a sword. Below, under a trefoiled arch, a shield of arms: *six clarions* (the ABBEY).

SIGILLUM.COMMUNE.MONASTERII/...TE.MARIE.DE.
KEYNESHAM   (BL)

Pointed oval, 65×40; red, tag. Nearly complete, deep clear impression, figures flattened. Also on E 25/69/1 (1534). BM 3346.

E 322/122   1539

abbot's seal: Morgan

M425. A gem: a figure, seated, facing R.

SECRETVM...ABBATIS   (Lom)

Oval, 28×23; dark green, tag. Complete, green impression, partly indistinct.

E 327/46   (c.1200)

KILBURN (Midd) Benedictine priory (F)
priory seal
M426. St John the Baptist, standing, pointing with his R hand to a long scroll hanging from his L hand inscribed ECCE ANGNUS DEI. The saint's L elbow seems to rest on a crutch.
SIGILL' CO...SCI.IO[HANNIS.B]APT' DE KENEBVRN (Lom)
Pointed oval, 58×40; dark green, tag. Deep but not sharp impression, part of R edge lost. Also on E 42/429 (c.1258). BM 3348.
E 42/428   Pl 5   (c.1258)

KILWINNING (Ayr) Tironian abbey
abbot's seal
M427. Under a panelled and gabled canopy resting on slender pillars, the Virgin, half-length, holding the Child on her L side; below, under an arch, the abbot, kneeling in prayer to L, holding a crozier.
S'ABBATIS DE/KILLWYNYN   (Lom)
Pointed oval, 50×30; mottled green, detached, on hemp cords. Complete, deep uneven impression. Laing 1065. BM 15359, which closely resembles this seal, reads KILWYNNYN.
SC 13/D55   (13c)

KINGS LANGLEY (Herts) Dominican house
friary seal
M428. Our Lord, seated on a low backless throne, blessing and holding an orb. Below, a king, in armour, crowned, kneeling to L, holding a church with a tall spire topped with a cross; on his L shoulder, a shield of arms: *three leopards* (ENGLAND); the field sown with trefoils.
[S'COV'ET FR'VM ORD' P...] DE.LAGG[ELE REGIS] (Lom)
Pointed oval, c.41×c.24; uncoloured, tongue. Deep uneven impression, flattened, edge damaged. Also on E 43/120 (1346), 121 (1329).
E 43/119   1331
prior's seal
M429. Our Lord, seated on a bench-type throne with arcaded front, blessing and holding an orb. Below, (L) a friar, half-length, praying to R; (R) a shield of arms: *three leopards* (ENGLAND). The field sown with trefoils.
+S' PRIOR' FR'VM ORD' PRED' DE LAGGELE REGIS (Lom)
Pointed oval, 41×23; uncoloured, tongue. Fine impression, small loss at points. Also on E 43/119 (1331).
E 43/118   Pl 7   1323
prior's seal
M430. On L, a friar, kneeling in prayer to R before the Rood; leafy branches in the field.
+NI/...RE . DARRETON   (Lom)

Oval, 19×15; dark green, tongue. Deep clear impression, part of R edge lost.
E 43/122   Pl 26   1350
prior's seal: John Astwode
M431. Under a pinnacled canopy with ogee arch, Our Lord, seated on a throne with fleur-de-lys finials, blessing with his R hand; background diapered with stars. Below, (L) a kneeling figure; (R) a shield of arms: *quarterly, France modern and England.*
...IS : FR'UM/OR...VE   (BL)
Pointed oval, 45×c.30; red, tongue. Two impression, flattened and broken, but complementary.
E 213/426   1401
prior's seal
M432. Under an elaborately pinnacled triple canopy, in a square panel, the Annunciation. Below, under a rounded arch, the king, robed, crowned, kneeling between two shields of arms: *quarterly, Old France and England.*
Traces remain of a legend within the circumference:
S'P'.../P...   (BL)
Pointed oval, 70×40; red, tongue. Deep clear impression, cracked, part of edge lost. BM 3409.
E 329/79   1515

KINGSTON UPON HULL (Yorks) Carthusian priory
priory seal
M433. In a canopied niche with tabernacle work at the sides, St Michael, standing, holding a long spear and a shield with a cross. Below, a shield of arms: *a fesse between three leopard's faces* (DE LA POLE).
...MICHIS.AR... IS : DE : KYNGESTON : SR : HVLL (BL)
Pointed oval, 50×30; dark green, detached, on tongue. Deep clear impression, upper and R edge lost. Has counterseal, **M434.**
SC 13/D158   Pl 7   (n.d.)
counterseal
M434. Under a crown, initial I (Lom) between branches.
No legend.
Oval, 14×11; dark green, detached, on tag, as counterseal to **M433.** Two impressions, one complete and clear.
SC 13/D158   (n.d.)
prior's seal: Roger Billington
M435. Under a double canopy, the Annunciation; below, under an arch, a figure, half-length, holding a book.
ANGELUS : DO/...   (BL)
Oval, 25×20; dark brown, tongue. Deep indistinct impression, edge damaged.
E 213/346   Pl 32   1412

KINGSWOOD (Glos, formerly Wilts) Cistercian abbey

abbey seal

M436. A hand issuing from R, holding a crozier. In the field, three pellets and, lower L, a branch.

...KING...WV...   (Lom)

Pointed oval, c.40×c.25; light green, tag. Large fragment of a deep indistinct impression.

E 327/46   (n.d.)

abbey seal

M437. Under a trefoiled arch in a gabled and crocketed canopy resting on slender columns, the Virgin, crowned and with nimbus, standing, holding the Child on her L side. Diapered ground outside the pillars. Below, under an arch, a monk, half-length, praying to R.

S' AB[BATIS]... ENTUS B/EATE...   (BL)

Pointed oval, 55×c.35; red, detached, on tag. Nearly complete, deep clear impression. Also on E 322/114 (1539). BM 3353.

SC 13/R30   Pl 11   (n.d.)

abbot's seal

M438. The abbot, standing on a corbel, mitred and holding a crozier and a book.

SIGILL' ABBATI/S DE KINGESWDE   (Lom)

Pointed oval, 45×28; dark brown, detached, on tongue. Complete, deep clear impression. Has counterseal, **M439.** BM 3355.

SC 13/D95   (n.d.)

counterseal

M439. A vested forearm issuing from R, the hand holding a crozier. Above the arm, a star in a crescent; on L, five slipped trefoils.

+CONTRASIG : ABBATIS DE KIGESWOD   (Lom)

Pointed oval, 35×20; dark brown, detached, on tongue, as counterseal to **M438.** Complete deep clear impression. BM 3356.

SC 13/D95   Pl 25   (n.d.)

KIRBY BELLARS (Leics) Augustinian priory

priory seal

M440. St. Peter, seated on a canopied throne, blessing and holding keys. On either side, curious decoration resembling water falling from a gutter into a basin. Below, a shield of arms: *a lion rampant crowned* (BELLARS).

...ECCLESSIE.BEATI... KIRKEBI . SVPER . WRETHEK (Lom)

Pointed oval, c.65×35; red, tag. Deep clear impression, flattened, edge broken. BM 3358.

E 25/70   Pl 48   1534

KIRKHAM (Yorks) Augustinian priory

priory seal

M441. Our Lord, with nimbus, seated, blessing and holding a book.

Legend lost.

Pointed oval, 70×c.45; uncoloured, tag. Very indistinct impression, edge lost. Has counterseal, **M442.** Also on E 326/11354 (1350). Clay, p.22, plate V, 1. BM 3360.

E 322/115   1538

counterseal

M442. In base, the Annunciation, both figures half-length; above, the Nativity. At the top, a bust of the Virgin, crowned.

...MARIA   (Lom)

Pointed oval, 35×24; uncoloured, on tag, as counterseal to **M441.** Complete, deep indistinct impression.

E 322/115   1538

KIRKSTALL (Yorks) Cistercian abbey

abbey seal

M443. In a niche with ogee arch and crocketed pinnacles, the Virgin, crowned, seated on a bench-type throne with arcaded front; on her L, the Child, standing on the throne, facing her, his R hand raised and his L hand grasping her robe; background of curling stems and leaves. On either side of the niche, the exergues have a diapered field containing (a monogram of TL?).

SIGILLV...MVNE.DE.KYRKESTAL   (Lom)

Round, 50; red, tag. Deep clear impression, parts flattened, R edge chipped. Clay, p.23, plate V, 5. BM 3364.

DL 27/126   Pl 10   1399

abbot's seal

M444. The abbot, standing on a corbel, vested for mass, holding a crozier and a book. On L, a cowled head, a cross above and a fleur-de-lys below; on R, another head, a fleur-de-lys above and a cross below.

...IS : DE KIRKESTALL   (Lom)

Pointed oval, 55×35; uncoloured, on red silk laces. Complete, deep clear impression. Also on DL 27/34 (1284). Has counterseal, **M445** BM 3366.

DL 27/199   Pl 22   1287

abbot's counterseal

M445. A sleeved forearm and hand issuing from R, holding a crozier, between (L) a star and (R) a crescent.

CONT' SIGILL' ABB'IS DE KYRK...L   (Lom)

Pointed oval, 33×22; uncoloured, on red silk laces, as counterseal to **M444.** Complete, deep clear impression. Also on DL 27/34 (1284).

DL 27/199   1287

KNAITH see HEYNINGS

KNARESBOROUGH (Yorks) Trinitarian house

prior's seal: Robert

M446. In a pointed oval with cusping, the Trinity, on

an arcaded throne. Below, under an arch with traceried spandrels, a man, seated under a tree, reading a book.

...ROB/TI.DE...RGHE (Lom)

Pointed oval, 55×c.38; red, tag. Deep clear impression, R side lost, edge damaged. BM 3378.

E 322/117 Pl 22 1538

KYME (Lincs) Augustinian priory
priory seal

M447. The Annunciation. On R, the Virgin, standing, a lily in a pot behind her; on L, the archangel, standing with bended knee on a mount.

[SI]GILLVM.PRIORIS.ET.CONVENTVS.DE.KI[MA] (Lom)

Round, 48; red, tag. Nearly complete, deep but very uneven impression. Also on E 25/71 (1534). Pedrick, plate VI, 11. BM 3383.

E 322/118 1539

LACOCK (Wilts) Augustinian abbey (F)
abbey seal

M448. Under a church-like canopy, the Virgin, crowned, enthroned, holding the Child on her L knee. The slender columns supporting the canopy rest on a lower gabled and arcaded canopy, below the Virgin's feet, under which, in a trefoiled arch, a canon kneels in prayer to L. The Virgin's throne rests on slim tapering turned legs and has two tall S-curved arms ending in human faces.

S' CONVENT:BEATE:MARIE:&:SANCTI:BERNARDI:D': LACOC (Lom)

Pointed oval, 70×45; pale green, tag. Nearly complete, deep clear impression. Also on E 40/6820 (1351), 11184 (1240–55); E 42/194 (1240–55), 344 (1300), 345 (1240–55) which has counterseal M449, 347 (1316);
E 322/119 (1539); WARD 2/28/78 (1240–55). BM 3389.

E 42/346 (1240–55)

abbess's seal: Ela, countess of Salisbury

M449. Under a canopy, the Virgin and Child, enthroned.

SIGILL'.ELE.ABBATISSE.DE.LACOK (Lom)

Pointed oval, 44×30; mottled green, tag. Complete, deep indistinct impression. Also on E 42/345 (1240–55) as counterseal to M448.

E 42/346 (1240–55)

LAMBLEY (Northumb) Benedictine priory (F)
priory seal

M450. The Holy Lamb; above, [AG]N/VS DEI. (Lom)
[+S] COMV...E...

Pointed oval, 45×30; dull red, tongue. Large fragment of a deep impression, head and banner lost.

E 213/71 1323

LANCASTER (Lancs) Dominican house
prior's seal: Nigel

M451. The Virgin, crowned, seated on a throne, holding the Child, with nimbus, on her L knee. Below, under an arch, (a praying figure ?). Foliage in the field on either side.

...FRIS...LL...ANCASTR (Lom)

Pointed oval, 40×25; dark green, tag. Deep clear impression, flattened, lower L quarter lost.

DL 25/345 1315

prior's seal

M452. St Martin, on horseback, riding to L, dividing his cloak with the beggar. Above, in an arched panel, the Virgin, half-length, holding the Child on her L side. Below, under an arch, the prior, praying.

...IOR BE MARIE LANC (Lom)

Pointed oval, 40×25; uncoloured, tongue. Deep uneven impression, edge much damaged.

DL 25/3472 1334

LANGDON (Kent) Premonstratensian abbey
abbey seal

M453. *Obv.* Under a cusped arch below a crocketed gable, in a niche with tabernacle work at the sides, the Virgin, crowned, seated, holding the Child on her L knee; below her feet, a deep moulding carved with quatrefoils.

SIGILL' [COMMVNE:M]ONASTERII:ECCE:[BE:MARIE:DE LA]NGEDON (Lom)

Rev. In a representation of Canterbury cathedral, the martydom of St Thomas Becket. On L, the four knights, in chain mail, standing, one of them holding a drawn sword above the head of St Thomas who kneels before the altar on R. Behind the altar Grim, standing facing the knights, holds a tall cross which dominates the scene and seems to check for a moment the knights' advance.

+:CAVSA:[DOMVS]XPI:[MORTEM]SIC[INTVLIT]ISTI (Lom)

Round, 66; red, tag. Nearly complete, fine impression. The late 13c matrix is in the British Museum (Tonnochy 844, plate XXIII). Pedrick, plate XIV. BM 3396.

E 322/120 Pl 21 1535

LANGLEY (Leics) Benedictine priory (F)
priory seal

M454. The Virgin, frontal, enthroned, holding the Child before her on her lap. The throne's sides curve outwards and terminate in carved knobs.

SIGILLVM SANCTE MA...ELEI (Lom)

Pointed oval, 45×30; dark green, tongue. Deep impression, edge damaged. Also on E 326/11601 (1358). BM 3404.

E 329/144 1284

priory seal

M455. The Virgin, crowned, seated on a bench-type throne, holding the Child, with nimbus, on her R knee. Below, the prioress, kneeling in prayer to R.

SIGILLU PRIORISSE & C...BEATE MARIE DE LANGLEY (BL)

Pointed oval, c.55×32; red, tongue. Deep impression, flattened, upper point lost, edge crumpled. BM 3407.

E 329/76　　Pl 37　　　　　　　　　　1542

prioress's seal: Christina de Wynton

M456. The Virgin, crowned, seated, holding the Child on her L knee.

AVE MARIA GRACIA PLE (Lom)

Pointed oval, 30×20; uncoloured, tag. Complete, indistinct impression.

E 329/205　　　　　　　　　　　　　(13c)

LANGLEY (Norf) Premonstratensian abbey

abbey seal

M457. The abbey church, with tall tower and spire. Legend illegible.

Round, c.50; uncoloured, tag. Uneven impression, R side lost. Has counterseal, **M458**.

E 42/430　　Pl 9　　　　　　　　　　(13c)

abbot's seal

M458. The abbot, standing, vested for mass, holding a crozier and a book; on either side, scrolls of foliage.

...IGILLVM.ABBATI[S... (Lom)

Pointed oval, c.45×30; uncoloured, on tag, as counterseal to **M457**. Deep clear impression, L part lost.

E 42/430　　　　　　　　　　　　　(13c)

LANGLEY see KINGS LANGLEY

LAUNCESTON (Corn) Augustinian priory

priory seal

M459. The priory church, shown as a rectangular building with hipped roof and a central tower with conical roof.

+SIGILLVM:SCI:STEPHANI:DE:LAN' (Lom)

Round, 40; red, tag. Complete, deep impression at centre, legend uneven. Also on E 25/76/1 (1534). BM 3420.

E 322/122　　Pl 5　　　　　　　　　　1539

LAUNDE (Leics) Augustinian priory

priory seal

M460. In a niche with traceried interior, under a vaulted canopy with lantern and pinnacles, St John the Baptist, with nimbus, standing, holding the Lamb; on either side, in niches with similar but lesser canopies, kneeling figures of (L) the founder, Richard Basset,

and (R) his wife Maud, daughter of Geoffrey Riddell. Below, two shields of their arms: (L) *three pales and a bordure* (BASSET); (R) *a chevron* (RIDDELL) impaling BASSET.

...ILL'.CO.../IOHIS BAPTISTE DE LANDS (BL)

Pointed oval, c.75×c.44; red, tag. Fine impression, part flattened, much broken at points and R side. Also on E 41/203 (1458). BM 3394.

E 25/72/2　　Pl 28　　　　　　　　　1534

LAVENDON (Bucks) Premonstratensian abbey

abbey seal

M461. Under a flattened trefoiled arch with a church-like building above, the baptism by St John of Our Lord, who is shown waist-deep in water and with a cruciform nimbus.

+SIGILL'...BAPTISTE D'LAVENDNNE (Lom)

Pointed oval, 55×35; red, tag. Deep clear impression, R edge lost. BM 3418.

SC 13/R31　　Pl 30　　　　　　　　　n.d.

abbot's seal: Augustine

M462. The abbot, standing, holding a crozier and a book.

...MI KARISSI... (Lom)

Pointed oval, c.35×25; dark green, tag. Large fragment of a deep impression, centre and L side only.

C 146/2280　　　　　　　　　　　　1233

LEDBURY (Worcs) Hospital

common seal

M463. The facade of a church, with spires, central gable and tower, and arcading. In the rounded doorway, a bishop, mitred, kneeling in prayer to R, holding a crozier. Above the doorway, in a large deep niche, a figure, crowned, enthroned, holding a sceptre and book. On either side of the niche, a deeply-sunk roundel, containing a demi-angel, wings outspread.

...GILL...EBV... (Lom)

Pointed oval, c.55×c.45; dull red, tag. Deep uneven impression, edge much damaged. Also on E 210/9659 (1549), 9720 (1550), 10153 (1515); E 212/138 (1511).

E 212/43　　Pl 5　　　　　　　　　　1516

LEEDS (Kent) Augustinian priory

priory seal

M464. *Obv.* Under a triple canopy with crocketed gables, the Virgin, crowned, seated on a bench-type throne, holding the Child on her L knee, between two censing angels. Below, under an arch, the prior and two canons, half-length, praying to R. Outside the canopy on either side, a three-towered castle with a cinquefoil above and a bell-like flower below.

...IGILLVM : COM/MVNE:EC...S (Lom)

Rev. Under a canopy resembling that on *Obv*, St Nicholas, enthroned, blessing and holding a crozier, between two canons, each standing and holding a book. Below, between two angels, the three children in the tub.

.../E:A[NNO]DNI/M:CC:NONOG':TERCIO   (Lom)
Round, 70; dark green, tag. Complete except for loss on one side, fine impression. Also on DL 25/299 (1337); E 42/431 (1479). The legend gives the date of the matrix, 1293. Pedrick, plate XXVI. BM 3425.
E 25/79/1   Pl 14   1534

LEICESTER (Leics) Austin Friars' house
common seal
M465. In a canopied niche with tabernacle work at the sides, St Katharine, crowned, standing on a corbel, holding up a sword in her R hand and resting her L hand upon her wheel.
...VILLE.LECEST...   (BL)
Pointed oval, 60×37; light brown, tag. Nearly complete, light impression, legend faint.
E 322/124   Pl 37   1538

LEICESTER (Leics) Dominican house
common seal
M466. Under a canopy with tabernacle work at the sides, St Clement, wearing tiara, standing on a carved corbel, blessing and holding a patriarchal cross with three bars.
S' COMUNE FRATRŪ PDICATOR' COVENTU LEYC   (BL)
Pointed oval, 58×35; light brown, tag. Complete, deep clear impression, heavily flattened. BM 3453.
E 322/125   Pl 37   1538

LEICESTER (Leics) Franciscan house
common seal
M467. The Noli Me Tangere scene. Our Lord, with nimbus, standing on L and St Mary Magdalene, kneeling on R; between them, a tree.
S' FRATRV MINOR' LEYCEST NOLI...TANGERE   (Lom)
Pointed oval, 38×24; light brown, tag. Complete, centre deep but rubbed, legend uneven. BM 3454.
E 322/126   1538

LEICESTER (Leics) St John the Baptist and St John the Evangelist, hospital
common seal
M468. An eagle, wings outspread, facing L. Legend lost.
Pointed oval, over 50×30; bronze-green, tag. Central fragment. Also on E 326/6747 (n.d.).
E 3298/198   1386

LEICESTER (Leics) St Leonard's, hospital
common seal
M469. St Leonard, seated, both arms extended. Legend lost.
Pointed oval, c.70×?; green, tag. Fragment. BM 3445.
DL 25/318   1352

LEICESTER (Leics) St Mary de Pratis, Augustinian abbey
abbey seal
M470. Under a cusped rounded arch resting on two columns, the Virgin, crowned and with nimbus, seated on a bench-type throne, holding the Child, with nimbus, on her L knee and a fleur-de-lys in her R hand. On either side, outside the columns, a tower with arcaded base and lantern top.
SIGILLVM SANCTE...DE PRATO   (Lom)
Round, 62; dark green, tag. Nearly complete, deep clear impression, cracked and chipped. Has counterseal, **M471**. Also on E 322/127 (1538–9). BM 3437.
E 25/77   Pl 28   1534
counterseal
M471. The abbot, half-length, holding a crozier in his R hand; around him, five canons, half-length.
+ PONIMVR A TERGO SIGNI TESTES SVMVS ERGO   (Lom)
Round, 38; dark green, on tag, as counterseal for **M470**. Complete, clear impression. BM 3437. The matrix appears to be of c.1200.
E 25/77   Pl 25   1534
seal of procurator of the revenues ?
M472. Between the busts of four canons, the abbot, seated, holding a crozier and a book.
+S' PCVRA...VENCIONVM ABBIS & VE...RE   (Lom)
Pointed oval, 40×c.20; bronze-green, tag. Deep impression, part of edge lost. Has counterseal, **M473**. Also on DL 25/311 (1311), where it is described as the common seal, improbably. The description here follows that of Birch in BM Catalogue; see BM 3440.
E 322/127   1538
counterseal
M473. Between two stars, the Virgin, seated, holding the Child on her L knee.
*AVE MARIA GRACIA   (Lom)
Round, 22; bronze-green, on tag, as counterseal to **M472**. Complete, clear impression. BM 3440.
E 322/127   1538

LEIGHS (Essex) Augustinian priory
priory seal
M474. In the upper part, the Last Supper: behind a table spread with a cloth, Our Lord, half-length, with nimbus, blessing, St John reclining on his bosom; on

either side, three apostles, each with nimbus. Below, St John as the Evangelist, with nimbus, standing on his eagle and holding a long scroll inscribed ...P'CIPIO VBV MANSIT/A...DEVM; on either side, three mitred heads; on L and R of his head IO/HS; the area enclosed by the curving scroll is diapered.

...ESAQVIL... (Lom)

Pointed oval, 60×43; red, tongue. Nearly complete, deep uneven impression, legend defaced. Also on E 42/485 (1532) which has counterseal M475.

E 25/76/2　　Pl 41　　　　　　　　1534

counterseal

M475. Under a canopy, the Virgin and Child, seated; below, under an arch, a figure, praying.
Legend lost.

Pointed oval, c.40×25; light brown, on tag, as counterseal to M474. Central fragment of a deep impression.

E 42/485　　　　　　　　　　　　1532

LEISTON (Suff) Premonstratensian abbey
　　abbot's seal: Philip
M476. The abbot, standing, vested for mass, holding a crozier and a book.

...PI.ABBATIS.DE.LEESTONA (Lom)

Pointed oval, 45×30; uncoloured, tag. Deep clear impression, R edge broken.

E 42/426　　　　　　　　　　(c.1200)

LENTON (Notts) Benedictine priory
　　priory seal
M477. The Trinity

...MONASTERII SCI... (BL)

Round, c.45; bronze-green, detached, on tag. Small lower fragment of a deep clear impression. BM 3458.

SC 13/R32　　　　　　　　　　　1524

LEOMINSTER (Heref) Benedictine priory
　　prior's seal: Walter
M478. A gem: under a crescent and a star, a man's head in profile to R.

+QVISQ' HVMI[LIS EST E]XALTABITVR (Lom)

Pointed oval, 35×25; dark green, tag. Nearly complete, deep impression.

E 329/186　　　　　　　　　　　1220

LEWES (Sussex) St Pancras, Cluniac later Benedictine priory
　　priory seal
M479. Under a canopy composed of a large rounded arch, with a small arch at each extremity and indication of roof and turrets above, the martyrdom of St Pancras. On R, the saint, kneeling to L; on L, the executioner, in

Roman(?) armour, standing, holding aloft his drawn sword.
Legend lost or illegible.

Round, c.60; uncoloured, varnished pink, on red and white laces. Upper half, cracked, of a deep impression mainly indistinct but with some fine detail, e.g. the face of the executioner. Has counterseal, M480. Also on E 42/349 (1319), 433 (1342), 434 (1319).

DL 25/9　　Pl 43　　　　　　　　1218

counterseal

M480. A gem: a man's(?) head facing R, the hair bound with a fillet.

+DEVM C... (Rom)

Round, 20; uncoloured, varnished pink, on red and white laces, as counterseal to M479. Complete, deep indistinct impression, L half cracked.

DL 25/9　　　　　　　　　　　　1218

　　prior's seal: Stephen
M481. The prior, seated on a bench with cushion, facing L, reading a book.

+SIG[ILL'.STE]PHAN[I]PRI[ORIS.SCI.P...II] (Lom)

Pointed oval, 50×35; uncoloured, on red and white laces. Nearly complete, deep but very rough impression. Has counterseal, M482. BM 3464.

DL 25/9　　　　　　　　　　　　1218

　　counterseal: Stephen de Hzi (Hussey ?)
M482. A stylised lily.

+SECRETVM STEPHANI.DE.HZI (Lom)

Round, 24; uncoloured, on red and white laces, as counterseal to M481. Complete, clear.

DL 25/9　　　　　　　　　　　　1218

　　prior's seal: John de Thyenges
M483. Under a canopy, the prior, standing on a corbel, vested for mass, holding a book before him. On either side, a small checker board of four squares, in allusion to the arms of WARENNE, the founder.

S'.FR'IS:JOH'IS/:PRIORIS:LEWENSIS (Lom)

Pointed oval, 65×38; dark green, tag. Nearly complete, deep clear impression. BM 3465.

DL 27/216　　Pl 48　　　　　　　1285

　　prior's seal: John de Montmartin
M484. The martyrdom of St Pancras. On R, the saint, kneeling to R; behind him, the executioner, standing, brandishing a sword.

[SE]CRETVM...P'ORIS.LE... (Lom)

Round, 25; dark green, tag. Deep blurred impression, damaged at top and foot.

E 42/348　　　　　　　　　　　1322

　　prior's seal: John de Cariloco
M485. Under a gabled and pinnacled canopy with tabernacle work at the sides, Our Lord, enthroned, blessing with his R hand and holding an orb with cross on his L knee. Below, under an arch, a figure, praying to L.

S' FR'IOHIS DE CARILO...O... (Lom)

Pointed oval, c.45×35; dark green, tongue. Deep clear impression but much lost on L and at foot. On a deed of his predecessor Peter de Joceaux. Also on E 40/14997 (1368).

E 42/433   1343

prior's seal: Hugh de Chintaco

M486. In a canopied niche with tabernacle work at the sides, the prior, standing, vested for mass, holding a crozier and a book.

S' FRIS HVGONIS:DE L...S (Lom)

Pointed oval, 50×35; dark green, tongue. Light impression, much flattened, edges damaged.

E 42/432   1359

LILLESHALL (Salop) Augustinian abbey
abbey seal

M487. The Virgin, with nimbus, frontal, seated on a bench-type throne with knobbed arms, holding the Child before her and a sceptre tipped with fleur-de-lys in her R hand.

SIGILL' E[CCLE]SIE BEATE MARIE DE LILLESHULL' (Lom)

Pointed oval, 60×37; light brown, tag. Complete, deep uneven impression, parts flattened. Also on E 40/6926 (1421). BM 3469.

E 322/128   Pl 48   1538

LINCOLN (Lincs) St Katherine's, Gilbertine priory (M and F)
priory seal

M488. Under a rounded arch resting on corbels, St Katharine, with nimbus, seated on a bench-type throne, holding a book before her and a sceptre in her R hand.

+SIGILL' ECLESIE BEATE KATERINE VIRGINIS LINCOLIE (Lom)

Pointed oval, 65×35; uncoloured, tag. Complete, deep clear impression. BM 3471.

DL 27/281   Pl 5   (13c)

priory seal

M489. St Katharine, crowned and with nimbus and flowing hair, standing on a corbel, holding a large two-handed sword, point downwards, in her R hand and a book(?) in her L hand; behind her to R, her wheel.

...OR': ET CONVENT...S SCE KATRINE LI... (Lom)

Pointed oval, c.55×35; red, tag. Deep impression showing detail, points and part of edge lost. BM 3472.

E 322/129   Pl 48   1538

seal ad causas

M490. St Katharine, crowned, standing on a corbel, holding a palm branch in her R hand and her wheel with her L hand.

...PRIOR' ET CO...E LINCOLN' AD CAUSAS (Lom)

Pointed oval, 53×37; red-brown, detached, on tongue. Deep uneven impression, lower edge lost. BM 3473.

SC 13/D105   Pl 11   (n.d.)

LINDORES (Fife) Tironian abbey
abbey seal

M491. The Virgin, frontal, seated on a bench-type throne, holding a flowering sprig in her R hand and the model of a church in her L hand; on her lap, the Child, with cruciform nimbus, seated, blessing with his R hand.

Legend lost.

Pointed oval, c.60×c.45; mottled green, tag. Deep clear impression, edge lost. BM 15374.

DL 27/39   Pl 11   1261

abbot's seal: Thomas

M492. In the centre, four small figures binding St Andrew to his cross. Above, in three adjacent niches under a canopy, the Virgin, crowned, seated, holding the Child on her L knee, between two standing angels. Below, under a gable and a trefoiled arch, a monk, kneeling in prayer to R.

S' THOME AB/BATIS LVNDOR (Lom)

Pointed oval, 50×30; mottled green, detached, on hemp cords. Complete, deep clear impression. Laing 1074. BM 15377.

SC 13/E58   (n.d.)

abbot's seal: Henry Orm

M493. Under a vaulted and pinnacled canopy with tabernacle work at the sides, the Virgin, seated, holding the Child on her L knee. Below, under an arch, a shield bearing the initials HO, between them a saltire and the slender trunk of a tree which rises and spreads its branches above the shield.

S' HENRICI ORM / ABBATIS DE LVNDOR (Lom)

Pointed oval, 58×35; brown, detached, on tag. Nearly complete, deep uneven, but clear, impression.

SC 13/E57   (n.d.)

LITTLE DUNMOW (Essex) Augustinian priory
priory seal

M494. Under a trefoiled arch with three edicules above (the central one domed), the Virgin, crowned, seated on a bench-type throne, holding the Child on her lap before her with her L hand and a slender sceptre tipped with a dove (which breaks the legend) in her R hand. The Child has a cruciform nimbus and raises his R hand, two fingers extended in benediction. The throne has some arcading on the plinth and criss-cross ornament on the upper cornice.

SIGILL'.ECCLESIE.S...VNMAW/IA (Lom)

Pointed oval, c.90×63; light brown, on plaited laces. Deep impression, much detail clear, points lost.

E 212/97   Pl 26   (13c)

priory seal

M495. Under a canopy, the Coronation of the Virgin. Below, under an arch, the prior, kneeling between two shields of arms: *a cross between four mullets* (the PRIORY).

SIGILLV:COE:ECCLIE:SCE:MARIE:DE:DUNMAWE   (BL)

Pointed oval, 60×35; red, tag. Complete, deep clear impression. BM 3082.

E 25/44/2   1534

LITTLE MALVERN (Worcs) Benedictine priory
   priory seal

M496. Under a triple canopy with vaulting, pinnacles, central lantern and tabernacle work at the sides, (centre) the Virgin, with nimbus, holding the Child, with nimbus, on her R side and a sceptre tipped with fleur-de-lys in her L hand, (L) St Giles, with nimbus, a faun at his feet, and (R) St John the Evangelist, with nimbus, holding a book; all standing on a plinth with dog-tooth moulding. Below, a shield of arms: *on a fesse between three cock's heads, a mitre* (bishop ALCOCK).

S'.COE.DOMUS.SIVE/PRIORATUS:MALVARNIE:MIOR'   (BL)

Pointed oval, 65×42; red, tag. Nearly complete, deep clear impression. BM 3605.

E 25/83/2   Pl 30   1534

LLANTHONY (LLanthony Secunda) (Glos)
Augustinian priory
   priory seal

M497. The Virgin, frontal, seated on a bench-type throne, her hands outstretched, holding an orb with cross in her R hand; before her, on her lap, the Child, with nimbus, seated and blessing with his R hand.

SIGI...AR...ONIE   (Lom)

Pointed oval, 65×c.45; green, on green and white plaited laces. Deep clear impression, parts rubbed, most of edge lost. Has counterseal, **M499.**

DL 27/7   Pl 8   (1207–16)
   priory seal

M498. In a canopied niche with tabernacle work at the sides, the Virgin, crowned, seated, holding a sceptre tipped with fleur-de-lys in her L hand and the Child, with nimbus, on her R knee, his R hand raised in blessing; below her feet, a lion passant.

SIGILLVM COMVNE PRIORIS & CONVENTUS ECCLIE BTE
MARIE LANTHON IUX GLOUCESTRM   (BL)

Pointed oval, 90×50; red, on plaited laces in metal skippet. Complete, deep clear impression. Also on E 25/74 (used by Llanthony, Monm), 75 (1534); E 322/121 (1538). BM 3415.

DL 27/329   Pl 26   1504
   prior's seal: Gilbert

M499. The prior, wearing cloak and hood, standing,

holding a book in his L hand and a crutched staff in his R hand.

SIGILL' GILBERTI PRIORIS LANTONIE   (Lom)

Pointed oval, 42×25; green, on green and white plaited laces, as counterseal to **M497.** Complete, deep clear impression, rubbed.

DL 27/7   Pl 9   (1207–16)

LONDON Austin Friars' house
   common seal

M500. In adjoining canopied niches, standing figures: (L) St Paul holding a sword; (R) a bishop, mitred, blessing and holding a crozier. Below, under an arch, a sleeping boar(?), curled up.

SIGILLM COMUNE FRM ORDINIS SCI AUGUSTINI LONDON
(BL)

Pointed oval, 55×35; red, detached, on tongue. Complete, deep very clear impression. Also on E 33/26/16 (1504). BM 3486.

SC 13/R34   Pl 25   (n.d.)

LONDON Blackfriars, Dominican house
   common seal

M501. Our Lord on the cross, between (L) St Mary and (R) St John, surrounded by an inner legend:
+ECCE FILIVS TVVS/ ECCE MATER TVA.

+S' CON...EDICATOR LVNDONIEN'   (Lom)

Pointed oval, 47×30; red, tag. Deep clear impression, points and part of R edge lost. BM 3499.

DL 27/62   Pl 36   1286
   common seal

M502. In a canopied niche with a corbel carved with foliage below, Our Lord on the cross, between (L) St Mary and (R) St John.

S' CONVENTVS FRATRU[M PREDICATOR' LONDONIARU']
(BL)

Pointed oval, c.55×c.30; red, tag. Large fragment of a deep uneven impression, cracked, flattened. Also on SC 13/C13 (n.d.) BM 3500.

E 322/132   1538
   prior's seal: William de Holham (Holhum)

M503. St John the Baptist, standing, holding a palm across his breast in his L hand and a long scroll in his R hand. On L, in the field, the letters IO.

...RV...LONDONIEN...   (Lom)

Pointed oval, c.32×c.24; dark green, tag. Deep clear impression, defaced, most of edge lost.

DL 27/62   Pl 36   1286
   master's seal: Simon

M504. Our Lord on the cross; on L, a kneeling figure.

+S' FRIS : SYMONIS : MAG'R...RDINIS : PREDICA/TORVM
(Lom)

Pointed oval, c.52×c.34; scarlet, in a bed of uncoloured

wax, on green silk tapes. Nearly complete, flattened.
DL 27/63   1352

master's seal: Raymond

M505. Our Lord on the cross; on L, a kneeling figure; the field hatched.
...PRE...   (BL)
Pointed oval, c.55×c.35; red, on green and red ribbons.
E 135/6/44   1397

master's seal: Thomas de Firmo

M506. Our Lord on the cross; on L, a kneeling figure; stars in the field.
...THOME...ORDIS...P'DIC...   (BL)
Pointed oval, c.50×c.30; red, detached, on purple cords. Clear impression, edge chipped.
E 135/6/45   1401

master's seal; Hugh

M507. Our Lord on the cross; on L, the prior, kneeling.
+S' FRIS : HVGONIS : MAG/RI : ORD : FRVM : P'DICATOR'
                                   (Lom)
Pointed oval, 50×30; red, backed with white, on green silk laces. Complete, clear impression, flattened.
BM 3501.
DL 27/142   Pl 50   1333

LONDON Carmelite house
common seal

M508. In two adjoining canopied niches, standing figures: (L) a saint, holding a sword and a church; (R) the Virgin, crowned, holding the Child on her R side.
S' CONVENTVS.FRM.CARMELI.LOND'   (Lom)
Round, 38; red, tag. Complete, deep clear impression, slightly flattened. Also on E 33/26/17 (1504).
BM 3571.
E 322/140   Pl 23   1538

prior's seal

M509. Under adjoining canopies, standing figures: (L) St Peter, holding keys; (R) St Paul, holding a sword. Above, in a compartment, the Virgin and Child, both half-length. Below, under an arch, the prior, half-length, praying to L.
S' PRIORIS ORDIS/CARMELI LOND   (Lom)
Pointed oval, 35×25; red, tag. Deep but uneven impression, points damaged.
C 148/21   1336

LONDON Charterhouse, Carthusian priory
priory seal

M510. Under a panelled canopy, with a flattened ogee arch and tabernacle work at the side, the Annunciation. Below, a crowned M between sprigs.
S' COMMVNE:DOMVS:MRIS:DEI:ORDIS:CARTUS':
LONDONIARUM   (BL)
Pointed oval, 50×30; dark green, tag. Deep clear

impression, nearly complete. Also on E 25/82/2 (1534), E 33/26/18 (1504, complete and fine); E 40/2109 (1525); E 212/123 (1528); E 322/133 (1537); E 326/4266 (1488); E 326/4274 (1404); E 326/5617 (1495–6); E 326/8003 (1421); E 326/8775 (1470); E329/206 (1525). BM 3502.
E 329/134   Pl 50   1380

prior's seal: John

M511. Under a canopy, the Annunciation. Below, under an arch, the prior, praying.
...MEI...   (BL)
Pointed oval, c.30×?; red, tag. Indistinct impression, edge damaged.
E 326/9889   1447

LONDON Crutched Friars' house
common seal

M512. A cross; a star above and a crescent below the R arm.
S' COIE...ORDIS...   (Lom)
Round, 25; dark green, tag. Clear impression, L half lost.
E 40/2666   1320

common seal

M513. In a circle cusped to a quatrefoil, with dog-tooth moulding and a lozenge in each spandrel, a cross formy between the letters FIAT.
SIGILL':COMUNE:DOMVS:SCI:CRUCIS:LONDON'   (BL)
Round, 33; red, tag. Nearly complete, deep clear impression.
BM 3507.
E 322/134   Pl 4   1538

LONDON Elsing Spital Cripplegate, Augustinian priory and hospital
priory seal

M514. In a canopied niche below a rose window, the Virgin, crowned, holding the Child on her L side and a flower in her R hand. On either side, a shield of arms: (L) (defaced); (R) *quarterly, France modern and England.* Diapered field. Below, under an arch, the prior, kneeling, with the words of his prayer above [EXORA NATV P ME PIA VIRGO BEATVM]
S' COM...HOSPITALIS:BEATE:MARIE:INFRA: CREPEL-
GATE:LONDON'   (BL)
Pointed oval, c.90×50; red, tag. Nearly complete, clear impression, heavily flattened. BM 3542.
E 25/47   1534

LONDON Greyfriars, Franciscan house
common seal

M515. On either side of a bush with a bird on it, two

friars, standing on a carved corbel, holding up a canopied edicule containing St Paul, seated, holding a sword and book; background diapered.

SIGILLVM : CONVENTVS : FRATRVM : MINORV : LONDONIE

(Lom)

Pointed oval, 64×37; red, detached, on red and white plaited laces, in silver skippet engraved S MINOR. Complete, fine impression. Also on E 322/135 (1538). BM 3519.

E 33/26/22   Pl 15   1504

LONDON Holy Trinity or Christ Church, Aldgate, Augustinian priory

priory seal

M516. Our Lord in majesty, enthroned on the rainbow, his R hand raised in blessing and his L hand resting on a book with a star above it.

SIGILLV:ECCL'E:SCE*TRINI[T]ATIS LVNDONI[E   (Lom)

Pointed oval, 70×40; dark brown, tag. Complete, clear impression, cracked. Has counterseal, **M520**. Also on E 40/1824 (with counterseal **M518**; 13c, temp. William, prior); E 33/26/20 (1504, with counterseal **M518**); E 40/1967 prix); E 40/1967 (1281); E 42/354 (1170–97); E 42/358 (after 1197); E 42/440 (1199–1221); E 42/449 (1223–52); E 42/450 (1197–1221); E 42/452 (with counterseal **M520**, 1260–4); E 42/453 (with counterseal **M519**, 1197–1221); E 210/8467 (with counterseal **M518**, 1296). BM 3563.

E 42/451   Pl 11   (1223–52)

priory seal

M517. In three adjoining niches with panelled canopies, the Trinity between standing figures: (L) the Virgin, crowned, holding the Child on her R side and a lily in her L hand; (R) a bishop, mitred and holding a crozier. Below, three shields of arms: (L) *quarterly, 1 and 4 France modern, 2 and 3 England*; (R) *a cross, in the dexter chief quarter a sword erect* (City of LONDON); (centre) held by an angel, the *scutum Dei triangulum* for the PRIORY).

S' COE MONASTERII SCE TRINIT...LONDON   (BL)

Pointed oval, 70×45; dark red, detached, on red and white cords, in silver skippet. Deep clear impression, slightly damaged at edge. Has counterseal, **M518**. *See* Francis Wormald's Note on the Illuminations, pp. xxii and xxiii, in G.A.J. Hodgett's edition of *The Cartulary of Holy Trinity Aldgate*, London Record Society 7, 1971.

E 33/26/20   (1504)

counterseal

M518. A pelican in her piety.

+MORS PELLICANI PASSIO XPI   (Lom)

Pointed oval, 30×18; dark red, on cords as counterseal to **M516**. Also on E 40/1824 (n.d.); E 210/8467 (1296).

E 33/26/20   (1504)

prior's seal: Peter of Cornwall

M519. St Peter, standing, holding keys and a book.

+SIGILL': PETRI : PR[IORIS...]E : TRINITATIS : LVND

(Lom)

Pointed oval, c.50×c.25; mottled green, on tag, as counterseal to **M516**. Deep clear impression, lower point lost.

E 42/453   (1197–1221)

prior's counterseal

M520. A bearded head (?)

+ANGELVS HO[C SI]GNAT   (Lom)

Round, 20; dark brown, on tag, as counterseal to **M516**. Also on E 42/452 (1260–4), as counterseal to **M516**.

E 42/451   (1223–52)

prior's seal

M521. Under a canopy, Our Lord (?), seated; below, under an arch, the prior, praying.

Legend lost or blurred.

Round, 25; dark green, tag. Deep impression, L side lost.

E 40/1508   1352

prior's seal

M522. In a border decorated with quatrefoils, the Trinity, between (L) a dove and (R) a quatrefoil; below, under an arch, the prior, praying.

S' PRIORIS SCE TRINITAT LONDONIEN'   (Lom)

Oval, 28×23; red, tag. Deep clear impression, flattened, edge damaged. Also on E 213/84 (1442).

E 42/441   1424

prior's seal: William (Clark)

M523. In a canopied niche, Our Lord, seated, crowned, blessing and holding an orb in his L hand. Below, a shield of arms: the *scutum Dei triangulum* (the PRIORY).

...ET... / ECCLIE CRIST...DON   (BL)

Pointed oval, c.40×c.28; red, tongue. Very deep clear impression, flattened, most of edge lost.

E 213/347   Pl 50   1435

proctor's seal: Nicholas Cornwall

M524. Above a canopy, a half-length figure; below, on L, an angel.

...SACESVIL +...(?)   (Lom)

Round, c.18; brown, tongue. Fragment.

E 42/454   (13c)

LONDON the Minories, Franciscan abbey (F)

abbey seal

M525. The Virgin, crowned, standing on a carved corbel, holding the Child on her L side and an apple in her R hand. On either side, a censing angel, standing, wings outspread. Above, an angel descends from clouds and touches the Virgin's crown.

*S' CONVENTVS:SOROR MINOR GRA BE MARIE
LONDONIAR'   (Lom)
Pointed oval, 65×43; red, tag. Complete, fine
impression, slightly flattened. Also on WARD 2/29/14
(1538). BM 3555.
E 42/442   Pl 6   1371
   abbess's seal
M526. The Coronation of the Virgin; below, an arch.
...ISSE SORO...   (Lom)
Pointed oval, c.50×c.35; red, tag. Clear impression,
edge broken.
LR 14/546   1534

LONDON New Temple, Templars' later Hospitallers'
house
   common seal
M527. The Holy Lamb, with nimbus, cross and
banner, facing R.
+SIGILLVM TEMPLI   (Lom)
Round, 30; dark green, tag. Complete, deep
impression. Used by Haimeric de St Maur, knight,
minister of the Temple. Also on DL 25/2348 (1190).
E 42/448   Pl 34   (c.1200)

LONDON St Bartholomew's Smithfield, Augustinian
priory
   priory seal
M528. St Bartholomew, with nimbus, blessing and
holding a tall cross in his L hand, shown half-length on
a church seen from W with rounded arches and a round
tower on either side.
Legend lost.
Round, c.65; green, tag. Very deep clear impression,
edge lost. Also on DL 25/139 (1263); E 42/353
(1259–60). BM 3488 (attributed to the Hospital,
though recording the legend as *SIGILL' CONVENTVS.
ECC... HOLO.../...DE.LVNDON). Has counterseal, M531.
E 40/13688   1302
   priory seal
M529. *Obv.* Between (L) a crescent and (R) a star, St
Bartholomew, enthroned, holding his knife erect in his
L hand. The throne has a long cushion, arcaded
decoration, and a high back with crocketed half-gables
with fleur-de-lys finials, resembling the thrones on the
Great Seals of Henry III and Edward I.
SIGILLVM:COMMVNE:PRIOR:ET:COVENTVS:SCI:BARTHOL-
OMEI:LONDON   (Lom)
   Rev. a masonry church with tiled roof standing in
a ship on waves, between (L) NAVIS and (R) ECCLIE.
The church shows three gables with lancet and rose
windows, a tiled roof, and a central tower with spire;
gables and spire have fleur-de-lys finials.
CREDIMVS:ANTE[DEVM PROV]EHI:PER:BARTHOLOMEVM
                                                     (Lom)

Round, 60; bronze-green, tag. Nearly complete, very
deep clear impression. Also on E 42/439 (1525);
E 326/7062 (1530); E 326/8523 (1452); E 329/141
(1393). BM 3492.
E 322/136   Pl 45   1539
   seal ad causas
M530. St Bartholomew, standing on a corbel, holding a
knife in his R hand and a staff in his L hand.
...TVM...THOL'I LOND' AD CAVS...   (Lom)
Pointed oval, 55×37; red-brown, tongue. Clear
impression, points lost, upper R edge damaged.
BM 3495.
E 329/127   Pl 4   1531
   prior's seal
M531. A ship, on waves, with bird-headed prow and
stern; on it, a stylised church between (L) a sun and (R)
a moon and the words NAVIS/ECCLIE.
...IORIS ECCLESIE SCI BARTOLOMEI   (BL)
Round, 50; dark green, on tag, as counterseal to M528.
Fine impression, upper R edge lost. Also on
DL 25/139 (1263) as counterseal. BM 3489.
E 40/13688   1302

LONDON St Bartholomew's, Augustinian priory and
hospital
   common seal
M532. St Bartholomew, standing, blessing and holding
a long cross.
+SIGILLVM: HOSPITA[LIS SANCTI BAR]TOLOMEI   (Lom)
Pointed oval, 70×48; uncoloured, varnished brown,
tag. Deep impression, edge damaged. Has counterseal,
M533. Also on E 42/438 (c.1213); DL 25/148 (1231–
7). BM 3487.
E 42/437   Pl 28   1265
   counterseal
M533. A gem: a splayed eagle.
+SIGILL' HOSPITAL S BARTHOL'   (Lom)
Oval, 34×23; uncoloured, varnished brown, on tag, as
counterseal to M532. Complete, clear. Also on
DL 25/148 (1231–7); E 329/145 (1338). BM 3491.
E 42/437   1265
   common seal
M534. Under a crocketed canopy with trefoiled arch
resting on corbels, St Bartholomew, standing on a
leopard couchant, holding up a knife in his R hand and
a book before him in his L hand. On either side, slung
from a tree, a shield of arms: *three leopards* (ENGLAND).
S': C...E : HO...TAL...TI : BARTHI : LONDON   (Lom)
Pointed oval, 75×c.45; red-brown, tag. Deep clear
impression, centre flattened, edge chipped. Also on
E 329/145 (large central fragment of a fine impression,
1338). BM 3490.
E 25/81   Pl 4   1534

LONDON St Giles without Cripplegate, Benedictine hospital

common seal

M535. St Giles, standing, vested for mass, holding a crozier and a book.

[SIG]ILLVM : SAN[CTI EGI]DII . INFIRMOR...　　　(Rom)

Pointed oval, 65×45; scarlet, tag. Deep clear impression, figure's head lost. Also on E 42/444 (1201–4); E 326/9030 (n.d.); LR 14/608 (n.d.). BM 3511.

E 42/443　　Pl 37　　　　　　　　　1392

LONDON St Helen's Bishopsgate, Benedictine priory (F)

priory seal

M536. A tall Latin cross with channelled moulding. On L, St Helen, crowned, standing, supporting the cross with her L arm and holding the three nails in her L hand. On R, a group of six women, standing or kneeling, stretching out their hands towards the cross. Below, under an arch, the head and shoulders of a monk, praying and looking up to L.

SIGILL' MONIALI[VM.SANCTE.HE]LENE LONDINIARVM
　　　　　　　　　　　　　　　　　　　　　　　(Lom)

Pointed oval, 75×50; dark green, tag. Fine impression, rubbed, edge chipped, lower part lost. Also on E 42/445 (1228–52) which has counterseal **M537**; E 42/446 (1534) (fine but incomplete); E 322/137 (1538). BM 3521.

E 329/155　　Pl 4　　　　　　　　1333–4

counterseal

M537. On L, St Helen, standing, facing R, holding a book in her R hand, her L hand raised; on R, an angel, his R arm raised in greeting, holding in his L hand a pendent scroll inscribed HIV...VA(?).

[SEC]RETI HELEN P'O...　　　　　　　(Lom)

Pointed oval, c.45×33; mottled green, on tag, as counterseal to **M536**. Fair impression, upper point lost, edge damaged.

E 42/445　　　　　　　　　　　(1228–52)

LONDON St Mary Graces, Cistercian abbey

abbey seal

M538. Under a pinnacled canopy, the Virgin, crowned, enthroned, holding the Child on her L knee. On either side, a roofed and gabled compartment containing: (L) a king, (Edward III, the founder), crowned, kneeling to R; (R) two monks, one offering a book to the Virgin. Below, a shield of arms: *quarterly, Old France and England*.

SIGILLVM COMVNE MONACHOR / BEATE MARIE DE GRACIIS　　　　　　　　　　　　　　(Lom)

Round, 35; red, on cords, in metal skippet. Complete,

fine impression. Also on C 148/54 (1538); E 42/447 (1364; E 329/158 (1534); E 33/26/23 (1504). BM 3549.

E 42/447　　Pl 49　　　　　　　　1364

abbot's seal: William Wardone

M539. Under a panelled canopy, the abbot, standing, vested for mass, holding a crozier and a book. On either side, tabernacle work and a shield of arms: (L) *quarterly, France and England*; (R) *England*.

S' FRIS [WILL'I]DE WARDONE...IS DE GRACIIS LOND'
　　　　　　　　　　　　　　　　　　　　　　　(Lom)

Oval, 30×20; dark green, tag. Fine impression, lower R edge lost. Also on E 41/458 (1363); E 213/26 (1371); E 213/65 (1396).

E 41/457　　　　　　　　　　　　1363

abbot's seal: John (Pecche)

M540. A leopard's face in front of a crozier.

S' ABB'IS / DE GRATIIS　　　　　　　　(BL)

Round, 15; dark red, tongue. Complete, deep clear impression, centre flattened.

E 213/31　　Pl 36　　　　　　　　1430

abbot's seal: Henry More

M541. Under a gabled and pinnacled canopy with a group of small figures above, the abbot, standing, mitred and vested for mass, blessing and holding a crozier. On either side, tabernacle work and a shield of arms: (L) *quarterly, France and England*; (R) the abbot's coat (defaced) impaling *a crozier in pale* (the ABBEY). Legend lost.

Pointed oval, c.60×c.40; red, tongue. Large central fragment of a deep clear impression, flattened. BM 3552

E 329/158　　　　　　　　　　　　1534

LONDON St Mary without Bishopsgate or Domus Dei, Augustinian hospital (M and F)

common seal

M542. The Virgin, crowned, seated on a bench-type throne, holding the Child, crowned, on her R knee.

...E BISOPEGATE LON...　　　　　　　(Lom)

Pointed oval, c.65×42; dark green, tag. Deep clear impression slightly flattened, most of R half lost.

E 42/355　　　　　　　　　　　(1244–8)

common seal

M543. The Virgin, crowned, frontal, enthroned, holding the Child on her R knee and a fleur-de-lys sceptre in her L hand. On R, a kneeling figure.

SIGILL' DOM DEI EX...[SOPEGATE.LONDO...]　(Lom)

Pointed oval, c.63×c.50; mottled green, on plum-coloured laces. Indistinct impression, L edge and foot lost. Also on E 42/355 (1244–8). BM 3539.

E 42/259　　Pl 50　　　　　　(c.1389–1400)

common seal

M544. The Assumption of the Virgin: the Virgin,

crowned and with nimbus, surrounded by rays and upborne by eight angels; below her feet, a cherub's head. Above, a vaulted canopy with lanterns and pinnacles. On either side, in a canopied niche, a bishop, with nimbus, mitred and holding a pastoral staff. Below, on a large corbel, a shield of arms: *a cross moline voided* (BRVNE).

SIGILLVM : COE : NOVI : HOSPITALIS : BE / MARIE : EX[TRA : BYSSH] OPPISGATE : LOND (BL)

Pointed oval, 80×50; red, tag. Nearly complete, deep clear impression, L edge chipped. Also on E 210/2066 (1538). BM 3541.

E 25/80   Pl 4   1534
    prior's seal: William Maior
M545. Under a cusped arch within a pinnacled canopy, the Virgin, standing, holding the Child on her L side; a figure, kneeling before her on R. Close to the Child's head, a sun and crescent moon.

...DEI . RI... (Lom)

Oval, c.25×c.18; red, tongue. Nearly complete, crumpled, flattened.

E 329/184   1531

LONDON St Thomas of Acon, hospital
    common seal
M546. St Thomas Becket, enthroned, mitred and vested for mass, holding a pastoral cross in his L hand and giving alms to a figure, kneeling, with outstretched hands, on L. Between them and above their hands, a large Greek cross.

+SIGILL'.COMMVNE.CAPITVLI.FRATRVM.BEATI.THOME. MARTIRIS.LOND' (Lom)

Round, 60; red, tag. Nearly complete, deep impression, fine except for the two faces, edge chipped. Also on E 25/1 (1534; fine, nearly complete); E 213/52 (1460). BM 3557.

E 322/139   Pl 49   1538

LONDON Savoy, hospital
    common seal
M547. St John the Baptist, standing, with radiant nimbus, holding the Holy Lamb and cross with banner, between (L) a slipped rose and (R) a portcullis.

+S...CAPELLA...HOSPITALIS.SAVOYE (Rom)

Round, 75; light brown, tag. Complete, deep impression, flattened, R edge crumpled. Also in C 110/25 (1528).

DL 27/331   Pl 23   1614

LONDON see also BARKING; BERMONDSEY; BOW; CLERKENWELL; SHOREDITCH; STRATFORD; SOUTHWARK; SYON; WESTMINSTER

LONGBRIDGE see BERKELEY

LOUTH PARK (Lincs) Cistercian abbey
    abbey seal
M548. Under a gothic canopy, the Virgin, crowned, standing, holding the Child on her L side; in the diapered field, sprigs of foliage. On either side, a tree.

S' COMMVNE:ABBIS ET CONVE[NTVS...D]PARCO LVD (Lom)

Round, 42; red, tag. Deep clear impression, partly flattened, L edge damaged. Also on E 135/10/20, no. 8 (c.1400).

E 42/455   Pl 49   1535

MAIDEN BRADLEY (Wilts) Augustinian priory
    priory seal
M549. A masonry building with a cross on the roof at either end; in the centre, a pillared tower with a conical roof, surmounted by a ball and cross.

SIG...DE : BRADELE (Lom)

Pointed oval, 70×50; red-brown, tag. Uneven impression, edge damaged. BM 3586.

E 329/124   Pl 12   1534
    prior's seal: John
M550. The Virgin, crowned, seated on a bench-type throne, holding the Child on her L knee; on L, a standing figure. Below, under an arch, the prior, kneeling.

...DE MAYDENE BRAD... (Lom)

Pointed oval, 35×30; dark green, tag. Fair impression, most of edge lost. BM 3588.

E 210/2976   (13c)
    prior's privy seal
M551. The Annunciation.

MATER DEI MEMENTO MEI (Lom)

Round, 23; uncoloured, tag. Nearly complete, clear impression.

E 329/85   1279

MALLING see WEST MALLING

MALMESBURY (Wilts) Benedictine abbey
    abbey seal
M552. In three adjoining canopied niches, (centre), the Virgin, seated, holding the Child on her R knee and a flowered sceptre in her L hand, between two saints, standing, with indistinct emblems. Below, under an arch, the abbot, half-length, holding a crozier, between two shields of arms: (L) *quarterly, France modern and England*; (R) *a griffin*.

S...COMM...MONASTERI/BE MRIE MALMESBV (Lom)

Pointed oval, 72×45; red-brown, detached, in metal skippet.

cracked. Also on
d there as 15c,

(n.d.)

(Lom)
ᴵ ᵣand
di
E 2   1380

MAL   ᴀT MALVERN; LITTLE
MALV.

MARKBY (Lincs) Augustinian priory
priory seal
M554. Under a canopy with crocketed gable and
cusped arch resting on two panelled piers, St Peter,
with tiara, standing on a carved corbel, blessing and
holding keys; the field diapered. On either side,
masonry on a hatched field.
S':PRIORIS:ET:CONVENTV...TI:PETRI:DE:MARKEBY (Lom)
Pointed oval, c.70×45; red, tag. Nearly complete, fine
impression, points lost.
E 25/83/1   Pl 42   1534

MARKYATE (Beds) Benedictine priory (F)
chapter seal
M555. On an arcaded bench-type throne above an
arch, the Trinity.
...TVLI . M...   (Lom)
Pointed oval, c.60×40; red-brown, detached, on tag.
Large central fragment of a very deep clear impression,
flattened. BM 3634.
SC 13/R36   (n.d.)

MARRICK (Yorks) Benedictine priory (F)
priory seal
M556. A seated figure (the Virgin and Child ?).
Legend lost.
Pointed oval, c.70×c.50; red, tag. Nearly complete,
almost entirely defaced.
E 322/149   1539

MARTON (Yorks) Augustinian priory
priory seal
M557. In a canopied niche, the Virgin, seated, holding
a fleur-de-lys sceptre in her R hand. Tabernacle work
at the sides containing two shields of arms: (L) *billety, a
lion rampant, queue fourche* (BULMER); (R) (defaced).
Below, under a rounded arch, a canon, half-length,
frontal, hands folded.

...OVEN...   (BL)
Pointed oval, c.50×c.30; red, detached, on tongue.
Large fragment of a deep clear impression.
SC 13/D159   Pl 27   (14c)
priory seal
M558. The Virgin, crowned, frontal, seated on a carved
throne between (L) a crescent and (R) a flaming sun;
decoration in the field.
SIGIL...LI : S...   (Lom)
Round, 50; red, tag. Large fragments of a deep
indistinct impression. Clay, p.25, plate vi, 2. BM 3620.
E 322/148   1535

MATTERSEY (Notts) Gilbertine priory
prior's seal
M559. St John the Baptist, standing, blessing with his
R hand and holding a tall cross in his L hand; on L, a
female figure, kneeling.
S' PRIORIS DE : MARESEYA   (Lom)
Pointed oval, c.45×25; uncoloured, tag. Nearly
complete, deep impression, flattened. BM 3623. Other
interpretations of the device are: (i) the Noli Me
Tangere scene; (ii) St Helen, to whom the priory is
dedicated, adoring the Cross.
E 322/150   Pl 39   1538

MELROSE (Roxburgh) Cistercian abbey
counterseal
M560. A sleeved forearm and hand issuing from L,
holding a crozier; on R, a star.
+CONTRA SIGILLVM DE MELROS   (Lom)
Round, 21; dark green, detached, on tongue.
Complete, deep clear impression. Laing 1077.
BM 15380.
SC 13/D75   (13c)
abbot's seal: Robert
M561. In a gothic housing, the Virgin, crowned,
standing, holding the Child on her R side. Below, a
shield of arms: *quarterly, 1 and 4 a chevron, 2 and 3 a fesse
between three annulets*.
SIGILLVM ROBERTI ABBATIS DE MELROS   (BL)
Pointed oval, 60×40; red, detached, on tongue (pieces
of hempen string also attached). Complete, uneven but
clear impression. Also SC 13/F38 (n.d.)
SC 13/F37   Pl 43   (n.d.)
abbot's seal
M562. In a canopied niche, centre and R, the Visitation
and on L, St John the Baptist, standing. Below, a shield
of arms: *a bull's head*.
...ATIS MONASTERII DE MELROS   (Rom)
Pointed oval, 65×40; red, detached, on blue and red
plaited laces. Deep indistinct impression, R side lost.
SC 13/F5   (n.d.)

MENDHAM (Suff) Cluniac priory

priory seal

M563. Lower part of a seated figure ?

...RIE DE M... (Lom)

Pointed oval, uncoloured, small fragment, on tag.

E 42/216 (13c)

prior's seal: Simon

M564. The Virgin, frontal, seated on a bench-type throne, holding the Child on her L knee.

+SIGILLVM SIMONIS PRIORIS DE MENDHAM (Lom)

Pointed oval, 40×25; uncoloured, tag. Complete, deep but not sharp impression.

E 42/216   Pl 37 (13c)

prior's seal: John

M565. Under a pinnacled canopy resting on slender columns, the Virgin, crowned, seated, holding the Child on her L knee. Below, under a trefoiled arch set in arcading a shield of arms (defaced) hung from a sprig.

S' FRIS IOHIS...MENDHAM (Lom)

Pointed oval, c.40×28; brown, tag. Deep clear impression from a fine matrix, points lost. BM 3626.

E 327/638   Pl 39 1308

MEREVALE (Warw) Cistercian abbey

abbey seal

M566. In a canopied niche, the Virgin, crowned, seated, holding the Child on her L knee, her feet on a carved corbel. On L, in the field, a hand holding a crozier; on R, a crescent between two stars.

...ABBATIS . ET CONVE...IREVALLI... (Lom)

Pointed oval, c.30×35; red, tag. Deep clear impression, flattened at centre, points and part of edge lost. BM 3628.

E 322/151 1538

MERTON (Surrey) Augustinian priory

priory seal

M567. Under a panelled canopy, a seated figure; the plinth inscribed ...XPS + REGN...; arcading below. Legend lost.

Pointed oval, c.45×30; red, double tongue. Small fragment of a clear impression.

E 135/2/18 1363

priory seal

M568. In base, a hand issuing from R, holding the stem of a lily with three flowers at the top and two below; on either side, a bird with a large bill.

[SIGILLV] DOMUS . BEATE . MARIE . DE . M[ERTON] (BL)

Pointed oval, 33×23; brown, tongue. Deep clear impression, part of edge lost. Also on E 326/9928 (1507). BM 3641, described as 'a doubtful seal', from a cast. Used here to seal a receipt for rents received by the priory and so possibly a seal *ad causas*.

E 329/179   Pl 32 1507

priory seal

M569. Under a church-like canopy, the Virgin, in an embroidered robe, crowned, seated on a bench-type throne, holding the Child, blessing and holding a book, on her L knee and a sceptre tipped with fleurs-de-lys in her R hand; below her feet, a corbel carved with foliage. On either side, a pointed-oval opening each containing a head, the L head bearded. The field is diapered.

SIGILL' : ECCLESIE : [SANCTE:M]ARIE : DE : MERI[TON]A :
(Lom)

Pointed oval, 88×50; brown, tag. Nearly complete, fine impression. Has counterseals, **M570** and **M571**. Also on E 210/1226 (1534); E 326/11,152 (1515); E 322/152 (1538) which has counterseal **M570**. Pedrick, plate I, 1. BM 3637. The matrix is known to have been brought into use in 1241.

E 329/378   Pl 9 1535

counterseal

M570. Initial M (Lom).

No legend.

Round, 12; brown, on tag, as counterseal to **M569**. Deep clear impression. Also on E 329/378 (1535; two impressions).

E 322/152 1538

counterseal

M571. Initial S (Lom).

No legend.

Round, 12; brown, on tag, as counterseal to **M569**. Deep clear impression. Also on E 329/378 (1535).

E 322/152 1538

MICHELHAM (Sussex) Augustinian priory

priory seal

M572. Under a canopy, Our Lord, seated on a bench-type throne, his R hand raised in blessing; on either side, scroll ornament.

Legend lost.

Pointed oval, c.50×40; brown, tag. Central fragment of a clear impression. Has counterseal, **M573**.

E 42/456   Pl 15 1376

counterseal

M573. A gem: an angel, walking to L.

+M . SI . VIS . AMARI . AMA (Lom)

Oval, 22×18; brown, on tag, as counterseal to **M572**. Complete, clear.

E 42/456 1376

MILTON ABBAS (Dors) Benedictine abbey

abbey seal

M574. *Obv.* A facade of the abbey church, with central and flanking towers. In a central niche, the Virgin,

crowned, seated, holding the Child, with nimbus, on her L knee; in the flanking niches, standing figures of mitred bishops. Above, two censing demi-angels.
...MARIE . MIDELTONENSIS . ECC... (Lom)
Rev. A facade of the abbey church. In two adjoining central niches, the Annunciation. Above, in a sunk trefoil in the central gable, a woman's head.
...TIS AVE P' TE PATET... (Lom)
Round, 70; red, detached, on tag. Deep clear impression, upper part lost, edges chipped. Also on E 322/153 (1538). Pedrick, plate XL. BM 3643, which gives the legend on *Rev* as PORTA SALVTIS AVE PER TE PATET EXITVS AVE VENIT AB EVA VE VE Q'TOLLIS AVE.
SC 13/R37 (n.d.)

abbot's seal: Richard (Maury)
M575. In two adjoining vaulted and canopied niches, standing figures of two mitred ecclesiastics: (R) blessing; (L) holding a pastoral cross.
Legend lost.
Pointed oval ?, c.60×c.40; red, tongue. Central fragment of a fine impression, slightly flattened.
DL 41/9/5, no. 8 1338

abbot's seal: John Bradley
M576. In a panel, a shield of arms: *three baskets of bread* (the ABBEY); above, a heron(?), feeding.
SIGILLV... (BL)
Oval, 18×15; red, tag. Complete, deep clear impression except for legend on R.
E 326/5427 1530

MISSENDEN (Bucks) Augustinian abbey
abbey seal
M577. Under a pinnacled canopy, with three trees growing from grass on either side, the Virgin, crowned, seated, holding the Child on her R side and a sceptre in her L hand. Below, under a rounded arch, standing figures of the abbot, holding a crozier, and two canons.
S'COE ABBIS CONVENT MONAST/BEATE MARIE DE MISSYDEN (BL)
Pointed oval, c.65×40; red, tag. Deep clear impression slightly rubbed, points and part of edge lost. Also on E 25/87 (1534). BM 3651.
E 329/94 Pl 47 1527

MONK BRETTON (Yorks) Cluniac later Benedictine priory
priory seal
M578. St Mary Magdalene, standing.
Legend illegible.
Pointed oval; c.70×c.50; uncoloured, detached, on tag. Complete, defaced. Also on SC 13/R38B (n.d.). Clay, p.27, plate VI. BM 3657.
SC 13/R38A (n.d.)

MONKS HORTON (Kent) Benedictine priory
priory seal
M579. St John the Evangelist, seated, holding a long scroll in his hands, his feet on a crouching man; the background diapered.
S' ECCLESIE S...WANGELISTE DE HORTON (Lom)
Round, 70; brown, on yellow cords. Clear impression, R edge chipped, large crack through centre.
E 41/233 1518

MONKS KIRBY (Warw) Benedictine priory
priory seal
M580. The Virgin, seated on a bench-type throne, holding the Child, with nimbus, on her L knee.
Legend lost.
Pointed oval, over 30×20; red, tag. Central fragment of a deep clear impression, flattened.
E 326/9876 1366

prior's seal
M581. The prior, vested for mass(?), standing, holding a long rod in his R hand and a book before him in his L hand.
...GILLVM PRIORIS DE KIRKEBI: (Lom)
Pointed oval, 37×28; uncoloured, tag. Nearly complete, deep impression, rubbed.
DL 27/31 1231

prior's seal: Maurice
M582. In a double canopied niche with tabernacle work at the sides, standing figures: (L) the Virgin, crowned, holding the Child on her L side; (R) a bishop, blessing and holding a crozier. Below, a shield of arms: (defaced, but apparently two coats impaled).
Legend lost.
Pointed oval (?), over 40×25; red, tongue. Large central fragment of a very deep clear impression, flattened.
E 326/7999 1352

prior's seal: William de Graulerio
M583. In a canopied niche with tabernacle work at the sides, the Virgin, with nimbus, seated on a bench-type throne with turned legs, holding the Child, with nimbus, on her L knee. Below, a shield of arms: *three ducks*.
...GVILLERMI DE GRAVL/ERIO PRI...RKEBY (Lom)
Pointed oval, 45×30; red, tag. Deep clear impression, flattened, upper point and L edge lost. The design shows French or Italian influence. The deed bears a fine notarial mark.
E 326/9876 Pl 32 1366

MONMOUTH (Monm) Benedictine priory
priory seal
M584. The prior, standing on a corbel, holding both

hands before him.

SIGILL' CONVENTVS SCE MARIE DE MONEM' (Lom)
Pointed oval, 60×35; dark green, on tag, in linen bag.
Nearly complete, deep clear impression. Has
counterseal, **M585**.
E 210/3415   Pl 15   (13c)

prior's seal: Florence

M585. Under a crescent, a double-headed eagle.
SIGILL' FLORENCI PRIORIS MONEM (Lom)
Pointed oval, 35×25; dark green, on tag, in linen bag,
as counterseal to **M584**. Complete, deep clear
impression. Also on E 329/46 (temp. Hen. III).
E 210/3415   Pl 40   (13c)

MONTACUTE (Som) Cluniac priory
priory seal

M586. Under a triple gothic canopy: (centre) the
Virgin, crowned, seated, holding the Child on her L
knee, between (L) a flaming sun and (R) a crescent; (L)
St Paul, holding a sword and a book; (R) St Peter,
holding keys. Below, under an arch, a monk, half-
length; on L, a sexfoil.
...MONTIS : ACVT... (Lom)
Pointed oval, c.60×40; red, tag. Deep indistinct
impression, heavily flattened, most of edge lost. Also on
E 326/5655 (1482), 8107 (1529). BM 3660.
E 322/158   1539

MOTTISFONT (Hants) Augustinian priory
priory seal

M587. The Holy Trinity. God the Father, enthroned,
holding with both hands a cloth from which Our Lord,
half-length, appears before him; above, the Holy Dove,
descending; on either side, (L) the sun and (R) the
moon.
+[SIGIL]L' ECCLESIE : SANCTE : TRINITATIS : DE :
[M]OTTESFVNT (Lom)
Pointed oval, 70×48; uncoloured, tag. Deep
impression with some sharp detail, cracked, edge
chipped. Has counterseal, **M588**. BM 3661.
DL 27/232   Pl 13   1277

prior's seal: Henry

M588. The Virgin, enthroned, holding the Child, with
nimbus, on her L knee. The throne has diaper
ornament on the front, and the arms are turned up into
wyvern's heads above which are scrolled branches. The
lower edge of the throne forms a trefoiled arch beneath
which the prior kneels in prayer to R.
*S' FRATRIS HENRICI . PRIORIS . DE . MOTESFONTE (Lom)
Pointed oval, 45×30; uncoloured, on tag, as
counterseal to **M587**. Complete, deep clear impression.
Pedrick, plate XXVII, 53. BM 3662.
DL 27/232   Pl 10   1277

MOUNT GRACE (Yorks) Carthusian priory
prior's seal: Nicholas Luff

M589. In a canopied housing, St Nicholas, seated,
mitred and vested for mass, blessing and holding a
crozier.
...OMUS : MONTIS : GRACIE (BL)
Oval, 25×20; dark brown, tongue. Deep clear
impression, rubbed, R side lost. Also on SC 13/R39
(n.d.). Clay, p.26, plate VI.
E 213/348   1412

MUCHELNEY (Som) Benedictine abbey
abbey seal

M590. Under richly pinnacled twin canopies, seated
figures: (L) St Peter (as Pope), with tiara, holding keys
and a cross; (R) St Paul, with nimbus, holding a book
and a sword. On either side, under a smaller canopy, a
smaller figure, bare-headed, robed, holding a shield of
arms: (L) two keys and a sword in saltire (the ABBEY);
(R) *a saltire*.
...MUNE . ABBATIS & CONVENTUS... (BL)
Oval, c.70×60; brown-red, tag. Deep impression,
flattened, most of edge lost. Also on E 25/88 (1534);
E 329/311 (1533). BM 3666.
E 329/6   1534

MUCH WENLOCK (Salop) Cluniac later
Benedictine priory
priory seal

M591. Under a double canopy, in a niche, standing
figures: (L) St Michael, trampling on the dragon: (R) St
Milburga. Above, in a niche, the Virgin and Child,
enthroned.
[SIGILL' ECCLESIE . CONVENTVALIS . MONA]CH[ORVM D'
WE[NLO... (Lom)
Pointed oval, c.60×40; red, tag. Deep impression,
distorted, edge much damaged. Has counterseal,
M592. Also on E 326/8011 (1536). BM 4290.
E 42/491   1458

counterseal

M592. St Milburga, half-length, frontal, holding a
crozier and book.
SANCTA [MILB]VRGA (Lom)
Round, 20; red, on tag, as counterseal to **M591**.
Complete, uneven and indistinct impression. BM 4290.
E 42/491   1458

prior's seal: Henry

M593. In a canopied niche with tabernacle work at the
sides, St Milburga, standing, holding a tall cross and a
book.
Legend lost.
Pointed oval, c.55×c.40; dark green, tongue. Heavily
flattened, cracked, edge lost.
E 42/387   (14c)

NEATH (Glam) Cistercian abbey
abbey seal
M594. Under a gothic canopy, the Virgin, seated, holding the Child on her L side. Below, a shield of arms: *three clarions* (GRAINVILLE).
[SIGIL]LVM:COMVNE:MONASTERII:BEATE:MARIE:DE:NE[-TH]   (Lom)
Pointed oval, 55×40; brown, tag. Nearly complete, clear impression. Also on SC 13/R41 (n.d.).
C 106/100   1536
abbot's seal: A
M595. The abbot, standing on a corbel, vested for mass, holding a pastoral staff in his R hand and a book in his L hand; on R, a crescent.
+SIGILLV . ABB...TH   (Lom)
Pointed oval, 40×c.25; bronze, tag. Fine impression, L edge lost. BM 3670.
DL 25/254   Pl 44   1266

NETLEY (Hants) Cistercian abbey
abbey seal
M596. under an ogival canopy, the Virgin, crowned, seated, holding the Child on her L knee. On R, in a niche, a monk, kneeling.
...DI DE...   (Lom)
Round, c.40; red, tag. Large fragment of a deep clear impression. BM 3674.
E 326/9332   1341
counterseal
M597. A vested forearm and hand issuing from R, holding a crozier, between (L) a crescent and two stars, and (R) a crescent and star.
CONTRAS' LOCI SCI EDWARDI   (Lom)
Pointed oval, 38×24; dark green, tag. Nearly complete, clear impression.
E 42/182   1303

NEW MINSTER see WINCHESTER

NEWBATTLE (Midlothian) Cistercian abbey
counterseal
M598. A vested forearm and hand issuing from R, holding a crozier.
+CONTRA . S' . DE . NEUBOTEL   (Lom)
Pointed oval, 36×22; mottled green, detached, on hemp cords. Complete, fine impression. Laing 1089. Also SC 13/D74 (n.d.). BM 15394.
SC 13/D56   Pl 14   (n.d.)

NEWBURGH (Yorks) Augustinian priory
abbey seal
M599. Under a trefoiled arch, the Virgin, crowned,

seated, holding the Child, with nimbus, on her L knee and a sceptre tipped with fleur-de-lys in her R hand. In the gabled canopy above the arch, three deeply-cut arches each containing a head. The throne rests on a trefoiled arch, below which stands the prior, holding a book, two canons on either side of him. On either side of the throne, a censing angel, kneeling.
SIGILLVM : CAPITVL[I : SANCTE : M]ARIE : DE : NOVOB[VRG']   (Lom)
pointed oval, c.70×47; uncoloured, tag. Complete except for lower point, deep uneven impression. Has counterseal, M600. Also on E 210/4928 (1438); E 326/330 (1439). Clay, p.26, plate VI. Pedrick, plate XLI, 81. BM 3679.
E 322/159   Pl 14   1539
counterseal
M600. A large gem: on L and R, two figures, seated, facing inwards; before each, a smaller figure, standing, making an offering.
S' SECRETAR CAPITVLI BEATE MARIE DE NOVOBVRGO
                                                                         (Lom)
Oval, 42×53; uncoloured, on tag, as counterseal to M599. Complete, faint impression. Also on E 210/4928 (1438). The reading of the legend's second word is uncertain; BM Cat. reads it as above, Clay (p.27, plate VI) reads SECRET.R'. BM 3678.
E 322/159   Pl 46   1539

NEWCASTLE UPON TYNE (Northumb) Austin Friars' house
common seal
M601. A mitred bishop or abbot, standing, holding a crozier; below, under an arch, a cross.
...TERE...   (Lom)
Oval, 34×c.25; red, tag. Upper and lower fragments of a clear impression.
E 322/160   1539

NEWCASTLE UPON TYNE (Northumb) Carmelite house
common seal
M602. In a circle, two kneeling ecclesiastics upholding a castle with three crenellated towers, the portal's double doors opened wide; the field sown with quatrefoils. On either side of the castle, a shield of arms: *three lions passant guardant*. Below the castle, the Virgin, crowned, enthroned, holding the Child on her L side.
*SIG...DE CARMELO NOVI CASTR' SVP' TYNAM   (Lom)
Round, 38; red, tag. Fine impression, slightly flattened, L edge lost. BM 3686.
E 322/164   Pl 14   1539

NEWCASTLE UPON TYNE (Northumb)
Dominican house
common seal
M603. In a niche with trefoiled arch above and
tabernacle work at the sides, the Virgin, seated, holding
the Child on her L knee. Below, under a trefoiled arch,
a pilgrim(?), with a high collar turned down at the back,
and a round cap, standing, holding a staff and scrip.
...[FRM.P'DICA]TOR'.N/OVI... [CAST]...   (Lom)
Pointed oval, 50×c.30; red, tag. Deep clear impression
of the centre, flattened, most of edge lost. Also on
E 327/217 (1476). BM 3684.
E 322/161   1539

NEWCASTLE UPON TYNE (Northumb)
Franciscan house
common seal
M604. The Virgin, crowned and with nimbus,
irradiate, standing on a shield of arms: *quarterly, France
modern and England*.
SIGILL...VS/MINO...CASTRO   (Rom)
Pointed oval, 50×30; red, tag. Clear impression,
flattened, cracked. BM 3685.
E 322/162   Pl 39   1539

NEWCASTLE UPON TYNE (Northumb) St
Bartholomew's, Benedictine priory (F)
prioress's seal: Margery
M605. Defaced fragment, uncoloured, double tongue.
E 213/86   1323

NEWCASTLE UPON TYNE (Northumb)
Trinitarian house
common seal
M606. Our Lord, enthroned, frontal, raising both
hands; on L, a cross formy.
...IS DE WALK...   (BL)
Pointed oval, c.45×c.35; red, tag. Large fragment of a
shallow impression.
E 322/163   1539

NEWENHAM (Devon) Cistercian abbey
abbot's seal: Leonard (Houndaller)
M607. In a canopied and vaulted niche, the Virgin,
seated, holding the Child on her R knee. On either
side, on the traceried pilasters supporting the canopy, a
shield of arms: (L) *a cross engrailed*; (R) *three mullets*.
Below, in a panel, the abbot, half-length, frontal,
praying.
...GILLVM . LEONARD...ABB : NYWEHAM   (BL)
Pointed oval, c.35×26; red, tongue. Deep clear
impression, edge lost at top and foot. BM 3695.
E 327/28   Pl 39   1411

NEWNHAM (Beds) Augustinian priory
priory seal
M608. *Obv*. Under a trefoiled arch resting on two
clustered columns with foliated capitals, St Paul, with
nimbus formed by the cusping of the arch, seated on a
bench-type throne, holding a sword and book, his feet
on a platform with BEDFORD inscribed on the plinth.
On either side, under a similar but smaller arch, a
group of five figures, seated or standing; above their
heads, (L) a crescent and (R) a sun. Above the arches,
two angels, each holding a book, one wing extended.
SIGILL':PRIORIS:ET:CONVENTVS:SANCTI:PAVLI:DE:NEWE-
NHAM   (Lom)
   Rev. A fanciful gothic facade identified by the
name RO/MA on either side of the central gable,
which contains a man's head set in a deeply sunk trefoil.
Below, under a trefoiled arch, St Paul, kneeling to R;
above him, the hand of God and his name PAVLVS;
behind him, on L, the executioner, holding a sword. On
either side, under an arch and a gable, a saint, with
nimbus, standing, his name inscribed on the frieze
above: (L) LVCAS; (R) TITVS.
MVCRO:FVROR:SAVLI:FVIT:EN[SIS:PA]SSIO:PAVLI   (Lom)
Round, 70; red, tag. Nearly complete, fine impression
of a fine 13c seal, centre slightly flattened on *Rev*.
Pedrick, plate XXXI. BM 3692.
E 25/89   Pl 20   1534

NEWSHAM (Newhouse) (Lincs) Premonstratensian
abbey
abbey seal
M609. St. Martial, preaching to three persons; above, a
star.
+SIGILL...   (Lom)
Round, 40; uncoloured, varnished, tag. Faint
impression, edge broken.
DL 25/325   (13c)

NEWSTEAD (Lincs) Gilbertine priory
priory seal
M610. The letter N with a cross formy above, the field
goutty.
No legend.
Round, 17; brown, tag. Complete, deep clear
impression. Used here as or in place of the priory seal.
E 322/166   1538

NEWSTEAD BY STAMFORD (Lincs) Augustinian
priory
priory seal
M611. Under a double canopy, the Coronation of the
Virgin; above the head of each figure, a star. Below,

under three rounded arches, a lion asleep under a tree. Field diapered.

SIGILLVM.CO[MVNE.PRIORATVS:NOVI:LO]CI [DE FO]...S (Lom)

Pointed oval, c.60×c.40; red, tag. Deep clear impression, points and most of edge lost. Also on E 40/8368 (1435), 9042 (1435).

E 25/91 Pl 14 1534

prior's seal

M612. The bust of a tonsured man with draped shoulders, facing L.

IHESVS... (Lom)

Oval, 25×20; red, tongue. Clear impression, edge broken.

E 101/568/53, no. 10 1305

NEWSTEAD (Notts) Augustinian abbey
abbey seal

M613. In a canopied niche with tabernacle work at the sides, the Virgin, seated on a bench with arcaded front, holding the Child, with nimbus, on her R knee. Foliage below, background diapered.

.../NOVO.LOC... (BL)

Pointed oval, c.75×c.45; red, tag. Lower fragment of a deep impression. BM 3732.

E 322/165 1539

NOCTON (Lincs) Augustinian priory
priory seal

M614. On R, St Mary Magdalene, crowned, standing; on L, the prior, kneeling before her; about them, trees and flowers.

SIGILLVM . CAPITV .../ DE . NOCTONE . PARK (Lom)

Pointed oval, c.45×26; red, tag. Deep impression, flattened, both points and adjacent edges lost. BM 3733.

E 25/90/2 Pl 44 1534

NORTHALLERTON (Yorks) Carmelite house
common seal

M615. In a canopied niche, the Annunciation. In two adjoining canopied niches, standing figures: (L) a saint; (R) St Edmund the King, holding his crowned and severed head.

S'...VM.ORD...MELI (Lom)

ROUND, 48; red, tag. Large central fragment of a deep clear impression. BM 3734.

E 322/168 Pl 39 1538

NORTHALLERTON (Yorks) St James's hospital
common seal

M616. In a canopied niche with tabernacle work at the sides, St James, standing on a corbel; on L and R, the letters A and T.

S' COMUNE.HOSPITALIS.SCI./IACOBI.DE.ALUERTONNE (BL)

Pointed oval, 60×40; light brown, tag. Deep impression, flattened, edge crumpled, points lost. BM 3735.

E 322/167 1540

NORTHAMPTON (Northants) Austin Friars' house
common seal

M617. In a mandorla, the Virgin, enthroned. Legend defaced.

Pointed oval, c.55×c.35; red, tag. Faint and uneven impression, heavily flattened, upper and lower parts lost. BM 3757.

E 322/169 1538

NORTHAMPTON (Northants) Carmelite house
common seal

M618. On R, a figure, standing, blessing and holding a tall cross; before him, in centre, a tree with a bird on it (?); below, on L, a smaller figure.

...COMUN... (BL)

Pointed oval, c.40×c.25; red, tag. Indistinct impression, flattened, most of edge lost. BM 3759.

E 322/174 1538

NORTHAMPTON (Northants) Delapré, Cluniac abbey (F)
abbey seal

M619. In a canopied niche with tabernacle work at the sides, the Coronation of the Virgin.

S' COE.ABATHIE.BE...PRATIS.IVX.NORHT (Lom)

Pointed oval, c.50×37; red-brown, tag. Deep impression, flattened, points lost. BM 3750.

E 322/70 1538

NORTHAMPTON (Northants) Dominican house
seal of the prior provincial

M620. In a canopied niche, two seated figures (the Coronation of the Virgin ?); below, a shield of arms (defaced).

...PRIOR PROV[INC/ALIS FR]... (BL)

Pointed oval, c.45×c.35; red, tag. Deep impression, defaced, heavily flattened, upper and lower parts lost. Described in the sealing clause as the common seal. BM 3758.

E 322/170 1538

NORTHAMPTON (Northants) St Andrew's, Benedictine priory

priory seal

M621. St Andrew, seated, blessing with his R hand, a book in his L hand resting on his L knee.

...SANCTI.A...OLI . DE . N... (Lom)

Pointed oval, c.60×c.as42; light brown, tag. Very large fragment of a deep clear impression. Also on E 42/279 (1233) which has counterseal **M622**; E 135/10/21 (1400). BM 3736.

E 322/172   Pl 39   1538

counterseal

M622. An eagle, displayed.

+TESTIMONIVM CONVENTVS (Lom)

Pointed oval, 25×20; dark green, on tag, as counterseal to **M621**. Complete, deep uneven impression. BM 3737.

E 42/279   1233

NORTHAMPTON (Northants) St James's, Augustinian abbey

abbey seal

M623. Under a canopy, St James, wearing a pilgrim's hat, standing on a corbel, holding a book and a long knobbed staff. Below, under an arch, the abbot, half-length, facing R, holding a crozier. On either side, ahead, facing inwards with a crescent and star above. Scallops in the field.

S' CONVENTVS : SCI : IACO/BI : EXTRA : NORHATONA (Lom)

Pointed oval, 70×43; red, tag. Complete, deep clear impression. Also on E 210/6933 (1297); E 322/173 (1538); E 135/10/21, no. 10 (1400). BM 3745.

E 25/92   Pl 14   1534

abbot's seal

M624. The abbot, standing, holding a crozier.

SIGIL...NORHAMT (Lom)

Pointed oval, c.55×c.35; dark green, tag. Upper fragment of a clear impression.

E 329/188   (13c)

NORTHAMPTON (Northants) St John the Baptist's and St John the Evangelist's, hospital

common seal

M625. Under a double canopy, standing figures: (L) St John the Evangelist, holding a book; (R) St John the Baptist, holding a staff; between them, the Holy Lamb on a disk.

...NORH (Lom)

Pointed oval, c.60×c.43; red, tag. Deep uneven impression, flattened, most of edge lost. BM 3752 is complete and clear; *see* Pedrick, plate L, 99 which is taken from the same cast.

E 25/93   1534

master's seal: William Rote

M626. Under a canopy, St John the Baptist, standing, holding the Holy Lamb on a disk; the background diapered with roses. Below, under an arch, a figure, praying.

S'IOH'...SERVPAV...(?) (Lom)

Pointed oval, 50×?; red, tag. Clear impression, R side lost.

E 42/161   1459

NORTH FERRIBY (Yorks) Augustinian priory

priory seal

M627. A round building, arcaded, with a conical roof topped by a cross.

SIGILL' TEMPLI DOMINI DE ANGLIA (Lom)

Pointed oval, 45×30; red, detached, on tag. Complete, deep indistinct impression. The seal's device no doubt refers to the status of the house as a cell of the Augustinian abbey of the Temple of the Lord at Jerusalem. Clay, p.16, plate II, 10. BM 4493.

SC 13/R22   Pl 43   (n.d.)

NORTH ORMSBY (Lincs) Gilbertine priory (M and F)

priory seal

M628. The Virgin, crowned, seated on a throne with turned legs, holding the Child on her L knee.

SIGILL'... (Lom)

Pointed oval, c.70×c.45; uncoloured, tag. Deep clear impression, cracked across, most of edge lost. BM 3797.

DL 25/324   Pl 47   1272

priory seal

M629. Under a canopy with side-shafts resting on her throne, the Virgin, crowned and with nimbus, seated, holding the Child, with nimbus, on her L knee. Above the Child's head, three roundels.

SIGILLUM.COE.DOM'.B...RIE.DE.ORMISBY (BL)

Pointed oval, c.45×30; uncoloured, tag. Deep uneven impression, edge chipped, and distorted. BM 3798.

E 322/185   1538

NORTON (Ches) Augustinian priory

priory seal

M630. The Virgin, crowned, seated, holding the Child on her L side and a palm or sceptre in her R hand. Traceried field above. Below, a carved triangular corbel.

S...VENT... (Lom)

Pointed oval, 50×c.25; red, tongue. Upper and lower fragments of a clear impression. Also on SC 13/R42 (n.d.). Dugdale records a prior Richard, as named in this deed, in 1391.

E 210/4419   (c.1391)

NORWICH (Norf) Benedictine cathedral priory
priory seal
M631. *Obv.* The cathedral church, showing three towers with pinnacles and spire, roof with lattice pattern, and richly decorated facade. Under a trefoiled arch below the central tower, a bishop (Herbert de Losinga, founder), standing; beneath his feet, the legend HERBERTVS FVNDATOR; on either side of him, an arcade of three arches each framing a monk's head. On either side of the central spire, a censing demi-angel; on L of the L tower, a crescent moon; on R of the R tower, a flaming sun.

+SIGILLVM : ECCLESIE : SANCTI : TRINITATIS : NORWICI
:   (Lom)

Rev. The cathedral church, richly decorated as on *Obv*, showing three arcaded gable ends above the pitched roof; under the central gable, in a double quatrefoil, Our Lord, half-length, hands raised; below, a portal of two arches framing the two figures of the Salutation. On the roof, two birds with long scroll-like tails.

EST:MIHI:NVMEN:IDEM:TRIBVS:VNI:LAVS:HONOR:IDEM:-
ET:BENEDICO:GREGI:FAMVLANTVR:QVI:MICHI:REGI
                                                        (Lom)
Round, 80; red, detached, on tag. Complete, fine impression, slightly crumpled at edge. A legend round the rim, only partly legible in this example, dates this matrix 1258:
(ANNO:DOMINI:MILLESIMO:DVCENTESIMO:QVINQVAGES-
IMO:OCTAVO:FACTVM:EST:HOC:SIGILLVM). Also on
E329/335 (1383); SC 13/C15 (n.d.). Pedrick, plate xxxiii. BM 2093.
E 25/94/1   Pl 13   1534

NORWICH (Norf) St Giles's, hospital
common seal
M632. St Giles, with nimbus, facing L, seated on a gothic chair; on L before him, a tree; at his knee, a fawn, wounded by an arrow. Below, under an arch, a mitre(?).
S'.MAGRI.&.FRM.HOSPI...CI:EGIDII.DE.NORWIC   (Lom)
Pointed oval, c.45×28; red, tongue. Deep clear but uneven impression, points lost. Also on E 322/178 (1547). BM 3779, shown in Pedrick, plate xxxix.
E 25/94/3   Pl 9   1534

NORWICH (Norf) St Paul's, Benedictine hospital
warden's seal
M633. On a pointed arch between pinnacles, St Paul, half-length, holding a sword and a book; below, a figure, half-length, praying to L.
*S' CVS...PITAL':SCI:PAVLI:DE:NORWICO   (Lom)
Pointed oval, 35×23; three impressions, two red, one

green, each on tongue. Deep but partly indistinct impressions.
E 213/349   (1432–9)

NOSTELL (Yorks) Augustinian priory
priory seal
M634. St Oswald the king, crowned, enthroned, his feet on a foot stool, holding a short sceptre tipped with a cross in his R hand and a sprig of foliage in his L hand.
SIGILLV...S' OSWALD' REGIS & M DE NOSTELT   (Lom)
Round, 62; mottled green, tag. Complete, fine impression. Also on DL 25/57 (1232–40). Has counterseal, **M635**. See *Collections for a History of Staffordshire*, New Series VIII, p.130 for a description in 1375, in Bishop Stretton's register, of an impression of 1231.
E 42/484   Pl 12   1280
counterseal
M635. The Virgin, crowned, frontal, seated on a bench-type throne, holding the Child on her lap before her with her L hand and a lily in her R hand.
+CONTRASIGILL' SANCTI OSWALDI DE NOSTLE   (Lom)
Pointed oval, 50×35; mottled green, on tag, as counterseal to **M634**. Complete, deep clear impression, much rubbed. Also on DL 25/57 (1232–40).
See note on **M634** above; Bishop Stretton's register describes this counterseal as having 'an image after the fashion of a Trinity'.
E 42/484   Pl 46   1280
prior's seal: Robert de Quixley
M636. Between two bishops, St Oswald, enthroned, holding a sceptre. Below, under a triple arch, the prior, standing between two canons.
...ORIS...(?)   (BL)
Pointed oval, c.50×c.30; red, tag. Damaged, edge chipped. Clay, p.28, plate VII.
E 43/658   1397
prior's seal: John de Huddersfield
M637. In an oval panel, a splayed eagle; on its breast, a shield, charged with an unclear device, apparently a decorative cross with two croziers or flowered sceptres in saltire behind.
...ENHO...(?)   (Lom)
Oval, c.28×23; dark red, tongue. Deep uneven impression, flattened, edge crumpled. Clay, p.28.
E 213/7   1428
prior's seal
M638. Under a richly pinnacled and buttressed canopy, St Oswald, enthroned, holding two sceptres. Below, under an arch, a canon, praying, between two shields of arms: (L) *a fesse between three lions* (?); (R) the emblems of the Passion?
Legend lost.
Pointed oval, c.55×c.30; two damaged and incomplete

impressions, one dark green, one red.

E 213/352   1434 and 1457

prior's signet?

M639. St Mary Magdalene, half-length, crowned, holding a flask in her L hand; on R, an ear of corn; on L, two indistinct objects.

*MARIA MA...LENA   (Lom)

Round, 18; dark brown, tongue. Deep indistinct impression, rubbed, L edge crumpled or lost.

E 213/351   1430

NOTLEY (Nutley) (Bucks) Augustinian abbey
    abbey seal

M640. Between (L) a star and (R; a crescent, the Virgin, crowned, frontal, seated on a bench-type throne, holding the Child on her L knee and a flower in her R hand.

...IGILLVM : SANC...MARIE : DE : NVT...   (Lom)

Pointed oval, c.65×43; red-brown, tag. Nearly complete, very deep clear impression, rubbed in parts. BM 3794.

DL 27/21   Pl 8   1364

    abbey seal

M641. In three canopied niches, standing figures: (centre) the Virgin, crowned and with nimbus, holding the Child, with nimbus, on her R side, and an apple in her L hand; (L) St John the Baptist; (R) a bishop. On either side, tabernacle work and a shield of arms: (L) *quarterly France modern and England*; (R) *a bend cotised between six lions rampant* (BOHUN). Below, a third shield of arms: *a lion rampant.*

SIGI/LLVM:C...MONAST':B'E:MARIE:ET:SCI:IOHANNIS:

BAPTISTE':DE:NOTTELE   (BL)

Round, 63; dark red, tag. Nearly complete, fine impression. Also on E 25/96 (1534); E 322/184 (1538); SC 13/F153 (n.d.). BM 3795.

DL 27/105   Pl 12   1394

    abbot's seal

M642. Under a double canopy, the Annunciation. Below, under an arch, a figure(?) (lost).

Legend lost.

Pointed oval, c.50×c.35; dull red, tongue. Deep clear impression, parts rubbed, edge lost.

E 213/63   Pl 39   1360

    abbot's seal: Richard Ridge

M643. Under a canopy with tabernacle work at the sides, the Virgin, crowned, standing on a carved corbel, holding the Child on her R side and a fleur-de-lys sceptre in her L hand.

...BEATE M...   (BL)

Pointed oval, c.45×c.30; red, tag. Deep impression, flattened, most of edge lost. BM 3796.

E 329/111   1531

NOTTINGHAM (Notts) Carmelite house
    common seal

M644. In a border of traceried cusping, on a diapered field, the Virgin, crowned, standing, turning to L, holding the Child on her R side. Behind her, on R, a tree; before her, on L, a figure, kneeling, holding up a shield of arms: *barry, and a label* (GREY of WILTON).

...CO... NITATIS DOM NOTINGHAMIS ORDINIS BEATE

MARIE DE CA...   (Lom)

Round, 47; red, tag. Nearly complete, deep but not sharp impression, edge chipped. BM 3791.

E 322/180   Pl 40   1539

NOTTINGHAM (Notts) Franciscan house
    common seal

M645. In a canopied niche with tabernacle work at the sides, St Francis, three-quarter length, frontal, standing, hands joined in prayer; before him a crenellated masonry parapet rising from waves.

SIGILLU.CONVENTUS:FRATRUM.MINOR'.NOTINGHAMIE

                                    (BL)

Pointed oval, 55×30; light brown, tag. Complete, fine impression lightly flattened. BM 3789.

E 322/179   Pl 39   1539

NUN COTHAM (Lincs) Cistercian priory (F)
    common seal

M646. The Holy Lamb with cross and banner.

ECCE AGNVS DEI   (Lom)

Oval, 30×25; light brown, tag. Complete, deep uneven impression, flattened.

E 322/181   1539

NUNEATON (Warw) Fontevraldine, later
Benedictine, priory (F)
    prioress's seal

M647. Under a canopy, the prioress, standing, holding a book before her.

[S'.CECIL]IE PR[IORIS]SE D[E E]TON   (Lom)

Pointed oval, 35×23; dark green, tag. Deep impression flattened, edges damaged. The deed names Cecilia, prioress, and William de Verny, prior, which according to VCH (*Warw.* Vol. II. pp.68–69) indicates a date of 1256–72, during which period Cecilia de Lexyngton and Cecilia de Sutton were successively prioress. Also on E 326/8008 (the same parties: 1256–72). BM 3792.

E 329/172   (1256–72)

    prioress's seal

M648. As **M647**, but with a fleur-de-lys on L. Legend lost.

Pointed oval (?); red, tag. Central fragment of a deep impression. Used by Agatha de Sutton (1290–7 in VCH), but possibly the seal of Cecilia de Lexyngton altered for her successor Cecilia de Sutton who preceded Agatha de Sutton as prioress.
E 329/123 (1290–7)

prioress's seal

M649. Under a canopy with crocketed gable, pinnacles and tabernacle work at the sides, the Virgin, crowned, seated, holding the Child on her L knee; on the plinth below her feet, AVE MARIA. Below, the prioress, kneeling in prayer to L, between two shields of arms: (L) three leopards (?); (R) *two bars, and three roundels in chief.*

...CA...PRIORISSE DE E... (Lom)

Pointed oval, 50×30; red, tag. Nearly complete, deep uneven impression, defaced, flattened. Also on E 326/7991 (1363; incomplete but clear), E 326/8198 (1413). Used here as the priory seal, and so described in the sealing clause.
E 322/182 1539

prior's seal: William (de Verny)

M650. A gem: a man's head facing R.

SIGILLVM WILLELMI (?) (Lom)

Oval, 28×22; dark green, tag. Indistinct impression especially of the legend, lower part lost.
E 329/172 (1256–60)

prior's seal: Walter

M651. Under a canopy and above a pointed arch, the Virgin seated, holding the Child on her L side; below, a figure, half-length, praying to L.

...DEI / MEMENTO MEI (Lom)

Pointed oval, c.35×25; red, tag. Clear impression, upper point and edge lost. Prior Walter is dated by VCH to c.1294. BM 3793.
E 329/123 (c.1294)

prior's seal: Robert de Rodburne

M652. Under a trefoiled arch, the Virgin, half-length, holding the Child. Below, under an arch with letter R in either spandrel, the prior, half-length, praying to R.

S'FRIS ROBER[TI] D'RODBORNE (Lom)

Pointed oval, 35×20; dark green, tag. Nearly complete, deep clear impression. VCH dates prior Rodburne to c.1328, and E 40/5785 shows him contemporary with Sibilla, prioress.
E 329/112 (c.1328)

NUNKEELING (Yorks) Benedictine priory (F)
priory seal

M653. St Helen, crowned, standing, holding a book before her in her L hand and a tall cross and a pendent scroll in her R hand.

S' SCANTE.HELE...ECCLIE D' KILLING (Lom)

Pointed oval, c.45×25; light brown, tag. Deep clear impression, lower point lost.
E 322/183 Pl 47 1539

NUTLEY see NOTLEY

OLD WARDEN (Beds) Cistercian abbey
abbey seal

M654. Under a deep vaulted canopy, the Virgin, crowned, seated, her feet resting on a carved corbel, holding a sceptre in her L hand and the Child, standing, on her R knee, his R hand raised in blessing. On either side, an elaborate penthouse containing a figure standing on a carved corbel, on L, an abbot holding a crozier.

S'.COMVE.ABBATIS.ET./COVENTVS.DE.WARDONA (Lom)

Round, 55; red, tag. Complete, deep clear impression, slightly rubbed. Has counterseal, **M655**. Also on E 135/10/21, no. 11 (1400). BM 4258.
E 322/253 Pl 43 1537

counterseal

M655. A shield of arms: *a pastoral staff between three pears* (the ABBEY).

SPES MEA IN DEO EST (Lom)

Round 22; red, on tag, as counterseal to **M654**. Complete, fine impression. BM 4259.
E 322/253 Pl 51 1537

ORFORD (Lincs) Premonstratensian priory (F)
priory seal

M656. The Virgin, seated on a bench-type throne, holding the Child on her L knee.
Legend defaced.
Pointed oval, c.50×c.33; red, tag. Central fragment of a deep indistinct impression, flattened. BM 3325.

ORMSBY see NORTH ORMSBY

OSNEY (Oxon) Augustinian abbey
abbey seal

M657. Under a gabled canopy, the Virgin, crowned, seated, holding the Child, with nimbus, on her L knee and an apple in her R hand. Below her feet, a plinth lettered DE OXONIA; and below this, under a rounded arch, an ox, walking to L.

SIGILLVM A...CONVENTVS ECCLESIE S...IE DE OSENAYA (Lom)

Pointed oval, 85×55; dark green, tag. Very deep clear impression, L and R edges lost. Also on E 326/8838 (1436); WARD 2/28B/15 (1523). Pedrick, plate xxv, 49. BM 3801.
E 25/99 Pl 33 1534

OTTERTON (Devon) Benedictine priory
prior's seal: Richard Blandoyt
M658. In a cusped circle, two (remaining of four or five) otters.
Legend lost or defaced.
Round, c.20; dark green, tag. Fragment of a deep clear impression.
E 327/332 (14c)

OWSTON (Leics) Augustinian abbey
abbey seal
M659. St Andrew, with nimbus, bound to his cross by two men pulling ropes on either side; above him, (centre) the Hand of God, (L) a star, and (R) a crescent enclosing a flame. Below, under an arch, the abbot, kneeling to R before an altar, holding a crozier.
SIGILL' ECL'IE SCI A...APL'I : OSOLVESTON (Lom)
Pointed oval, c.65×43; red-brown, tag. Deep clear impression, partly flattened, points lost. Also on E 326/8817 (1371). BM 3808.
E 25/100 Pl 30 1534
abbot's seal: Robert Kirkby ?
M660. Under a canopy with ogee arch, the abbot, standing, vested for mass, holding a crozier in his R hand.
Legend lost.
Pointed oval, c.35; brown, tongue. Upper fragment of fair impression. BM 3809.
E 329/264 1474

OXFORD (Oxon) Franciscan house
warden's seal: John de Claxton
M661. A friar, seated, hands outstretched, his feet on a footstool, between two seated groups of five friars.
Legend lost.
Pointed oval, c.40×c.25; orange, tongue. Central fragment of a deep clear impression.
E 213/30 Pl 26 1305

OXFORD (Oxon) St Frideswide's, Augustinian priory
prior's seal: Robert Downham
M662. Under an elaborate canopy, St Frideswide, crowned, standing; on either side, canopied niches containing (lost). Below, under an arch, a figure, half-length, praying.
Legend lost.
Pointed oval, c.65×c.40; red, tongue. Large central fragment of a deep clear impression, flattened.
E 213/350 1456

OXFORD (Oxon) St John the Baptist's, hospital
common seal
M663. A cross formy fitchy; above, an eagle rising with head turned back.

S' FRAT...OSPITAL...IOHANNIS . DE . OXEN... (Lom)
Oval, 50×38; dark green, tag. Clear impression, edge chipped. BM 3817.
E 135/19/66 1375

PAISLEY (Renfrew) Cluniac abbey
abbot's seal: Robert Shaw
M664. Under a canopy, St James, with nimbus, standing on a decorated corbel, holding a staff in his L hand; above his L shoulder, a scallop. Below, on a crozier, a shield of arms: *three covered cups* (SHAW).
SIGILLVM.ROBERTI/ABBATIS DE PASLETE (Lom)
Pointed oval, 63×42; red, set in uncoloured wax, detached, on red and blue plaited laces. Complete, deep clear impression. The legend is shown on two scrolls.
SC 13/E59 Pl 25 (n.d.)
abbot's seal
M665. On L, St Mirinus (?), kneeling before an altar on which are a chalice and a cross; behind it, on R, a crozier. Above, clouds and a figure descending.
+SIGILLVM ABBATIS DE PASSELET (Lom)
Pointed oval, 40×25; mottled green, detached, on hemp cords. Complete, deep but partly indistinct impression. BM 15409.
SC 13/D57 (n.d.)

PEEBLES (Peebles) Holy Cross, Trinitarian house
abbot's seal: John Turnbull
M666. Under a canopy, the Virgin, crowned, seated, holding the Child on her R knee; on either side, fronds. Below, a shield of arms: *a bull's head caboshed* (TURNBULL).
S' IOHIS TVRNBVL / ABBATIS DE PEBL (BL)
Pointed oval, 55×38; brown, detached, on tag. Complete, deep indistinct impression.
SC 13/E60 (n.d.)

PENTNEY (Norf) Augustinian priory
seal ad causas
M667. On R, Our Lord, with nimbus, standing, blessing and holding a tall cross; above his head, a crescent enclosing a star. Before him, on L, St Mary Magdalene, kneeling; above her, the inscription NOLI/ MET'/ANGERE. Between them, a tree under whose roots the prior, half-length, prays to L.
*S'ECCLESIE.SCE.MARIE.MAGDALENE.DE.PENTENEYE.A-D.CAUSAS (Lom)
Pointed oval, 65×40; light brown, tongue. Complete, deep clear impression, partly flattened. Also on E 42/462 (1511) which has counterseal M668. BM 3820.
E 25/101/2 Pl 30 1534

counterseal

M668. Between flowers, a figure, kneeling in prayer to L.

...ATE... (Lom)

Oval, 22×18; red, on tag, as counterseal to **M667**. Badly cracked and defaced.

E 42/462 1511

PERSHORE (Worcs) Benedictine abbey
abbey seal

M669. The Virgin, crowned, seated on a bench-type throne with panelled front, holding the Child on her L knee and a fleur-de-lys sceptre in her R hand; beside her head, (L) a crescent and (R) a sun. Beside the throne, standing figures: (L) St Paul holding a sword, above him, a star; (R) St Peter holding keys, above him, a star and a quatrefoil. Below, under a trefoiled arch, St Eadburga, holding a chalice and book.

...LL':BEATE:MARIE:ET:SCE:EADB[VRGE:VIR]GINIS:PERSO-RENSIS:ECCLES[IE] (Lom)

Pointed oval, 85×55; red, tag. Deep clear impression, points and part of edge lost. Also on SC 13/R43 (n.d.) BM 3822.

E 25/102/6 Pl 2 1534

PETERBOROUGH (Northants) Benedictine abbey
abbey seal

M670. In a square-topped niche, under a shallow conical canopy with a large finial, St Peter, with nimbus, seated on a bench-type throne, frontal but with his head in profile to L, raising his R hand and looking towards an altar in an adjacent arched housing with a pyramidal top. On R, a buttress pierced with two rounded arches.

...VEM (Lom)

Round, c.70; uncoloured, tag. Deep but partly indistinct impression, most of edge lost.

E 327/152 Pl 12 (1177–93)
abbey seal

M671. *Obv.* In a canopied niche, St Peter, wearing a tiara, seated on an arcaded throne, holding a key and pastoral cross; under his feet, an animal. On either side, a similar but smaller canopied niche containing: (L) an altar, with a chalice covered with a corporal and with a cover suspended above; (R) an abbot, holding a crozier. Above the central canopy, two shields of arms: *two keys in saltire* (the ABBEY).

TV:PRO:ME:NAVEM:LI[QVI]STI:SVSCIPE:CLAVEM (Lom)

Rev. Under a triple canopy (as on *Obv*) resting on a boat on waves, the boat having carved heads at prow and stern, St Paul, holding a sword upright by its point and a key, between (L) St Andrew holding his cross and (R) St Peter holding a key and a book. Above

the canopy, letters R, R and F, F.

SIGNVM:BVRGENSE:C[RV]CE:CLAVE:FVLGET:ET:ENSE (Lom)

Round, 70; uncoloured, tag. Complete, deep clear impression.

Pedrick plate XXXIX. BM 3830.

E 25/102/10 1534
abbot's seal: Robert (de Lindsey)

M672. The abbot, standing, vested for mass, holding a book and a crozier; to L of his head, a crescent.

+SIGILL' ROBER...I PETRI (Lom)

Pointed oval, 65×40; dark green, tag. Deep clear impression, most of edge lost. BM 3835.

E 327/666 (1214–22)
abbot's seal: Adam (de Boothby)

M673. Under an elaborate ogee-arched canopy resting on leopard's-faced corbels, the abbot, standing, vested for mass, holding a crozier and a book, between two cusped roundels containing: (L) St Peter's head with crossed keys above; (R) St Paul's head with crossed swords above.

...RI* (Lom)

Pointed oval, c.60×c.40; dark green, tag. Fragment of a deep clear impression. Also on DL 25/30 (1330, fragment).

E 329/142 Pl 4 1325
abbot's seal: William Genge

M674. In a circle, between four lunettes of tracery, a shield of arms: *two keys in saltire between four crosses crosslet fitchy* (the ABBEY).

...WILLELMI:ABBATIS:DE:BVRGO:SCI:P... (BL)

Round, 28; red, tongue. Deep clear impression, upper edge lost.

E 42/179 Pl 6 (1396–1408)
abbot's seal: Richard (Ashton)

M675. In a cusped quatrefoil, the bust of a man wearing a conical hat with knob; on his breast, a shield of arms: *two keys in saltire* (the ABBEY); from behind his shoulders spring fronds of oak.

BV...SALVE /...T (Lom)

Round, c.20; red, tongue. Complete, deep impression, edge distorted.

E 329/211 1448
abbot's seal: Robert Kirton

M676. Under a canopy, St Peter, standing, facing R, holding a book and keys; before him, on R, a kneeling figure.

Legend lost.

Pointed oval, c.40×c.25; red, tongue. Large central fragment of a poor impression. BM 3839.

E 329/157 1518
abbot's seal: John (Borowe)

M677. In three adjoining vaulted and canopied niches, (centre) St Peter, with tiara and nimbus, seated, blessing and holding keys, between standing figures: (L) St Paul, with nimbus, holding a sword; (R) St Andrew, with nimbus, holding his cross. Below, under an arch, the abbot, half-length, mitred and holding a crozier, between two shields of arms: (L) quarterly, Old France and England; (R) *two keys in saltire between four crosses formy fitchy* (the ABBEY).

S'DNI:IOHIS...BATIS / DE BURGO : SCI : PETRI (BL)
Pointed oval, 75×48; red-brown, detached, in metal skippet. Complete, deep clear impression, cracked. Also on SC 10/2502 (n.d.). BM 3840.
SC 13/O62   Pl 6   (1528–40)

PILL (Pemb) Tironian priory
  priory seal
M678. In an elaborate canopied niche with tabernacle work at the sides, the Virgin, crowned, standing, holding the Child with nimbus, on her R arm and a fleur-de-lys sceptre in her L hand. Below, under an arch, the prior, half-length, praying to L.

SIGILLU COMUNE PRIORATUS/BE.MARIE...DE PILL' (BL)
Pointed oval, 60×35; light brown, tongue. Nearly complete, deep uneven impression. Also on E 40/13435 (1531).
E 25/103/2   1534

PILTON (Devon) Benedictine priory
  priory seal
M679. *Obv*. In a vaulted and canopied niche, the Virgin, crowned, standing on a carved corbel, holding the Child on her R arm, and a fleur-de-lys sceptre in her L hand. On either side, in a similar but smaller niche, an angel, standing, swinging a censer.

VI...ROGA...TOTUM . SEMPER . TIBI . DO . ME (BL)
    Rev. In a vaulted and canopied niche, King Athelstan, crowned, standing on a decorated corbel, holding a sceptre and an orb. On either side, in a similar but smaller niche, a tree on which is hung a shield of arms: (L) *an eagle displayed*; (R) *per saltire, an orb with a trefoiled cross topped with a crown*.
HOC.ATHELSTANUS.AGO.QUOD [P'SENS.SI] GNAT [IMA]GO (BL)
Round, 60; red-brown, tongue. Fine impression, slightly flattened, two fragments on R (of *Obv*) lost. BM 3841.
E 25/102/2   Pl 53   1534

PIPEWELL (Northants) Cistercian abbey
  abbey seal
M680. In a canopied niche, the Virgin, seated, holding the Child on her L knee. On either side, under a crocketed canopy, a man's head, facing inwards; below,

a sprig of foliage. Below, under an arch, a bust of the abbot, praying to R, holding a crozier.

...IE . DE . PIPP... (Rom)
Pointed oval, c.50×c.35; red, tag. Deep impression, heavily flattened, most of edge lost. Also on SC 13/R40 (n.d.). BM 3843.
E 322/193   1538
  abbot's seal
M681. The abbot, standing on a corbel.
S...ELA (Lom)
Pointed oval, c.45×c.30; dark green, tag. Indistinct impression, most of edge lost.
E 210/8474   1297
  abbot's seal
M682. The Annunciation. Below, under an arch, the abbot, kneeling in prayer.
...PE...RIELI...AVE (BL)
Oval, 30; brown, tag. Clear impression, R side lost, edge damaged.
C 146/10039   1386

PLYMPTON (Devon) Augustinian priory
  priory seal
M683. St Peter and St Paul, each with nimbus, seated on a bench-type throne: (L) St Peter, holding a book in his R hand and two upright keys in his L hand; (R) St Paul, holding a book in his L hand and a sword upright by the tip in his R hand. Below their feet, a corbel carved with foliage.
SIGILLVM.ECCLESIE.AP'LOR...RI.ET.PA...PLIMTONA (Lom)
Pointed oval, 70×55; red, tag. Nearly complete, deep impression, partly flattened, legend indistinct. Also on E 329/199 (1537) which has counterseal **M684**; E 25/103/1 (1534). BM 3846.
E 322/194   Pl 25   1539
  counterseal
M684. The Virgin, seated, holding the Child on her L knee and a lily with a bird perched on it in her R hand.
[SIGILLV]M : SANCTE : MARIE : DE : PLIM... (Lom)
Pointed oval, c.50×35; bronze, on tag, as counterseal to **M683**. Large fragment of a deep clear impression. Also on E 25/103/1 (1534). BM 3846.
E 329/199   1537

POLESWORTH (Warw) Benedictine abbey (F)
  abbey seal
M685. In three adjacent canopied niches, standing figures: (centre) the Virgin, crowned, holding the Child on her R arm and a sceptre in her L hand; (L) St John the Evangelist, with nimbus, holding a cup with devil; (R) St Edith, with nimbus, holding a crozier and book. Below, under an arch, a shield of arms: *a fesse double cotised between [six] crosses crosslet*.

SIGILLU:COE:ABBISSE:ET...VENTS:MONIZ:DE:POLLESWO-
RTH (BL)
Pointed oval, 70×42; red, tag. Complete, deep clear
impression, lower point lost. BM 3850.
E 322/196 Pl 6 1539

POLSLOE (Devon) Benedictine priory (F)
 priory seal
M686. St Katharine, standing on a carved corbel,
holding her wheel. On L and R, parts of the broken
wheel. Diapered field.
SIGILLVM . SANCTE . [CA]TERINE . DE . POLS... (Lom)
Pointed oval, c.55×35; red, tag. Deep impression, parts
flattened, points lost. BM 3849.
E 322/195 Pl 49 1539

PONTEFRACT (Yorks) Cluniac priory
 priory seal
M687. The eagle of St John the Evangelist, rising
regardant, holding in its talons a scroll with inscription
(defaced).
+SIGI[LI':SCI:IOH...EL'TE:DE:PONTE]FRACTO (Lom)
Pointed oval, c.65×c.45; light green, tag. Clear
impression, most of edge lost. Has counterseal, **M688.**
Also on DL 25/65 and 66 (both 1283). BM 3852.
DL 25/45 (c.1219)
 counterseal
M688. The bust of St John the Evangelist
VIRGO EST ELECTVS A DOMINO (Lom)
Oval, 32; light green, on tag, as counterseal to **M687.**
Complete, clear impression, flattened. Also on DL 25/
65 and 66 (both 1283).
DL 25/45 (c.1219)
 prior's seal: Stephen
M689. The eagle of St John the Evangelist. Diapered
field.
...ONTE... (Lom)
Pointed oval, c.45×c.30; red, tag. Deep clear
impression, most of edge lost.
DL 25/75 1341
 prior's seal: Henry, or John Tunstall
M690. St Michael and the Dragon?
...E.FRACT... (BL)
Pointed oval, c.55×c.25; red, tag. Fragments of a fine
impression, rubbed.
E 43/656 1397

PORTSMOUTH (Hants) God's House or St John's
and St Nicholas's hospital
 common seal
M691. A cross flory, supported at the base by two
angels, wings outspread; on L, the sun; on R, the moon.
Above, a hand, issuing from clouds. Below, the
hospital.

SIGILLUM+COMUNE [DOMUS] DEI+DE+PORTISMOWTH
(BL)
Pointed oval, 45×30; red, tag. Nearly complete, deep
clear impression, defaced at lower edge. BM 3855.
E 322/198 Pl 49 1540

PRITTLEWELL (Essex) Cluniac, later Benedictine,
priory
 priory seal
M692. Under a double canopy, the Annunciation; on
L, the archangel holding a scroll lettered AVE MARIA
(Lom).
Legend lost.
Pointed oval, c.55×c.35; uncoloured, tag. Central
portion of a deep impression, partly indistinct.
BM 3858.
DL 25/250 1343
 priory seal
M693. Under a vaulted canopy, the Assumption of the
Virgin, who stands, crowned and irradiate, her hands
joined in prayer. The shafts of her canopy are
supported by four angels, two on either side, each in a
canopied niche. Below, under a rounded arch set in
masonry, St John the Evangelist, half-length, holding a
cup with devil in his R hand and a palm branch in his L
hand; on L the letter I and on R the letter O.
SIGILLUM : PRIORIS & COVETVS/MONASTERII BTE MARIE
DE PRITWE... (BL)
Pointed oval, 60×37; dark brown, tag. Fine impression,
slightly rubbed, points lost. BM 3859.
E 212/75 Pl 37 1513
 prior's seal: Nicholas de Cokefield
M694. In a canopied niche, the Virgin, crowned,
seated, holding the Child on her L knee. Below, under
an arch, the prior, kneeling in prayer to R.
S' FRIS [.NICHOLAI.POR]IS.DE [PRITEWELLE] (Lom)
Pointed oval, 50×30; dark green, tag. Fragments of a
deep clear impression. Has counterseal, **M695.**
BM 3860.
DL 25/249 1281
 **prior's signet or counterseal: Nicholas de
 Cokefield**
M695. A head.
S...HOLAI (Lom)
Pointed oval, 50×c.30; dark green, on tag, as
counterseal to **M694.** Deep impression, flattened,
lower part lost.
DL 25/249 1281

QUARR (IOW, Hants) Cistercian abbey
 abbey seal
M696. Under a canopy, the Virgin, seated on a
bench-type throne, holding the Child on her L knee.
...IA VIRG...OTVO LANO... (Lom)

Oval, c.23×17; brown, tag. Lower fragment of a deep impression.

E 329/183   1358

abbot's seal

M697. The Annunciation.

...ACIA PLEN...   (Lom)

Pointed oval, 30×20; dark green, tag. Deep impression, lower edge lost.

E 329/170   1305

abbot's seal

M698. In a canopied niche, the abbot standing, vested for mass, holding a crozier in his R hand and a book in his L hand. In the exergue on L, the letter W.

...QVARR...   (Lom)

Pointed oval, c.45×c.30; green, tag. Points and R edge lost, legend blurred, fine impression of abbot's figure.

E 41/458   Pl 25   1363

RAMSEY (Hunts) Benedictine abbey

abbey seal

M699. The abbot, wearing a girded alb and a cope, standing, blessing and holding a crozier.

SIGILLVM SCI BENEDIC[TI RA]MESENSIS ECCL'E   (Rom)

Pointed oval, 85×60; green, tag. Nearly complete, fine impression, slightly rubbed. Has counterseal, **M702**. Also on E 42/368 (1316), 370 (n.d.), 371 (1363), 372 (1293). VCH *Hunts* Vol. I, Plate I. BM 3866.

E 42/367   Pl 46   (1214–16)

counterseal

M700. Under a pinnacled canopy upon slender columns, the Virgin, crowned, seated, holding the Child on her L knee. Below, under an arch, a monk, kneeling in prayer to R.

AVE MARIA GRACIA /...ENA...   (Lom)

Pointed oval, c.50×30; red-brown, detached, in metal skippet. Deep clear impression, lower and L edge lost. Also on SC 13/R45A and B (both n.d.). BM 3869.

SC 13/O68   (n.d.)

abbey seal

M701. In a canopied niche with tabernacle work at the sides, the Virgin, crowned, seated, holding the Child on her L knee and a sceptre in her R hand. On either side, a shield of arms: (L) (defaced); (R) *on a bend [three ram's heads]* (the ABBEY).

...API...   (BL)

Pointed oval, c.65×45; uncoloured, tongue. Deep indistinct impression, most of edge lost.

E 327/602   1528

abbot's seal; Richard (de Selby)

M702. On R, an abbot, (St Benedict ?), frontal, seated, vested for mass, holding a crozier in his L hand and with his R hand offering another to a man, in monastic habit, who stands in a reverent attitude on L, facing the abbot.

...RICARDI : DEI : GRACIA : ABB[AT]IS : SANCTI : BENEDICTI : DE : RAMMES...   (Lom)

Pointed oval, 70×45; green, on tag, as counterseal to **M699**. Complete, deep clear impression, part of legend obscured by a thumbprint. VCH *Hunts*, Vol. I, plate I. Pedrick, plate XLV, 90. BM 3870.

E 42/367   Pl 3   (1214–16)

abbot's seal: Hugh (Foliot)

M703. The abbot, standing on a corbel, vested for mass, holding a crozier.

...VM...ON...ACIA...ESEIE   (Lom)

Pointed oval, 70×40; dark green, detached, on tag. Fine impression, headless, edge much damaged. Also on E 42/373 (1216–32).

SC 13/R44   (1216–31)

abbot's seal: Ranulf

M704. The abbot, standing, vested for mass, holding a crozier and a book. Background of diaper filled with crescents. Below, under a trefoiled arch, two rams on an island.

...G...LPHI : DE/I GR...RAMES...   (Lom)

Pointed oval, 75×45; dark green, tag. Deep clear impression, much damaged. Has counterseal, **M705**. BM 3871.

E 42/369   1247

abbot's counterseal: Ranulf

M705. The Annunciation. Below, under an arch, a figure, praying to R.

AVE M[ARIA . GRAC]IA : PLENA : [D]OMIN[VS TECVM]   (Lom)

Pointed oval, 56×35; dark green, on tag, as counterseal to **M704**. Clear impression, much broken, central part lost. BM 3871.

E 42/369   1247

abbot's seal: Hugh (de Sulgrave)

M706. The abbot, standing, vested for mass, holding a crozier and a book. On either side, in a diapered field, an oval panel containing a head; above and below each panel, a lozenge containing a head.

Legend lost.

Pointed oval, c.60×45; uncoloured, on tag. Central fragment (headless) of a deep indistinct impression. Has counterseal, **M707**. Also on E 210/6174 (n.d.)

E 42/464   (1254–67)

abbot's privy seal: Hugh (de Sulgrave)

M707. On L, an abbot, standing, vested for mass, holding a crozier and a book, facing a mitred bishop (St Ivo) who holds a crozier and blesses him.

+TE BENEDCVS HVGO SALVET TE PROTEGAT YVO   (Lom)

Pointed oval, 45×26; uncoloured, on tag, as counterseal to **M706**. Complete, clear. BM 3872.

E 42/464   Pl 8   (1254–67)

abbot's seal: (H)ugh de Sulgrave

M708. A figure, standing, vested for mass.

Legend lost.
Pointed oval, c.65×c.40; dark green, tag. Large central fragment of a fine impression from a deep and finely cut matrix. Also on E 210/6174 (n.d.).

E 40/14300   Pl 8   1267

abbot's seal: William (de Godmanchester)

M709. The abbot, standing, vested for mass, holding a crozier and a book. On either side, a deeply sunk roundel containing a monk's head. Background of diaper filled with crescents.

+SIGILL'.WILL'I: DE [...ABB]ATIS : RAMSEYE   (Lom)
Pointed oval, 60×40; dark green, tag. Deep clear impression, lower part lost. BM 3873.

E 42/370   Pl 8   (1268–85)

abbot's seal: John (de Sawtry)

M710. The abbot, standing, vested for mass, holding a crozier and book. Below, a ram; above, indications of a canopy.

...HIS...D...   (Lom)
Pointed oval, c.60×45; dark green, tag. Large fragment of a deep impression.

E 42/372   1293

abbot's seal: Simon (of Eye)

M711. Under a canopy, the abbot, standing, vested for mass, holding a crozier and a book. On either side, two lozenges each containing a head.

S': SIMONIS : DEI : G...   (Lom)
Pointed oval, c.70×45; dark green, tag. Deep clear impression, top and lower parts and L side lost. BM 3875.

E 42/463   Pl 8   1342

abbot's seal: Robert (de Nassington)

M712. Under an elaborate canopy, between two shields of arms (defaced), the abbot, standing, vested for mass, holding a crozier. Below, the abbot, half-length, praying to R, holding a crozier.
Legend lost.
Pointed oval, ?×?; uncoloured, tongue. large central fragment of a clear impression. BM 3876 (?).

E 42/373   1342

abbot's seal: Richard (de Sherringdon)

M713. Under an elaborate canopy, the abbot, standing, vested for mass.
Legend lost.
Pointed oval, over 60×over 20; dark green, tag. Central fragment of a clear impression.

E 42/371   1363

prior's seal

M714. The prior, standing, holding a book before him.
...RAM...   (Lom)
Pointed oval, c.32×22; mottled green, tag. Deep impression, headless, most of edge lost.

E 210/6174   (13c)

READING (Berks) Benedictine abbey

abbey seal

M715. *Obv.* In three adjoining canopied niches, the Virgin, crowned, seated, holding the Child on her L knee, between standing figures: (L) St James as a pilgrim; (R) St John the Evangelist, on an eagle, holding a long scroll and palm branch. On either side in the exergue, an inscription ANNO:MILLENO/TRICETENO:FABRICAT'. The gabled canopies are richly decorated with cusps, pinnacles and tracery, and the plinth, corbel and background with curling foliage.

S' CO/E ECCE COVETVAL' RADYNG' FVDATE [I HONORE]
SCE MARIE ET APOSTL'OR IOHIS ET IACOBI   (Lom)

Rev. In three adjoining canopied niches, King Henry I as founder, crowned, seated, holding a sceptre and a model church, between (L) St Peter, holding keys and a book, and (R) St Paul, holding a sword and book. On either side, in the exergue, the inscription (completing that on *Obv*)

SIGNVM:BIS:DENO:B'QRTO:CONSOCIAT'. The rich decoration repeats that on the *Obv*.

ENS./R/EX-HENRICVS VMME:DEITAT':AMICVS
ECVR':DEGIT ENTVM:DOM:ISTE:PEREGIT   (Lom)

Round, 85; bronze-green, tag. Completed except for small chip at foot of *Obv*, fine impression. In the legend of *Rev* a final S acts twice as the initial S of the next word; the first word ENS appears to be an error for DNS and is so shown in VCH *Berks*, Vol II, p.73. The inner legend dated the matrix at 1328. Also on E 40/13433 (1538); and in C 109/70 there are four impressions, three dated 1350–1, fine but broken, and the fourth which is described here. BM 3882 records the inscription IN PRINCIPIO upon St John's scroll, but no inscription appears in any of the impressions noticed here.

C 109/70   Pl 46   1537

abbot's seal: Joseph

M716. The abbot, standing, blessing and holding a crozier.
Legend lost.
Pointed oval, c.65×c.40; uncoloured, tag. Large central fragment of a deep indistinct impression.

E 210/3128   (1173–80)

abbot's seal: Henry

M717. In a canopied niche, the abbot, standing on a carved corbel, vested for mass, holding a crozier and a book. Outside the niche, (L) a hand blessing, (R) a bell above an eagle, with scallops above and below the hand and the eagle.

...HENRICI DE... A...ABBA...   (Lom)
Pointed oval, c.65×c.40; green, tag. Fine impression, L edge and upper part lost.

C 109/70   1350

READING (Berks) Franciscan house
warden's seal
M718. Under a triple canopy, Our Lord, half-length, blessing and holding a cross, on the roof of a church with initials T and O in the gables. Below, under a trefoiled arch, a figure, half-length, frontal, praying.
SIGILLU GUARDIANI FRATRU MINORU RADINGISPointed oval, 45×30; red, detached, on pink tapes, in metal skippet. Complete, deep impression, partly indistinct.
SC 13/O65 (15c)
common seal
M719. Figures under a canopy?
...NV...R...G (Lom)
Pointed oval, c.40×c.28; red, tag. Fragments of a clear impression.
E 322/279 1538

REIGATE (Surrey) Augustinian priory
priory seal
M720. Our Lord on the cross, with the Virgin and St John standing by. Below, a shield of arms: *checky*.
...MMVNE : PRIORATVS : SAN[CTE CRVCIS] DE...
Round, 50; red, tag. Clear impression, upper edge lost.
E 40/13494 1535

REPTON (Derb) Augustinian priory
priory seal
·**M721**. God the Father, with nimbus, seated on a bench-type throne, his R hand raised in blessing, holding a book in his L hand.
SIGILL': SANT[E : TRINITATIS : DE : R]APENDON (Lom)
Pointed oval, 50×35; green, tag. Deep clear impression, rubbed, lower edge lost. Also on E 135/10/21, no.15 (1400); E 322/200 (1538); SC 13/R46A and B (both n.d.). Has counterseal, **M722**. BM 3894.
C 109/86/48 Pl 8 (n.d.)
prior's seal: Peter
M722. Our Lord, seated on a bench-type throne with knobbed arms, his R hand raised in blessing. Below, under a trefoiled arch, a praying figure.
S[IGILLVM] PETRI PRIORIS DE R[A]PENDONE (Lom)
Pointed oval, 30×20; red, on tag, as counterseal to **M721**. Nearly complete, clear impression.
C 109/86/48 (13c)
prior's seal: Ralph de Derby
M723. In a cusped border, a figure, half-length, mitred, blessing and holding a crozier; below, under an arch, the prior, praying to R.
...BERTIS PATER MERITIS TE PROTEGE SEMPER (Lom)
Oval, 25×20; brown, tag. Complete, deep clear impression of centre, legend blurred.
C 109/86/47 1364

REVESBY (Lincs) Cistercian abbey
abbey seal
M724. Between four stars, a hand and sleeved forearm issuing from R, holding a crozier.
+SIGILLVM ABBATIS D' SCO LAVRENTIO (Lom)
Pointed oval, 40×25; orange, tag. Complete, deep clear impression.
DL 25/322 1208
abbot's seal: Henry May
M725. In a niche with vaulted canopy and tabernacle work at the sides, the Virgin, crowned, seated, holding the Child on her L knee and a sceptre in her R hand. Below, under an arch, the abbot, kneeling in prayer to L, holding a crozier.
S' HENRI...MAY / AB... (BL)
Oval, 44×35; dark red, tongue. Deep sharp impression, R edge lost.
E 135/10/20, no. 7 (c.1400)

REWLEY (Oxon) Cistercian abbey
abbot's seal
M726. The abbot, standing, vested for mass, holding a book; on L, a figure, half-length, above a shield of arms: *quarterly France modern and England, a label of three points*.
Legend lost.
Pointed oval, c.50×c.25; green, tag. Large central fragment of a clear impression.
E 41/457 1363

RICHMOND (Yorks) Franciscan house
common seal
M727. St Francis, standing on a corbel, preaching to the birds, holding a book in his L hand before him, his R hand raised with pointing finger. On either side, a tree with birds perching on it; on either side of his head, under a trefoiled arch, a shield of arms: *a saltire* (NEVILLE).
S'.COMVNE.FRATRVM.MINOR[VM.RI]CHIMVD (Lom)
Pointed oval, 45×30; light brown, tag. Complete, deep clear impression, slightly flattened, L edge damaged.
BM 3904.
E 322/201 Pl 29 1539

RIEVAULX (Yorks) Cistercian abbey
abbey seal
M728. Under a crocketed arch, the abbot, standing, vested for mass. Above, under an arch and between pinnacles, the Virgin, crowned, seated on a bench-type throne, holding the Child on her L knee. On either side of the abbot, under a crocketed gable, two monks, standing looking inwards; above, (L) a flaming sun and (R) a crescent moon.
...ALLIS (Lom)

Pointed oval, 63×c.35; uncoloured, tongue. Large fragment of a deep clear impression. Also on E 322/202 (1538) which has counterseal **M729**; SC 13/R47 (n.d.). Clay, p. 30, plate VIII; the legend is there shown as S'ABBATIS:ET:CONVENTVS:SANCTE:MARIE:RIEVALLIS.

E 43/108   1331
    counterseal
M729. A gem? St George, on horseback, holding a shield and spear, slaying the dragon.
No legend.
Oval, c.20×c.30; red, on tag, as counterseal to **M728**. Lower L fragment of a deep clear impression.
E 322/202   1538
    abbot's seal; William
M730. Under a canopy, the abbot, standing, vested for mass, holding a crozier and a book; on either side, a shield of arms: (L) *three water bougets* (ROOS); (R) *a lion rampant* (MOWBRAY).
SIGI...   (BL)
Pointed oval, c.50×c.20; green tag. Clear impression, most of edge lost. Clay, p. 30–31, plate VIII.
E 41/458   1363

ROBERTSBRIDGE (Sussex) Cistercian abbey
    abbey seal
M731. *Obv.* In a canopied niche with elaborate decoration, the Coronation of the Virgin. Below, under three arches, the abbot, holding a crozier, kneeling in prayer to R between the heads of two monks.
S':COE:ABBATIS:ET:CONV/ENTVS:DE:PONTE:ROBTI (Lom)
    Rev. The church, with tall central spire and two gables each with cross finial, standing on a bridge of three tall pointed arches with cusping and, at either end, a round crenellated tower; in the upper field, the letters PR.
HEC:PRESENS:CELLA:DOMVS:EST:DE:MATRE:PVELLA
                                                 (Lom)
Round, 56; red, tag. Complete, with one lug remaining and vestiges of three more; very deep clear impression, flattened. BM 3912.
E 322/203   Pl 53 (rev)   1539

ROCESTER (Staffs) Augustinian priory
    priory seal
M732. In a canopied niche, the abbot, standing, vested for mass, holding a crozier and a book; by his head, two annulets; below, on either side, curls of foliage. Above him, in a compartment in the canopy, the Virgin, seated on a panelled bench-type throne with a pinnacle at either end, holding the Child on her L knee, between two censing angels. On either side of the abbot, under an arch, a group of monks looking inwards; above them,

a six-pointed star with pellets between the spoints.
S' CO...STR...   (Lom)
Round, c.60; red, tag. Deep clear impression, most of edge lost. BM 3916.
E 322/206   Pl 52   1538

ROCHE (Yorks) Cistercian abbey
    abbey seal
M733. In a canopied niche, the abbot, standing, holding a book before him in his L hand; on either side, in a smaller canopied niche, a standing figure.
Legend lost or defaced.
Pointed oval, c.55×c.35; red, tag. R side of an indistinct impression. BM 3917.
E 322/204   1538

ROCHESTER (Kent) Benedictine cathedral priory
    priory seal
M734. *Obv.* St Andrew, with nimbus, being tied to his cross by five executioners.
+EGO:CRVCIS:CRISTI:SERVVS:SVM   (Lom)
    Rev. The W front of the cathedral, the centre forming a large niche containing Our Lord, with nimbus, enthroned, holding a cross and a book; below, the head and shoulders of a man supporting his footstool.
SIGILLVM SANCTI ANDREE APOSTOLI ROFFENSIS ECCL'E
                                                 (Lom)
Round, 75; bronze, tag. Completed, fine impression, slightly flattened. Also on E 33/26/31 (1504). Both these impressions show a legend round the seal's rim which has been read as ...DOMINVS...VANITATIS++HISS VITA (Lom). BM 2167.
E 25/104/1   Pl 40   1534

ROMSEY (Hants) Benedictine abbey (F)
    abbey seal
M735. St Elfleda as abbess, standing, holding a crozier and a book.
SIGIL' S' MARIE...[R]OMES'[E CL']E   (Lom)
Pointed oval, 60×40; orange, tag. Clear impression, edge chipped. Also on SC 13/F123 (n.d.). BM 3927.
E 326/11100   Pl 16   (c.1130)

ROYSTON (Herts) Augustinian priory
    priory seal
M736. In two adjoining canopied niches with tabernacle work at the sides, standing figures: (L) St John the Baptist; (R) St Thomas Becket, blessing and holding a patriarchal cross. Below, under a rounded arch set in masonry, the prior, half-length, frontal, praying.

SI[GILLV]:COMUNE:P'ORAT...DO...THOME : DE : RO... (BL)
Pointed oval, 75×47; red, tag. Deep impression, cracked, flattened, parts of edge lost. BM 3931.
E 25/104/2   1534

RUFFORD (Notts) Cistercian abbey
abbot's seal
M737. The abbot, standing, vested for mass, holding a crozier; on L, a star.
+SIGILLVM . ABBATIS : RVFFORDIE (Lom)
Pointed oval, 42×24; dark green, tag. Complete, deep clear impression. BM 3933.
DL 27/35   Pl 18   (1258–1311)

SAFFRON WALDEN (Essex) Benedictine priory, later abbey
abbey seal
M738. St James, with beaded nimbus, standing, holding a tall cross and a book, a scrip slung from his R shoulder. In the field, three scallops.
SIGILLVM : ECCLESIE : SANCTI : IACOBI : DE : WALDENA (Lom)
Pointed oval, 75×45; dark green, tag. Complete, deep clear impression, slightly rubbed. Also on DL 25/1947 (1329); DL 27/6 (1199–1213) which has counterseal, M741, and 17 (1343); E 327/672 (n.d.). Pedrick, plate XLIII, 86. BM 4241.
E 25/112/2   Pl 48 from DL 27/6   1534
seal ad causas
M739. The abbey church, shown with central tower and tall steeple; above the roof, on either side, a star and a scallop.
...: COVENTVS : DE : WALEDENA AD C...S (Lom)
Pointed oval, 45×25; red, tongue. Nearly complete, deep clear impression.
DL 25/251   Pl 27   1393
prior's seal: Roger
M740. The prior, standing.
...DE WALEDE... (Lom)
Pointed oval, c.55×35; uncoloured, varnished brown, tag. Incomplete and indistinct.
E 42/385   (1165–89)
abbot's seal: Robert
M741. A gem: a winged figure; above and below, an escallop.
+SIGILL' . ABBATIS . DE . WALDENA (Lom)
Pointed oval, 40×25; uncoloured, on tag, as counterseal to M738. Complete, light but clear impression. Also on DL 25/1947 (1329); DL 27/17 (1343); E 25/112 (1534); E 327/672 (n.d.).
DL 27/6   (1199–1213)
abbot's seal: William
M742. In a richly traceried circle, a shield of arms: on a

bend cotised three escallops, in sinister chief a pierced mullet (the ABBEY). The bend is hatched.
+S...Y : ABB... (BL)
Round, c.30; red, tongue. Fine impression, most of edge lost.
E 213/20   Pl 27   1401
abbot's seal: John
M743. In two adjoining vaulted and canopied niches, standing figures: (L) the Virgin, crowned, holding the Child on her R side and a fleur-de-lys sceptre in her L hand; (R) St James the Greater, wearing a pilgrim's hat and holding a staff. Below, under an arch, the abbot, half-length, frontal, holding a crozier, between two shields of arms: (L) a bend cotised between six lions rampant (BOHUN); (R) on a bend cotised three escallops, in sinister chief a pierced mullet (the ABBEY).
S'IOHI...ABBA / ...STERII DE WALDEN (BL)
Pointed oval, c.65×40; two impressions on attached documents, one dark green, deep clear impression but cracked and edge broken, the other red, lower fragment of a clear impression.
E 213/21   1409 and 1412

ST ALBANS (Herts) Benedictine abbey
abbey seal
M744. St Alban, with nimbus, seated on a bench-type throne with a cushion, holding a tall cross in his R hand, and a palm branch in his L hand.
SIGILLVM SCI ALBANI ANGLORV P'TOMARTIRIS (Lom)
Pointed oval, 80×55; dark brown, detached, on red and yellow laces, in metal skippet. Complete, deep clear impression. Also on E 40/5461 (1364); E 42/248 (c.1194) which has counterseal, M745, and 394 (1188–95); E 135/3/11 (1537); E 322/208 (1539); WARD 2/200/1 (1531). BM 3939.
The ivory matrix (with small alterations, see BM 3942) is in the British Museum, Tonnochy no. 852; see also VCH Herts, IV, p. 367 and Plate I.
E 33/26/2   Pl 6   (12c)
counterseal
M745. A gem: a man's head, laureate, facing R.
+SIGNACVLVM+SECRETOR' (Lom)
Oval, 35×28; dark green, on tag, as counterseal to M744. Complete, indistinct impression.
E 42/248   (c.1194)
abbot's seal
M746. In a canopied niche, Our Lord, seated, both hands raised in blessing, between two smaller canopied niches containing standing figures: (L) St Alban with palm branch; (R) a king (Offa?). Below, under an arch, the abbot, kneeling in prayer to L, between two shields of arms: (L) a saltire (the ABBEY): (R) three crowns.
...SCI... (Lom)
Pointed oval, c.75×c.35; red, tag. Very deep clear

impression, most of edge lost. Apparently from a mid-14c matrix used by successive abbots. Also on E 40/13612 (1538). BM 3951.

WARD 2/200/1   1531

ST ANDREWS (Fife) Augustinian priory
prior's seal
M747. St Andrew, with nimbus, on his cross; the space between his feet filled with quatrefoils. On either side, an angel, with nimbus, standing, holding a candlestick. Below, under a pointed arch, a monk, kneeling in prayer to R.

+S' I/OHIS.P'ORIS.SCI.ANDREE.AP'LI.IN.SCOCI/A   (Lom)

Pointed oval, 50×33; brown, detached, on hemp cords. Complete, fine impression in a bed of green wax. Laing 1107 (1266). BM 15428.

SC 13/E43   Pl 2   (n.d.)

prior's seal: John Haddington
M748. St Andrew, with nimbus, standing between candlesticks. Below, under an arch, the prior, kneeling in prayer to R.

S' IOHIS P'ORIS ECC/E SCI ANDREE I SC[OCIA]   (Lom)

Pointed oval, 50×30; dark green, detached, on tag. Nearly complete, deep clear impression. Laing 1108 (1296). BM 15429.

SC 13/C52   (n.d.)

ST BENET OF HULME (Norf) Benedictine abbey
abbey seal
M749. St Benedict, with nimbus, seated on a throne with low curved back and tower-like ends, blessing and holding a book in his L hand.

SIGILL...BENEDIC...   (Lom)

Round, 65; red-brown, tongue. Deep clear impression, large pieces lost on L and R. BM 3300.

E 25/65/2   Pl 7   1534

abbot's seal
M750. In a canopied niche with tabernacle work at the sides, the abbot, standing, holding a crozier and a book. Below, a shield of arms: *a crozier in pale between two crowns* (the ABBEY).

SIGILLUM.DOMINI.../ABBATIS.SCI.BENEDCI.DE.HULMO
                                                (BL)

Pointed oval, 75×48; light brown, detached, in metal skippet. Complete, deep uneven impression, cracked, legend partly indistinct.

SC 13/O60   (n.d.)

ST DENYS see SOUTHAMPTON

ST DOGMAELS (Pemb) Tironian abbey
abbey seal
M751. Under a canopy whose two slender side-shafts rest on a bench-type throne, the Virgin, crowned, seated, holding the Child, crowned, on her L knee. Below, under an arch, a monk, half-length, praying to R.

S'...IS DE KEMMEYS   (Lom)

Pointed oval, c.45×30; light brown, tongue. Deep uneven impression, flattened on R, points lost.

E 25/40   1534

ST GERMANS (Corn) Augustinian priory
priory seal
M752. A figure (St German?), seated on a carved bench-type throne, blessing and holding an orb(?). Legend lost or defaced.

Pointed oval, c.55×c.40; red, tag. Large fragment of an indistinct impression. Also on E 25/57/2 (1534). BM 3955.

E 322/209   1539

ST NEOTS (Hunts) Benedictine priory
priory seal
M753. Under a church-like canopy, the Virgin, crowned, enthroned, holding the Child on her L knee, giving a crozier with her R hand to the prior, kneeling on L. Diapered background.

SIGILLVM PRIORIS [ET CONVENTVS] ECCLESIE SCI NEOTI
                                                (Lom)

Pointed oval, c.70×44; red-brown, tag. Deep impression from a rather crude matrix, lower point and edge lost. BM 3958.

E 25/90/1   Pl 2   1534

ST OSYTH (Essex) Augustinian priory
priory seal
M754. In three adjoining niches with prominent canopies, standing figures: (centre) St Osyth; (L) St Peter; (R) St Paul. Below, under an arch, a demi-angel, holding a shield of arms: (defaced but including *three crowns*).

...DE CHICH   (BL)

Pointed oval, c.70×c.50; red, tag. Deep uneven impression, cracked, defaced, R edge lost. Also on E25/101/1(1534). BM 2949.

E 322/55   1539

counterseal
M755. In a cusped panel, St Osyth, standing, holding her severed head before her.

*CEI SELTCELE...MOESTASCOE (?)   (Lom)

Oval, 20×15; red, detached, on tag. Complete, deep impression but legend unclear. BM 2949 gives legend as *LEL SEIT CEL E...PAR M...TASEL.

SC 13/R48   (n.d.)

SALISBURY (Wilts) St Nicholas's, Harnham Bridge, Augustinian hospital
common seal
M756. St Nicholas as bishop, vested for mass, blessing and holding a crozier; below his feet, a fleur-de-lys.
...VS HOSPIT...ATI NICHOLAI . S... (Lom)
Pointed oval, 50×32; uncoloured, tag. Deep impression, cracked across, upper edges broken.
BM 3960.
DL 27/10 1238

SANDLEFORD (Berks) Augustinian priory
priory seal
M757. The head and shoulders of St John the Baptist, facing R, his hands raised in prayer.
S...SCI IOH...APTIS... (Lom)
Pointed oval, c.55×c.35; red, tag. Complete, deep impression, much blurred and flattened.
E 327/216 1457
prior's seal: Robert
M758. St John the Baptist, standing; before him, on R, a clerk, kneeling.
...PRIORIS DE SANDELF... (Lom)
Oval, 25×21; red, tag. Deep clear impression, R edge missing.
E 327/122 Pl 38 1348

SAWLEY (Yorks) Cistercian abbey
abbot's seal: Walter
M759. The abbot, standing on a corbel, holding a crozier and a book.
+SIGILLVM : ABBATIS : DE : SALLAIA (Lom)
Pointed oval, 42×30; orange, tag. Nearly complete, deep clear impression. The last two words of the legend are reversed. Clay, p.31, plate VIII, 7. BM 3965.
DL 25/56 (c.1236)

SCONE (Perth) Augustinian abbey
abbot's seal
M760. Under a three-towered canopy resting on corbels (R) the abbot, kneeling before (L) St Michael, who stands on the dragon and holds a long spear and a shield charged with a cross.
SIGILLVM ABBATIS DE SC/ONA (Lom)
Pointed oval, 53×35; mottled green, detached, on hemp cords. Complete, deep impression, much rubbed. Also on SC 13/D66 (n.d.). Laing 1127.
BM 15448.
SC 13/F30 (13c)

SELBY (Yorks) Benedictine abbey
abbey seal

M761. St German, vested for mass, seated on a throne, blessing and holding a crozier.
...ILLV...[ANI.S]... (Lom)
Pointed oval, c.70×c.50; buff-green, tag. Clear impression, most of edge lost. Has counterseal, **M762**. Also on E 40/11064 (1483). Clay, p.32, plate VIII, no. 10 from a nearly complete impression showing the legend as [SIG]ILLVM.SCI.GERMANI.SELEBIENSIS.ECLE.
BM 3981.
DL 25/55 Pl 33 (1232–40)
counterseal
M762. A gem: a bust of the emperor Honorius; in the field DN.HONORIVS.AVG.
+CAPVD NOSTRVM CRISTVS EST+ (Lom)
Oval, 40×25; buff-green, on tag, as counterseal to **M761**. Complete, clear impression. Also on E 40/11064 (1483). Clay, P. 32. BM 3981.
DL 25/55 Pl 37 (1232–40)
abbot's seal: Richard
M763. St German, frontal, enthroned, mitred and vested for mass, holding a crozier in his L hand, giving a crozier with his R hand to a monk who kneels on L before him.
+RICARDI DEI GRA MINISTER HVM[ILIS EC]CL'IE : SCI : GERMANI DE SELEBI (Lom)
Pointed oval, 65×43; uncoloured, painted crimson, tag. Complete except for lower point, deep impression. Also on DL 27/215 (n.d.). Clay, p. 32, plate VIII, 11 (from this impression).
DL 27/214 Pl 48 (1194–1214)
abbot's seal: Geoffrey
M764. Under a vaulted and traceried canopy, St German, seated, vested for mass, blessing and holding a crozier. Below, under an arch, the abbot, half-length, mitred, praying to R, holding a crozier.
...IS...CVRA . GER/... (Lom)
Pointed oval, 59×40; dark green, tongue. Deep clear impression, nearly all edge lost.
E 43/109 Pl 37 1355
abbot's seal: John de Shirburn
M765. In a canopied niche with tabernacle work at the sides, the abbot, seated, blessing and holding a crozier; below, arcading.
Legend lost.
Pointed oval, c.60×c.40; red, tongue. Fine impression, from a fine matrix, rubbed, edges and lower part lost.
E 135/10/21, no. 3 1400
abbot's seal: Robert Selby
M766. In a canopied niche with rich tabernacle work at the sides, St German, mitred and holding a crozier, standing on a plinth inscribed SCVS GERMANUS. Below, a shield of arms: *three swans*.
...ILLVM . ROBTI . SELBY / ABB...DE . SELBY (BL)
Pointed oval, 70×40; red-brown, detached, in tin

skippet. Nearly complete, deep clear impression, cracked.
SC 13/O63   Pl 38   (1526—40)

SEMPRINGHAM (Lincs) Gilbertine priory (M and F)
seal ad causas
M767. The Annunciation, both figures standing.
S PRIORIS ET CONVENTVS SCE M...E SEMPINGHAM AD
CAVSAS   (Lom)
Pointed oval, 55×35; red, detached on tag. Two deep clear impressions, both cracked and damaged. BM 3990.
SC 13/R50 A and B   Pl 11   (n.d.)

SEWARDSLEY (Northants) Cistercian priory (F)
priory seal
M768. The Virgin, crowned, frontal, seated on a decorated throne, holding the Child, with nimbus, on her lap.
Legend lost.
Pointed oval, c.70×c.45; uncoloured, tag. Indistinct impression, edge all lost.
E 210/2057   1342

SHAFTESBURY (Dors) Benedictine abbey (F)
abbey seal
M769. *Obv.* In a quatrefoil, the Coronation of the Virgin; on either side, a candlestick; above, the Dove; below, under an arch, the abbess, half-length, praying to R, holding a crozier.
SIGILL' [SCE] MARIE. ET.SCI.E[DWARDI.REGIS.ET]
MARTIRIS.SCHEF[TONIE]   (Lom)
      Rev. The abbey church, with central tower and spire and two lower flanking towers. Under an arch below the central tower, St Edward, standing, his name S' EDW/ARDVS inscribed on the string-course at the sides.
SA[LVE.S]TELLA.MARIS.TV.NOBIS.AV[XILLIARIS.GEMMA.]
PVELLARIS.REGIA.DONA.PA[R]IS   (Lom)
Round, 75; uncoloured, tag. Nearly complete, deep but not sharp impression, edge chipped. BM 4004.
E 322/211   1534

SHEEN (Surrey) Carthusian priory
priory seal
M770. The Nativity. Joseph, Mary with nimbus, the ox and the ass surround the Child who lies irradiate and with nimbus. The stable is shown as a pitched roof supported on four long poles, set in a wattled enclosure with a gate at the front. Above, under the Star of Bethlehem, a demi-angel holding a scroll inscribed

GLORIA IN EXSELSIS. Below, a shield of arms: *quarterly, France modern and England.*
SIGILLUM:COME:DOMUS:IHU:DE:BETHLEEM:IUXTA:SHE-
NE:ORDINIS:CARTUUS   (BL)
Pointed oval, 70 × 40; dark green, detached on red and white cords. Complete, deep clear impression. Also on E 40/4756 (1483), 4758 (1531); E 41/149 (1531); E 329/312 (1416). BM 4005.
E 25/104/4   Pl 5   1534
prior's seal: John Buckingham
M771. Monogram IHS (in BL) with a collar of SS. No legend.
Round, 18; red, tongue. Complete, deep impression, badly flattened at edge.
E 213/39   1430

SHERBORNE (Dors) Benedictine abbey
abbey seal
M772. The abbey church, showing porch, apse and two flanking towers with conical roofs.
+S[IGILLV.SCE.MARIE.SCYBVRNE]NSIS.ÆCCL'Æ   (Rom)
Round, c.55; red, tag. Deep clear impression, R and lower part lost. In the legend C and S are of angular form. BM 4009.
E 322/212   Pl 33   1539
abbot's seal: John de Saunde
M773. The Virgin, half-length, holding the Child on her R side, above a church with pinnacled turrets at the sides. Below, under a trefoiled arch, the abbot, half-length, praying to L, holding a crozier.
...DEI...MEM...   (Lom)
Pointed oval, c.35×25; red, tag. Clear impression, most of edge lost. BM 4012.
DL 34/1/3   1268

SHOREDITCH (Haliwell) (Midd) Augustinian priory (F)
chapter seal
M774. St John the Baptist, half-length, rising from waves, blessing and holding a book.
[+SIGILL'.CAPIT]VLI [SCI.IOHA]NIS . DE [HALIWELLE]
                                                          (Lom)
Round, 56; uncoloured, varnished, on tag. Deep clear impression, parts flattened, edge much broken. Has counterseal, **M755**. Also on E 42/419 (1225); E 327/309 (1537). BM 3246.
E 42/352   Pl 37   1224
prioress's seal
M775. A lady, standing, her L hand extended, holding her mantle with her R hand.
+SIGILL' MATILDIS PRIOR' DE.HALIW'   (Lom)
Pointed oval, 35×22; uncoloured, on tag, as counterseal to **M774**. Complete, deep clear impression.

Also on E 42/419 (1225). BM 3247.
E 42/352   1224

SHREWSBURY (Salop) Benedictine abbey
  abbot's seal: Thomas
M776. Under a Renaissance-style canopy, (lost).
SI[G]ILL...   (BL)
Pointed oval, c.70×?; red, tag. Small upper fragment.
SC 10/50, no. 2506   1531

SHREWSBURY (Salop) St Giles's, hospital
  common seal
M777. St Giles, standing, vested for mass, holding a
crozier and a book. Beneath his feet, a hind.
[+S'] COMMVNE DOMV[S.SCI.E]GIDII.SALOP...   (Lom)
Pointed oval, c.50×34; uncoloured, tongue. Deep
impression, points lost. Also on E 213/353 (1367).
E 213/14   1370

SIBTON (Suff) Cistercian abbey
  abbot's seal: Laurence
M778. The Holy Lamb with cross and banner.
+SE[C]RE [TVM...] AGN' IDEMQ' SERAT   (Lom)
Round, 26; uncoloured, detached from tag. Clear
impression, R side lost.
E 42/426   (c.1200)

SIXHILLS (Lincs) Gilbertine priory (M and F)
  priory seal
M779. In a cusped border, the Virgin, half-length,
holding the Child on her L side. Below, under an arch,
a monk, half-length, praying to R.
+LACTANS VIRGO DEVM PROTEGE...   (Lom)
Pointed oval, 40×25; light brown, tag. Nearly
complete, deep indistinct impression, L part defaced.
E 322/215   1538
  prior's seal: John
M780. Under a canopy, a praying figure.
Legend defaced.
Pointed oval, (?); brown, tongue. Central fragment.
E 101/568/63, no. 7   1302

SNELSHALL (Bucks) Benedictine priory
  priory seal
M781. The prior, wearing a flat cap, standing, holding
a crozier and book.
S' PRIORIS:ET C...DE : SNELLESHAL   (Lom)
Pointed oval, c.50×c.30; red, tag. Nearly complete,
clear impression. BM 4037.
E 25/105/2   1534

SOPWELL (Herts) Benedictine priory (F)
  priory seal
M782. The Virgin, seated on a bench-type throne with
ornamental finials, holding the Child on her L knee and
a sceptre with fleur-de-lys in her R hand.
...MARIE...SANCTVM ALBA...   (Lom)
Pointed oval, 70×50; bronze-green, twisted tag. Clear
impression, head and upper R part lost. From a matrix
of c.1200.
E 42/380   (n.d.)
  priory seal
M783. The Coronation of the Virgin. Below, under an
arch, a figure, kneeling in prayer to L.
Legend lost.
Pointed oval, (over 35×over 25); red, detached, on tag.
Central fragment of a deep clear impression.
SC 13/R51   (n.d.)

SOUTHAMPTON (Hants) St Deny's, Augustinian
priory
  priory seal
M784. Under a small ogival canopy, St Denys, standing
on a corbel. Diapered background.
Legend lost or defaced.
Pointed oval, c.60×c.35; dark green, tag. Central
fragments of a fine impression, rubbed. Has
counterseal, **M785**. Also on
E 326/9329 (1385).
E 326/8036   1351
  prior's seal: Richard
M785. In a canopied niche with hatched interior and
tabernacle work at the sides, St Denys, standing,
holding a palm branch before him in his R hand and a
crozier in his L hand. Below, under an arch, (lost).
[S'FRIS RICAR]DI DE...RD PORIS...   (Lom)
Pointed oval, c.55×c.35; red, on tag, as counterseal to
M784. Lower fragment of a fine impression. Also on
E 326/9329 (1385).
E 326/8036   1351

SOUTHWARK (Surrey) St Mary Overy, Augustinian
priory
  priory seal
M786. A king, in a long robe with jewelled girdle and
long pointed sleeves, wearing a crown of early pattern
with long pendent straps ending in trefoils, enthroned,
holding in his outstretched hands a long scroll inscribed
EGO...MISERI CORDIE.
+SIGILLVM SCE MARIE SVDWERKENSIS ECCL'E   (Lom)
Pointed oval, 70×47; dark green, varnished, tag.
Complete, clear impression. Also on E 42/472 (1212).
BM 4047.
E 42/468   Pl 7   (12c)

priory seal

M787. The Virgin, crowned and with nimbus, seated on a bench-type throne, holding a fleur-de-lys in her R hand and the Child, with nimbus, blessing and holding an apple, on her L knee; beneath her feet, a tiny dog, walking to R. The figures are contained in a mandorla inscribed on the rim

AVE.MARIA.GRACIA:PLENA:DNS:TECVM:BENEDICTA (Lom) and upheld by four angels, each with nimbus, the upper two supported by clouds.

SIG...IE:SAN...RCHA (Lom)
Round, 60; red, tag. Deep clear impression, flattened, edge chipped. Also on C 146/2394 (1457). Has counterseal, M788. BM 4050.

E 329/411   Pl 6   1376

counterseal

M788. A demi-angel, full-face, with nimbus, issuing from clouds, holding a globe.

AVE : MATER : MISERICORDIE (Lom)
Round, 33; red, on tag, as counterseal to M787. Complete, fine impression, rubbed. Also on C 146/2394 (1457).

E 329/411   Pl 43   1376

prior's seal: Bartholomew Linsted *alias* **Fowle**

M789. Under a canopy with tabernacle work at the sides, the Virgin, crowned, frontal, seated, holding the Child on her L side. Below, under an arch, a half-length figure.

AVE:GRACIA / [PL]EN[A] : MARIA (BL)
Oval, 25×20; red, tongue. Deep clear impression, edge and foot damaged.

E 213/43   Pl 35   1531

SOUTHWICK (Hants) Augustinian priory
priory seal

M790. The priory church, with masonry walls, transept and central tower.
Legend lost.
Round, c.55; uncoloured, tag. Large central fragment of a deep clear impression. Has counterseal, M792 BM 4060.

E 326/8901   1189

priory seal

M791. In a canopied niche with tabernacle work at the sides, the Virgin, crowned, standing, holding the Child on her R side and a sceptre tipped with fleur-de-lys in her L hand. Below, under an arch, a standing cloaked figure. On either side, a shield of arms: (L) *quarterly, France modern and England*; (R) (defaced).

SIGILLVM.CO...PRIORATUS.[ET]ECCLIE.BE[ATE.M]ARIE.D-E... (BL)
Pointed oval, c.60×40; red, tag. Deep sharp impression, cracked, parts flattened, edge damaged. BM 4064.

E 322/219   Pl 7   1538

counterseal

M792. A splayed eagle, holding pendent from its talons a circular gem, concave, showing a seated figure.

SPIRITVS DEI... (Lom)
Pointed oval, 41×26; uncoloured, varnished, on tag, as counterseal to M790. Complete, uneven impression. Perhaps the seal of prior G named in the deed.

E 326/8901   Pl 38   1189

SPALDING (Lincs) Benedictine priory
priory seal

M793. *Obv.* The Virgin, crowned, seated on a bench-type throne, holding the Child on her L knee.
Legend lost or defaced.
    Rev. St Nicholas, standing, blessing and holding a crozier.

SIGILL...OLAI SPALDING (Lom)
Pointed oval, c.70×c.50; uncoloured, tongue. Large fragment of a deep indistinct impression, from a matrix of early 13c style. BM 4065.

E 25/105/3   1534

prior's seal: Simon (de Hautebarge or de Hunton)

M794. The prior, standing on a carved corbel, holding a book before him.

+SIGILLVM SYMONIS :: PRIORIS SPALDINGIE (Lom)
Pointed oval, 53×30; uncoloured, detached, on tag. Complete, fine impression. BM 4067.

SC 13/D148   (1229–52)

STAFFORD (Staffs) Franciscan house
warden's seal: John

M795. The Virgin, crowned, standing, holding a cross with leaves (?) in her L hand.

*S' FRI...M...IE (Lom)
Pointed oval, 40×c.30; dark green, tag. Deep clear impression, cracked across, most of edge lost.

E 135/6/61   1479

STAFFORD See also BASWICH

STAMFORD (Lincs) Austin Friars' house
common seal

M796. The Annunciation, both figures standing.

S' COMVNITATIS . F...M : NORAMT... (Lom)
Pointed oval, c.50×c.35; red, tag. Deep indistinct impression, flattened, cracked, upper and lower parts lost. The reading of the later part of the legend is very uncertain; R.C. Fowler (in the Card Catalogue) read not F...M : NORAMT..., as here, but F...OR... BM 4974.

E 322/221   1538

STAMFORD (Lincs) Carmelite house
common seal
M797. Under a pinnacled canopy with tabernacle work at the sides, a figure, standing, holding a palm branch. Legend defaced.
Pointed oval, 50×34; red, tag. Deep indistinct impression, flattened, upper and lower edges lost. BM 4077.
E 322/224   1538

STAMFORD (Lincs) Dominican house
common seal
M798. Under a canopy, half-length figures: (L) the Virgin, holding the Child: (R) a saint. Below, under a trefoiled arch, a friar, kneeling in prayer to R.
...OS...RRE   (Lom)
Pointed oval, c.40×25; light brown, tag. Deep but very indistinct impression, points lost. BM 4075.
E 322/222   1538

STAMFORD (Lincs) Franciscan house
common seal
M799. The Assumption. The Virgin stands in a mandorla upheld by angels; below, an embattled bridge over water.
Legend defaced.
Pointed oval, c.45×c.30; red, tag. Deep but very indistinct impression, most of edge lost. BM 4076.
E 322/223   1538

STAMFORD (Northants) Benedictine priory (F)
priory seal
M800. St Michael, standing, holding a decorated buckler on his R arm and a long spear in his L hand; beneath his feet, the dragon.
+:SIGILLVM [SANCTI[MICHAELIS ARCHAN[GE]LI DE
STANFOR   (Lom)
Pointed oval, 65×45; dark green, tag. Nearly complete, deep clear impression from a fine matrix. Also on E 326/6819 (1528). The legend runs anti-clockwise and some letters are reversed.
E 329/113   Pl 50   (13c)
prioress's seal (?)
M801. St Michael, standing on the dragon, holding a sword and shield; facing him on R, a figure, half-length, praying to L.
[OR]O IOH'ES.T.MICHAEL ME P'TEGE PEST[E]   (Lom)
Round, 19; dark green, tag. Nearly complete, deep clear impression. Used by Isabel de Maltby, prioress, but apparently not her seal. BM 4073.
E 329/105   Pl 34   1371
prioress's seal: Agnes Leyke
M802. St John the Baptist, standing, holding the Holy

Lamb and cross with banner; in the field, IOHES DOMINUS (BL).
No legend.
Oval, 18×16; red, tag. Complete, deep impression, partly blurred.
E 212/3   1422
prioress's seal: Margaret Stainburn
M803. An eight-pointed star.
No legend.
Round, 13; red-brown, tag. Nearly complete, clear impression.
E 327/251   1527

STANLEY (Wilts) Cistercian abbey
abbey seal
M804. Under a double canopy, between lunettes of tracery, standing figures: (L) the Virgin, holding the Child on her L side; (R) St John the Baptist, holding the Holy Lamb and banner. Between them, a tall plant. Above the canopy (R) the sun and (L) the moon.
*S' COMVNE . ABBIS . ET . CONVENTVS . DE . STANLEYE .
IN WILT   (Lom)
Round, 45; dark green, on blue and red plaited silk laces. Complete, deep clear impression, a little rubbed. Also on E 40/6794 (1362); E 42/215 (1342), 382 (1363); E 326/11781 (1354). BM 4079.
E 329/91   Pl 21   1363
abbot's seal: Nicholas
M805. A sleeved forearm and hand issuing from R, holding a crozier.
+SIGILLVM ABBATIS STANL'   (Lom)
Pointed oval, 40×18; mottled green, on white and purple plaited laces. Complete, faint impression. BM 4080.
E 327/309   (c.1201)
abbot's seal: Richard
M806. In a beaded border, the abbot, standing on a carved corbel, vested for mass, holding a crozier and a book, between (L) the sun and (R) the moon.
[SIGI]LL' : ABBATIS DE STAN[LEIA]   (Lom)
Pointed oval, 35×25; dark green, tag. Clear impression, upper part lost. Also on E 212/46 (1280). BM 4081.
E 329/19   (13c)
abbot's seal: William de Combe
M807. Under a panelled canopy, the abbot, standing, [between the letters W and C]. Below, a shield of arms: *crusilly fitchy, a bend ermine.*
S' FRIS WIL...E COMBE... BIS DE...   (Lom)
Pointed oval, 48×32; red, tag. Deep clear impression, centre and much of edge lost. BM 4082.
E 326/11781   1354
abbot's seal
M808. In a canopied niche with tabernacle work at the

sides and a pattern of roses within, (R) St Anne, seated, teaching (L) the Virgin, standing, to read from a book which they hold between them. Below, under an arch between arcading, the abbot, kneeling in prayer to R, holding a crozier.

...S . DE . STANLEIE (BL)
Pointed oval, 60×c.40; dark green, on tag above which a later hand has written Stanlegh. Very deep clear impression, most of edge lost. Also on E 41/457 (1363).
E 41/458   Pl 55   1363

STANLEY PARK see DALE ABBEY

STONELEIGH (Warw) Cistercian abbey
abbey seal
M809. Under an elaborate canopy, the Virgin, crowned, seated on a bench-type throne, holding the Child on her L knee and a sceptre in her R hand. On either side, a compartment containing a standing figure: (L) (lost); (R) an abbot.
...COE : ABB...EY (BL)
Pointed oval, c.50×35; green, tag. Clear impression, most of edge lost.
E 42/469   1381
abbot's seal: John Clerkenwell
M810. Under a panelled canopy, the abbot, standing. On R, a shield of arms: *a fesse between six crosses crosslet*.
SIGILLVM IOHIS CLE...STONLE (BL)
Pointed oval, c.50×c.30; red, tag. Clear impression, part of edge lost.
E 326/8073   1495

STONELY (Hunts) Augustinian priory
priory seal
M811. In a canopied niche with diapered interior, the Virgin, crowned, seated on a bench-type throne, holding the Child on her L knee. On either side, a branch. Below, under a trefoiled arch, the prior, praying to L.
S' COMVNE CANONIC...MARIE : DE : STONLE... (Lom)
Pointed oval, c.45×33; red, tag. Deep and very clear impression, points and part of edge lost. BM 4109.
E 25/105/4   Pl 34   1534

STRATA MARCELLA (Mont) Cistercian abbey
abbot's signet
M812. A shield of arms: *a lion rampant holding a flag*. No legend.
Oval, 15×12; brown, tag. Complete, clear.
E 210/6238   1527

STRATFORD (Essex) Cistercian abbey
abbey seal
M813. In a canopied niche with rich tabernacle work at the sides, the Virgin, crowned, seated, holding the Child on her L knee.
...LLVM.CON...STRATFORDE (Lom)
Round, 43; red, tag. Deep impression, clear where not flattened, points lost. BM 4114.
E 322/226   Pl 55   1538
abbot's seal
M814. A sleeved forearm and hand issuing from R, holding a crozier; on L, a tall ornamental tree.
+SIGILLVM . ABBATIS . DE . STRATFOR (Lom)
Pointed oval, 47×31; dark green, varnished, tag. Complete, clear impression. The tall stylised tree may represent the Long Thorn, whose memory was preserved in the abbey's name of Stratford Langthorne. BM 4115.
E 42/470   (c.1200)

STRATFORD-AT-BOW see BOW

STUDLEY (Oxon) Benedictine priory (F)
priory seal
M815. The Virgin(?), seated on a bench-type throne, holding a flowering sceptre in her R hand.
SIGILLVM SCTE/MARIE DE STODELEYA (Lom)
Pointed oval, 65×40; light brown, tag. Nearly complete, deep indistinct impression. BM 4091.
E 25/107   Pl 21   1534
priory seal
M816. In a canopied niche resting on a corbel, the Annunciation. The Virgin, with nimbus, sits on R; the archangel kneels on L, holding a wand and a scroll; between them, the lily rises and spreads like a tree.
...ENTV...MARIE . D' STODLEY (BL)
Pointed oval, c.60×c.38; light brown, tag. Deep uneven impression, flattened, points lost. BM 4092.
E 322/225   1539

SULBY (Northants) Premonstratensian abbey
abbey seal
M817. The Virgin, with nimbus, seated on a bench-type throne, her feet on a corbel, holding the Child, with nimbus, on her L knee and a long flowering branch in her R hand.
SIGILL' CONVENTVS S...TE MARIE DE SVL... (Lom)
Pointed oval, c.50×33; light brown, tag. Nearly complete, deep clear impression slightly rubbed. Also on DL 27/125 (1342); E 326/11254 (1460). BM 4125.
E 322/230   Pl 55   1538

SWEETHEART (Kirkcudbright) Cistercian abbey
abbot's seal
M818. The abbot, standing on a corbel, mitred and holding a crozier; on L, a star.
+S' ABBATIS . DE . DVLCI CORDE (Lom)
Pointed oval, 48×32; mottled green, detached, on hemp cords. Complete, deep clear impression. Laing 1129. BM 15452.
SC 13/D58 (n.d.)

SWINE (Yorks) Cistercian priory (F)
priory seal
M819. The Virgin, crowned, seated on a bench-type throne, holding a lily in her R hand, her L hand extended.
SIG...LVM SCE MARIE DE SVINE (Lom)
Round, 45; red, detached, on tag. Two impressions, both deep and clear, flattened, part of edge lost. Also on SC 13/R52 (n.d.) fainter. BM 4133.
SC 13/R53 A and B   Pl 21 (n.d.)
prioress's seal
M810. The Virgin, crowned, seated on a bench-type throne, holding the Child on her L knee. Below, under an arch, the prioress, kneeling in prayer to L.
S' PRIORISSE SCE M/ARIE DE SWIRA (Lom)
Pointed oval, 50×30; light brown, tag. Nearly complete, very uneven impression, blurred and flattened. BM 4135.
E 322/231 1539

SYON (Midd) Bridgettine abbey (M and F)
seal ad causas
M821. Under a canopy with tabernacle work at the sides, the Virgin, crowned and with nimbus, seated, holding the Child, with nimbus, who stands on her L knee, and a long leafy branch with three roses in her L hand. Below, under an arch, the Virgin, veiled and with nimbus, stands on L and supports St Bridget, crowned and robed, who kneels facing R, her hands raised in prayer; on either side, a shield of arms: (L) *a cross* (hatched, and the field patterned with foliage); (R) *quarterly, France modern and England.*
S'.COMUNE MONASTERII/SCI SALVATOR[IS D]E SYON LONDON DIOC.AD.CA'S (BL)
Pointed oval, 65×40; red, tag. Nearly complete, fine impression. Also on E 33/26/27 (1504; fine); E 41/187 (1504); E 326/8121 (1427), 11229 (1538); E 329/167 (1462). BM 4022.
DL 27/128   Pl 50 1460
steward's seal: Henry Chadderton
M822. A lady, frontal, kneeling between the words SIRRA AVANT.
No legend.

Oval, 12×10; red, tag. Complete, clear impression.
E 329/204 1427

TANDRIDGE (Surrey) Augustinian priory
priory seal
M823. Under a double canopy, two standing female saints.
Legend lost.
Pointed oval, over 25?; red, double tongue. Central fragment of a defaced impression.
E 135/2/18 1363

TARRANT KEYNSTON (Dors) Cistercian abbey (F)
abbey seal
M824. On L, the Virgin, crowned, standing on a corbel, holding the Child, with nimbus; before her, on R, the abbess, kneeling, hands upraised; between them, a flowering tree.
SIGILLVM : CONVENTVS : DE : TARENT (Lom)
Pointed oval, 50×28; red, tag. Complete, deep uneven impression, sharp where not rubbed. BM 4139.
E 322/233   Pl 40 1539

TAUNTON (Som) Augustinian priory
priory seal
M825. Beneath adjoining canopies, standing figures: (L) St Paul, holding a sword; (R) St Peter, holding keys and a model church. Diapered background.
S'SCORV.APO[STOLOR.PETRI.ET.PAVLI.TANTO] NIESIS. ECCLIE (Lom)
Pointed oval, c.60×45; red, tag. Deep clear impression, parts flattened, lower part lost. Also on E 25/108/2 (1534). Pedrick, plate XLII, 84. BM 4142.
E 322/235   Pl 47 1539

TAVISTOCK (Devon) Benedictine abbey
abbey seal
M826. Under an elaborate canopy resting on corbels, the Virgin, crowned, seated on a bench-type throne, holding the Child on her L knee; on either side, a censing angel. Below, under a trefoiled arch between pinnacles, St Rumon, seated, mitred, blessing, and holding a crozier, between two kneeling figures.
[SIGILLV]M ECCLESIE SCE MA/RIE ET SCI RVMONI TAVISTOCH (Lom)
Pointed oval, c.80×55; red, tag. Nearly complete, deep uneven impression, details clear in the parts not heavily flattened. Also on E 326/10395 (1523). BM 4144.
E 322/236   Pl 13 1539

TEWKESBURY (Glos) Benedictine abbey
abbey seal
M827. In three adjoining canopied niches, the
Assumption of the Virgin between standing figures: (L)
St Peter, with nimbus, holding a book and keys; (R) St
Paul, with nimbus, holding a book and a sword. The
Virgin, with folded hands, stands in a mandorla of
clouds upheld by a demi-angel above; the canopy above
her includes a small niche containing the Holy Trinity.
Below her feet, a demi-angel, holding a shield of arms
(defaced) between two lions.
.../ SCE . MARIE . DE...BVRI   (BL)
Pointed oval, c.75×c.50; bronze, tag. Large fragment
of a deep impression, heavily flattened. Also on
E 42/383 (1537), 473 (1526). VCH *Glos*, Vol II, plate I.
BM 4148.
E 25/109/1   1534
abbot's seal: Henry Beeley
M828. The Annunciation. On R, the Virgin, standing,
facing L; on L, the archangel, kneeling, holding a scroll
inscribed AVE MARIA. On either side, in a compartment,
a standing robed figure. Below, an arch.
Legend lost.
Pointed oval (?), over 40×30; dark green, tag. Central
fragment of a deep clear impression.
E 42/473   1526
abbot's seal: John Wakeman
M829. Under an elaborate canopy, the Annunciation.
Legend lost.
Pointed oval, c.70×c.30; brown, tag. Central fragment
of a clear impression.
E 42/383   1537

THAME (Oxon) Cistercian abbey
abbey seal
M830. In a vaulted niche with elaborate canopy, the
Virgin, crowned, standing, holding the Child on her R
side and a flowering branch in her L hand. On either
side, in a similar but smaller niche, a standing female(?)
figure.
...OMVNE :...MARIE : D...   (Lom)
Pointed oval, 60×43; red, tag. Deep impression, parts
clear, cracked, flattened, upper and lower parts lost.
BM 4154.
E 322/232   1539
abbot's seal
M831. The abbot, half-length, frontal, in habit and
cowl, his L hand on his breast, holding a crozier in his
R hand.
+[SIGILL'] ABBATIS DE TAMA   (Lom)
Pointed oval, 40×5 ; orange, tag. Deep indistinct
impression, R edge damaged. BM 4155.
E 212/28   Pl 12   (temp. Hen. III)

abbot's seal: Richard
M832. The abbot, standing on a carved corbel, blessing
and holding a crozier.
+SIGILL RI...DE THAMA   (Lom)
Pointed oval, 35 × c.25; bronze, tag. Clear impression,
R edge damaged. BM 4156.
E 40/4864   (1259–83)
prior's seal: T
M833. A stylised lily.
+...M VERI NVNCIVS   (Lom)
Pointed oval, 35×32; orange, tag. Clear impression, R
edge broken.
E 212/28   (temp. Hen. III)

THANINGTON (Kent) St James's, Benedictine
priory and hospital (F)
common seal
M834. Under a rounded masonry arch with towers
above, St James, with nimbus, standing, holding a pen
and book.
+SIG...   (Lom)
Pointed oval, c.75×c.45; red-brown, tag. Large central
fragment of a fine impression from a matrix of 12c style,
flattened.
E 21/10592   1551

THELSFORD (Warw) Trinitarian house
common seal
M835. Almost all lost; the fragments show a diapered
field with a tree(?) on L and a standing figure on R.
...VO...   (Lom)
Round, (?); red, tag. Fragment of a clear impression.
E 322/237   1538

THETFORD (Norf) Holy Sepulchre, Augustinian
priory
priory seal
M836. Under a trefoiled arch resting on corbels, Our
Lord, with nimbus, rising from the sepulchre, blessing
and holding a cross. Below, two sleeping soldiers.
...CCLESIE...THETE'   (Lom)
Pointed oval, c.50×c.30; red, tongue. Deep
impression, partly indistinct, upper point and R part
lost. BM 4161.
E 25/109/2   Pl 14   1534

THETFORD (Norf) St Mary's, Benedictine priory
priory seal
M837. The Virgin, crowned, and with nimbus, seated
on a bench-type throne, holding a flower in her R hand;
the Child, with nimbus, sits on her L knee, blessing and
holding a book. Diapered field.

[S]IGILLVM PRIORIS ET CONVENTVS MONACHORVM
THETFO... (Lom)
Pointed oval, 90×50; red, tag. Nearly complete, deep
uneven impression, upper point lost. Also on SC/R54
(n.d.). BM 4157.
E 322/240   Pl 40   1540

THOBY (Essex) Augustinian priory
priory seal
M838. St Leonard, standing.
...NARDI DE TOBI (Lom)
Pointed oval, c.50×c.30; dark red, tag. Indistinct
impression, R side lost. BM 4163.
E 326/9040   1317
prior's seal: Henry Thoby
M839. A gem: a winged horse, flying to R; below, a
dog(?) running.
...GILL' H'RICI PRIORIS D' GI... (Lom)
Oval, 30×23; dark green, tag. Clear impression, upper
L part lost.
E 42/384   Pl 53   1240

THORNEY (Cambs) Benedictine abbey
abbot's seal: Nicholas (Islip)
M840. In a vaulted and canopied niche with tabernacle
work at the sides, the Virgin, crowned, seated, holding
the Child on her L knee and a sceptre in her R hand.
Below, under an arch, the abbot, half-length, holding a
crozier.
S' NICHOLAI...AT:/ABBI... DE : THORNEY (BL)
Oval, 35×27; dark red, detached, on tongue. Nearly
complete, deep sharp impression, rubbed.
SC 13/A159   Pl 53   (1396–1402)
abbot's seal: Robert Blythe or Moulton
M841. In a vaulted and canopied niche with tabernacle
work at the sides, the abbot, standing, holding a crozier
and a book. Below, under an arch, a shield of arms:
three croziers (the ABBEY).
S'.ROBI.MULTON.DEI.GRA:/...TIS.DE.THORNEY (BL)
Pointed oval, 62×38; light brown, detached, in metal
skippet. Complete, deep mostly clear impression,
cracked.
SC 13/O38   Pl 3   (1513–39)

THORNHOLME (Lincs) Augustinian priory
priory seal
M842. The Virgin, seated on a bench-type throne, her
feet resting on a corbel, holding the Child, with
nimbus, on her L knee and a lily in her R hand.
Legend lost.
Pointed oval, c.60×c.40; uncoloured, tag. Large
central fragment of a deep clear impression from a
matrix of early 12c style. Has counterseal, M843.

BM 4168.
E 25/110/2   Pl 15   1534
counterseal
M843. A gem: a nude figure, seated, and a column.
+FRANGE LEGE TEGE (Lom)
Oval, 25×22; uncoloured, on tag, as counterseal to
M842. Complete, clear.
E 25/110/2   1534
prior's seal: Thomas
M844. Under a crocketed canopy, figures(?). Below,
under an arch, a figure(?).
Legend lost.
Pointed oval, (?); red, tongue. Fragments of a deep
impression. Also on E 101/568/55, no.4 (1304).
E 101/568/46, no.9   1304

THORNTON (Lincs) Augustinian abbey
abbey seal
M845. The Virgin, crowned, seated, the Child on her
lap before her, holding a fleur-de-lys sceptre in her R
hand and an orb with cross in her L hand.
...LLVM : SCE : MAR... (Lom)
Pointed oval, c.65×c.45; light brown, tag. Deep
impression, flattened, most of edge lost. Has
counterseal, M846. Also on DL 25/73 (1291),
fragment. BM 4176.
E 25/110/1   Pl 15   1534
counterseal
M846. A gem: a nude figure, standing; beside him, an
amphora.
+SECRETVM (Lom)
Oval, 20×17; light brown, on tag, as counterseal to
M845. Complete, clear. BM 4176.
E 25/110/1   1534
abbot's seal: Thomas
M847. The Virgin, seated, holding the Child on her L
side and an apple in her R hand.
Legend defaced.
Pointed oval, 43×25; brown, tongue. Indistinct
impression.
E 101/568/45, no. 7   1304
abbot's seal
M848. Under a double canopy, two standing figures,
holding: (L) a crozier; (R) a cross. Above, the Virgin
and Child, both half-length. Below, under an arch, the
abbot, half-length, praying to R.
SIGILLU...ABBATIS DE THORNTON (BL)
Pointed oval, 55×c.30; red, tongue. Clear impression,
lower edge damaged.
E 135/10/20, no. 13   (15c)

THURGARTON (Notts) Augustinian priory
priory seal
M849. St Peter, seated on a bench-type throne,

blessing and holding keys. Below, under an arch, the prior, half-length, praying to R.

[S']ECCLE.BEATI.PETR[I AP]OSTOLI DE THVRGARTON (Lom)

Pointed oval, c.65×39; light brown, tag. Complete except for points, deep clear impression, flattened. Has counterseal, **M850**. BM 4188.

E 322/241   Pl 15   1538

counterseal

M850. Two hands draped at the wrist issuing from the L inner edge of the field; the R hand holds upright St Peter's two keys, the L hand points with extended forefinger.

+PETRE TIBI DABO CLAVES REIGNI CELORVM (Lom)

Pointed oval, 35×25; light brown, on tag, as counterseal to **M849**. Complete, partly indistinct. At the top is the mark of a loop or handle. BM 4188.

E 322/241   Pl 47   1538

prior's seal: William

M851. In a canopied niche, St Peter, wearing a tiara, seated, blessing and holding keys in his L hand. Below, the prior, kneeling in prayer to R, between two shields of arms: *billety, a fesse dancetty* (DE AYNCOURT, founder).

S : FRIS : WILL'I : P'ORIS : DE : THVRGARTON (BL)

Pointed oval, 50×30; red set in brown, on green silk laces. Complete, very deep clear impression. BM 4190.

SC 7/64/9   1389

TICKHILL (Yorks) Austin Friars' house

common seal

M852. Under an arch, three standing figures surrounded by a crowd (friars preaching to a congregation?); the upper part is defaced but perhaps shows a seated figure.

...GILLVM ORDINIS... (Lom)

Pointed oval, c.55×c.35; red, tag. Indistinct impression, heavily flattened. BM 4191 (?)

E 322/242   1538

TILTY (Essex) Cistercian abbey

abbey seal

M853. In a vaulted and canopied niche, the Virgin, crowned, seated, holding the Child, standing, on her L knee and a fleur-de-lys sceptre in her R hand. On either side, a compartment with penthouse canopy containing (L) the abbot and two monks and (R) three monks.

[SIG':COMUNE.MONASTERII] BEATE [MARIE.DE.TI]LTEYE (BL)

Round, 45; red, tag. Complete, deep but not sharp impression, flattened. BM 4192.

E 322/243   1536

abbot's seal: (Nicholas)

M854. The abbot, standing, vested for mass, holding a crozier and a book.

+SIGILLVM ABBATIS DE TILETEIA (Lom)

Pointed oval, 45×25; green, tag. Complete, clear impression.

E 40/15346   (n.d.)

abbot's seal: Simon

M855. A sleeved forearm and hand issuing from R, holding a pastoral staff; in the field, a star above a crescent.

...DE TILETEIA (?) (Lom)

Pointed oval, 30×c.20; brown, tongue. Clear impression, flattened, R edge lost.

C 146/10064   1526

TINTERN (Monm) Cistercian abbey

abbey seal

M856. Under a canopy, the Virgin and Child, seated. Below, under an arch, the abbot.

...BEATE... (BL)

Pointed oval, c.65×c.40; red, tag. Central fragment. BM 4193.

E 326/9180   1514

TIPTREE (Essex) Augustinian priory

priory seal

...MARIE DE... **(Lom)**

Round, c.50; green, tag. Central fragment of an indistinct impression.

E 40/14525   (13c)

prior's seal: Benedict

M858. Under a cusped arch, the Virgin, holding the Child, both half-length; on either side, three pellets. Below, under an arch, the prior, half-length, praying to L; on R, a pellet.

S' BENEDICTI PRIORIS D'TIPPETRE (Lom)

Pointed oval, 34×21; dark green, tag. Complete, clear impression. Has counterseal, **M859**.

E 42/384   1240

counterseal

M859. The Holy Lamb.

+ECCE AGNVS DEI (Lom)

Round, 20; dark green, on tag, as counterseal to **M858**. Complete, clear impression.

E 42/384   1240

TONGLAND (Kirkcudbright) Premonstratensian abbey

abbot's seal

M860. A sleeved forearm and hand issuing from R, holding a crozier; on L, a branch(?); on R, above the hand, a star.

+ SIGILLVM ABBATIS DE TVNGELAND (Lom)
Pointed oval, 35×20; mottled green, detached, on
hemp cords. Complete, deep uneven impression. Laing
1133. BM 15453.
SC 13/D59 (13c)

TORKSEY (Lincs) Augustinian priory
priory seal
M861. In a canopied niche with a corbel below, a
figure, standing, holding a staff; background diapered.
...BE . /... ONARDI . D'... (BL)
Pointed oval, c.45×c.30; light brown, tag. Deep
impression, flattened, upper edge and lower points lost.
E 25/110/3 1534

TORRE (Devon) Premonstratensian abbey
seal ad causas
M862. Our Lord, on the cross, between (L) St Mary
and (R) St John; above, (L) a star and (R) a crescent.
Below, in a quatrefoil, the Virgin, holding the Child,
with nimbus, both half-length, between (R) a star and
(L) a crescent; beneath them, under an arch, the head
and shoulders of the abbot, praying to L.
SIGILL' ABBATIS ET C...T' DE TORRE AD CAVSAS (Lom)
Pointed oval, 55×33; red, tag. Complete except for
points, deep uneven impression, flattened. Pedrick,
plate xxviii, 55. BM 4201.
E 322/246 1539

TORTINGTON (Sussex) Augustinian priory
priory seal
M863. Under a canopy, the Noli Me Tangere scene:
Our Lord stands on R; St Mary kneels on L under a
leafy branch; between them, the Dove descends. In
base, the letters MEI.
...DE TOR...GTONA (Lom)
Pointed oval, 38×25; red, tongue. Deep uneven
impression, cracked, edge damaged.
E 212/136 1359

TOTNES (Devon) Benedictine priory
priory seal
M864. In a panel with gothic frame, the Education of
the Virgin Mary (?): a female figure sits on R
brandishing a birch and holding out an open book to a
young girl who stands on L before her. Background
diapered.
S' PRIOR...[ONVENTV]...DE TOT... (Lom)
Pointed oval, c.65×48; red, detached, on tag. Deep
clear impression, flattened, most of edge lost. Also on
C 124/21 (two impressions, 1443 and 1493).
SC 13/R55 Pl 15 (n.d.)

TUPHOLME (Lincs) Premonstratensian abbey
abbey seal
M865. The Virgin, seated on a bench-type throne,
holding the Child, with nimbus, on her L knee and a
lily in her R hand.
Legend lost.
Pointed oval, c.50×c.35; uncoloured, detached. Large
central fragment of a deep impression. Has
counterseal, **M866**.
SC 13/R56 Pl 53 (n.d.)
counterseal
M866. A gem: a standing figure.
...ARI...EGE (Lom)
Oval, c.26×20; uncoloured, detached, as counterseal to
M865. Deep indistinct impression, lower part lost.
SC 13/R56 (n.d.)

TUTBURY (Staffs) Benedictine priory
priory seal
M867. Under a canopy, St Paul, standing on a corbel,
holding a sword and a book; the field diapered. On
either side, a shield of arms: (L) ENGLAND; (R) *vairy*
(FERRERS, founder). In a niche in the canopy, two
seated figures (the Coronation of the Virgin ?).
Legend lost.
Pointed oval, c.50×c.35; dark green, tongue. Deep
clear impression, much rubbed, edge and L side lost.
This may be a seal ad causas, though described as
sigillum comune in the sealing clause.
E 135/10/21, no. 13 1400
priory seal
M868. *Obv.* In a vaulted niche with triple canopy above
and tabernacle work at the sides, the Coronation of the
Virgin. The Virgin, crowned, seated between (R) God
the Father, crowned, and (L) Our Lord, with nimbus;
above her head, the Dove, with nimbus. On either side,
a shield of arms: (L) *a saltire between four crescents*; (R)
vairy (FERRERS, founder).
SIGILLUM.COMUNE:ABBATIS.ET.CONVENTUS.MONESTII...
(BL)
Rev. Under a large vaulted canopy, the Virgin,
crowned, seated, holding the Child who stands on her
R knee. On either side, under a similar but smaller
canopy, an angel, standing on a masonry parapet.
Below, under an arch, the prior, frontal, kneeling in
prayer.
...S.PIA./SERVOS.INTENDE.MARIA (BL)
Round, 65; red, tag. Deep clear impression, lightly
flattened, part of edge lost. BM 4218.
E 322/247 1538
prior's seal: Walter
M869. Under a church-like canopy, (L) the Virgin,
standing on a fluted corbel, holding the Child on her L

side and an apple in her R hand, and (R) a clerk, kneeling in prayer before her; above, a roundel and a cinquefoil. On either side, three roundels.

S' FRIS/GAL...ESBVRI (Lom)
Pointed oval, c.43×25; brown, tongue. Fine impression of a fine seal, cracked, damaged, most of edge lost. BM 4219.
DL 27/96   Pl 12   1302

prior's seal: Robert
M870. Under a canopy, the Virgin, crowned, seated, holding the Child on her L knee.

DATETAM...RVINA (Lom)
Pointed oval, 30×20; red, tongue. Deep clear impression, edge chipped.
DL 25/978   1316

TYNEMOUTH (Northumb) Benedictine priory
    priory seal
M871. In adjacent canopied niches with tabernacle work at the sides, standing figures: (L) the Virgin, crowned, holding the Child on her L side; (R) St Oswin, crowned, holding a sceptre and a long spear. Above, in a hexagonal compartment, the bust of a female saint (?) with curling hair and embroidered garment, between two stars. Below, two lion's faces set in curvilinear tracery.

SI/GILL[VM CO]E : PRIORATVS : SCE : [MARI]E : ET: BI :
OSWINI : D[E : TINEMVTHA] (Lom)
Pointed oval, 75×47; mottled green, tag. Nearly complete, fine impression from an elegant 14c matrix. Also SC 13/R57 (n.d.). BM 4226.
E 322/244   Pl 20   1539

prior's seal: Richard
M872. St Oswin, crowned, half-length, holding a sceptre and a book. Below, an arch with inscription ...VE
DEI MEM... (Lom)
Legend lost.
Pointed oval, (?); green, tag. Central fragment of a clear impression. BM 4227 (?).
E 210/1741   1331

TYWARDREATH (Corn) Benedictine priory
    priory seal
M873. In a vaulted and canopied niche with tabernacle work at the sides, St Andrew, standing, holding a saltire cross in his R hand. Below, under an arch, the prior, half-length, frontal, praying.

SIGILLU:PRIORIS:ET:CONVENTUS:ECCLIE:/SCI:AND...
TYW... (BL)
Pointed oval, c.70×40; red, tag. Deep uneven impression, much of L side lost.
E 25/110/4   1534

ULVERSCROFT (Leics) Augustinian priory
    priory seal
M874. Under a canopy, the Virgin, crowned, seated, holding the Child on her L knee and a sceptre in her R hand. On either side, under a crocketed gable, a censing angel. Below, under an arch, the prior, half-length, praying to R.

S' CANONICORVM SCE MARIE VLVISCROFT (Lom)
Round, 50; brown, tag. Complete, deep impression, much detail indistinct. Also on E 25/111 (1) (1534); E 322/249 (1539). BM 4228.
E 329/384   Pl 34   1384

prior's seal: Roger
M875. In a canopied niche with panelling at sides, the Virgin, seated, holding the Child on her L knee. Legend lost.
Pointed oval, over 45×20; red, tongue. Central fragment of a deep, clear impression.
DL 25/313   1352

UPHOLLAND (Lancs) Benedictine priory
    prior's seal?
M876. An oval gem: a man on horseback. Above, the nurder of St Thomas. Below, two shields of arms: (L) *three leopards and a label* (LANCASTER); (R) *a lion rampant* (HOLLAND, founder).
...ART... (Lom)
Pointed oval, c.60×c.45; brown, tag. Incomplete and indistinct impression from an unusual matrix of 13c style.
DL 25/3592   1478

USK (Monm) Benedictine priory
    priory seal
M877. Under a church-like canopy, the Virgin, crowned, seated on a bench-type throne resting on a large corbel, holding the Child, with nimbus, on her L knee. On L of the Virgin's head, a crescent; on R, a star.

S' : SCE : MARIE : ET...VENTVS : DE : VSK (Lom)
Pointed oval, c.60×36; red, tongue. Centre deep and clear, legend faint, points lost. BM 4231.
E 25/111/2   Pl 54   1534

VALE ROYAL (Ches) Cistercian abbey
    abbey seal
M878. Between two crowns, the abbot, standing on a corbel, holding a crozier and a book.
S' ABB'IS ET COVENT MON/AST'[II D'VALLE REGALI]
(Lom)
Pointed oval, 55×33; red, tag. Complete, deep impression. The legend is indistinct and the latter part of the reading is conjectural. BM 4232.
E 322/250   Pl 24   1538

abbot's seal

M879. In adjoining canopied niches, the Virgin, crowned, seated, holding the Child on her R knee and a sceptre in her L hand, between (L) a saint, standing, holding a crozier and a book, and (R) (lost). Below, under an arch, the abbot and two shields of arms: (L) ENGLAND, (R) (lost).

...IS . DE . VALLE REGALI　　　　　　　　　(BL)

Pointed oval, c.50×c.as30; light brown, tag. Deep clear impression, rubbed, R part lost. BM 4236.

E 135/3/16　　　　　　　　　　　　　　1509

VALLE CRUCIS (Denbigh) Cistercian abbey
abbey seal

M880. In a canopied niche, the Virgin, crowned, seated, holding the Child on her R knee; field diapered. Below, a shield of arms: *checky*.

SIGILLV COMMVNE DOMVS BE MARIE　　　(BL)

Pointed oval, c.48×c.32; light brown, tag. Complete, deep indistinct impression.

E 326/10141　　　　　　　　　　　　1534

WALDEN see SAFFRON WALDEN

WALSINGHAM (Norf) Augustinian priory
priory seal

M881. *Obv.* The priory church, shown with tall central tower and four transeptal towers, each with conical roof; a large rounded central portal contains the head and shoulders of a bearded man, praying to R.

+SIGILLVM : ECCLIE . BEATE . MARIE . DE . WALSINGHAM
　　　　　　　　　　　　　　　　　　　(Lom)

Rev. The Virgin, crowned and with nimbus, enthroned, holding the Child, with nimbus, on her L knee and a fleur-de-lys sceptre in her R hand. The throne has a high back with arched top between two slender pillars; from a point above the Virgin's head curtains fall and part in wavy lines on either side of the throne.

AVE . MARIA . GRA...PLENA . DOMINVS . TECVM　(Lom)

Round, 70; uncoloured, tongue. Complete, very deep but not sharp impression. There are indications of a legend on the outer rim of the seal. Also on E 40/12251 (1529) *Obv* only; E 326/5367 (1351). BM 4248.

E 25/112/3　　　Pl 53 (rev)　　　　　　1534

WALSOKEN (Norf) Holy Trinity, hospital
common seal

M882. Under a panelled canopy, the Holy Trinity. Below, a shield of arms (defaced).

Legend lost.

Pointed oval, c.65×?; brown, tag. Central fragment, indistinct. Also on DL 25/1848 (1479).

C 146/5225　　　　　　　　　　　　1470

WALTHAM HOLY CROSS (Essex) Augustinian abbey[1]
abbey seal

M883. Two angels, each with nimbus and wings outspread, facing each other and upholding with both hands the Holy Cross, which they place upon a mount.

...C.EST...LTHAAM　　　　　　　　　　(Lom)

Pointed oval, c.70×c.48; uncoloured, varnished brown, tag. Deep, clear but not sharp impression, numerous surface cracks, parts rubbed, most of edge lost.

E 42/97　　　　　　　　　　　　(1184–1201)

abbey seal

M884. The same design as **M883** but with some difference in detail: the cross shows (faintly) an overall interlaced pattern, and the mount below is clearly not the same.

...OC...　　　　　　　　　　　　　　(Lom)

Pointed oval, c.70×c.48; uncoloured, tag. Deep clear impression, sharp in places, cracked across, damaged at foot, most of edge lost. Has counterseal, **M885**.

DL 27/91　　　Pl 55　　　　　　　　1251

counterseal

M885. A gem: a nude warrior, wearing a helmet, standing, holding a spear; on his back, a shield.

+ANTE . S...L' . SCE . CRVCIS . DE . WALTHAM　(Lom)

Oval, 35×22; uncoloured, on tag, as counterseal to **M884**. Complete, very indistinct impression, cracked.

DL 27/91　　　　　　　　　　　　1251

abbey seal

M886. The same design as **M883** and **M884** but not identical with either: the cross is decorated with a wavy interlaced pattern and rests on a mount which has reverted to the earlier design as in **M883**.

+HOC . EST . SIGILL' ECCLES[IE SAN]CTE CRVCIS DE WALTHAAM　　　　　　　　　　　　　(Lom)

Pointed oval, c.70×c.48; dark green, tag. Fine impression, points lost, edge chipped. Much of the drapery is more finely cut in this version and the design has acquired an elegance not visible in earlier impressions. Has counterseal, **M887**.

E 42/137　　　Pl 54　　　　　　　　1350

counterseal

M887. In the centre, a large round gem, 32 mm in diameter: two heads, the hair bound with a fillet, facing each other; above, a crown, elongated over both heads; below and between, three stars and a crescent. Above, a

[1]The seals here catalogued as **M883** to **M890** are discussed by Sir William St John Hope, 'The Seals of the Abbey of Waltham Holy Cross', *Proceedings of the Society of Antiquaries of London*, 2nd series, Vol. XXVIII, (1916), pp. 95–102, and by Roger H. Ellis, 'The Seals of Waltham Abbey', in *Studi in onore di Leopoldo Sandri*, Roma 1983, vol. 2, pp. 473–6 and plate.

small (8 mm) gem: a man on a dolphin. Below, an oval gem (12×14 mm): a tiger(?), walking to R.

+HOC : CARTE : FEDVS : CVM:/TOVI : FIRMAT : HAROLD' (Lom)

Pointed oval, c.70×c.48; dark green, on tag, as counterseal to M886. Complete, fine impression. BM 4250.

E 42/137   Pl 55   1350

abbey seal

M888. *Obv.* In a traceried border, a pointed oval design with legend, identical with or closely resembling **M886**. The border bears no legend.

Rev. a pointed oval design with legend apparently identical with that of **M887**, enclosed in a border decorated with two shields of arms: (L) *three leopards* (ENGLAND) and (R) *a cross engrailed* (the ABBEY), each supported by two elongated lions rampant. The border bears no legend.

Round, 83; bronze-green, tag. Nearly complete, fine impression, cracked, traces of four lugs. Also on E 322/252 (1540). Pedrick, plate XXXV. BM 4250. A fine impression of this seal is in the muniment room of Jesus College, Cambridge.

E 41/452   Pl 56 (obv)   1532

abbot's seal: Reginald de Maidenhith

M889. The abbot, standing on a corbel, vested for mass, blessing and holding a crozier; in the field, the inscription RE/GI/NA/LD'.

[...INALDI DEI] GRA ABBIS ECCE SCE CRVCIS D[E... (Lom)

Pointed oval, c.55×c.35; green, tag. Clear impression, upper part lost. BM 4256. A contemporary description of this seal, transcribed from E 135/5/32, is given by R.C. Fowler in *Transactions of the Essex Archaeological Society*, New Series, Vol. XIII, pp. 247–8.

DL 25/180   1281

abbot's seal: John Sharnbrook

M890. In a canopied niche, the abbot, standing, mitred and vested for mass, blessing and holding a crozier. Above, two angels, supporting the Holy Cross; on either side, on a canopied balcony, an angel.

S IOHANNIS . DEI . GRA . ABBATIS/MON . SCE . CRVCIS . DE . WALTHAM   (BL)

Pointed oval, 80×45; red, detached, in tin skippet. Complete, fine impression.

SC 13/O35   Pl 21   (1507)

WARDEN see OLD WARDEN

WARE (Herts) Benedictine priory

prior's seal: William

M891. The prior, standing on a carved corbel, vested for mass, holding a book before him, between (L) a flaming sun and (R) a crescent moon.

+SIGILLVM WILL'I PRIORIS D' WARES   (Lom)

Pointed oval, 38×24; red, tag. Complete, deep uneven impression. Has counterseal, M892.

E 42/386   Pl 4   (13c)

prior's privy seal: (William)

M892. The head of a clerk, in profile to L.

+SECRETVM PRIORIS   (Lom)

Round, 18; red, on tag, as counterseal to M891. Nearly complete, deep indistinct impression.

E 42/386   (13c)

prior's seal: Ralph

M893. In adjoining canopied niches, standing figures: (L) St Peter; (R) a saint, with nimbus, holding a crozier. On either side in the field, roses.

...RADVLP...RIS . DE...   (Lom)

Pointed oval, c.45×28; brown, tag. Central fragment of a deep clear impression. BM 4263.

E 326/8506   1306

prior's seal: John

M894. Under a double-vaulted canopy, standing figures: (L) St Peter, holding a key; (R) a saint, with nimbus, holding a crozier.

Legend lost.

Pointed oval, c.45×c.30; dark green, tongue. Central fragment of a fine impression.

DL 25/315   1352

WARE (Herts) Franciscan house

warden's seal

M895. On R, the founder (Baldwin de Wake), in armour, kneeling, holding a shield of his arms: *two bars, in chief three roundels*; on L, his wife, kneeling. They look upwards in adoration at (lost) with rays and stars issuing therefrom; behind each of them an oak-tree. Below, under the corbels on which they kneel, a friar, half-length, praying to L.

S' GUARDIAN...MINORVM DE WARE   (Lom)

Pointed oval, c.50×33; red, tag. Damaged and distorted impression of a fine seal. BM 4264.

E 329/103   1409

WARWICK (Warw) Dominican house

common seal

M896. In a canopied niche, a seated figure (the Virgin and Child?)

Legend lost.

Pointed oval, c.50×c.33; red, tag. Large fragment of a very indistinct impression, cracked. BM 4269.

E 322/254   1538

WARWICK (Warw) St Michael's, hospital

common seal

M897. St Michael, standing, holding a spear and shield.

SIGILL': HOS... (BL)
Pointed oval, c.50×c.30; red, tag. Large fragment of a
deep uneven impression.
E 40/5036 1510

WARWICK (Warw) St Sepulchre's, Augustinian
priory
common seal
M898. The Holy Sepulchre, shown as a chest on four
feet, with pitched and diapered roof on which stands a
large patriarchal cross; on either side, a tower with
arcaded ornament and spire; below, the letters IHS.
+SIG...ATR...PVLCHR / WARWIKE IN ANGLIA (Lom)
Round, 60; red, tag. Complete except for chipping of R
edge, fine impression. BM 4266.
E 25/113 Pl 18 1534

WATTON (Yorks) Gilbertine priory (M and F)
seal ad causas
M899. Under a canopy, the Virgin, crowned, seated,
holding the Child, with nimbus, on her L knee. On
either side, a nun, kneeling. Below, under a trefoiled
arch, the prior, kneeling in prayer to R.
S' PRIORIS ET CONV...TONA AD C... (Lom)
Pointed oval, c.55×45; red, tag. Clear impression,
flattened, points lost, edge damaged. Also on
E 135/10/21, no. 17 (1400). BM 4270.
E 322/255 1539

WAVERLEY (Surrey) Cistercian abbey
abbot's seal
M900. Under an arch resting on lion-faced corbels,
against a diapered ground, the abbot, standing, vested
for mass, holding a crozier and a book, between two
shields of arms: (L) England; (R) *a sword and a key in
saltire* (the ABBEY).
[...BIS WAVERLEYE] (Lom)
Pointed oval, c.45×30; red, tongue. Fragment of a fine
impression. Also on E 41/457 (1363).
E 213/356 1422

WELBECK (Notts) Premonstratensian abbey
abbey seal
M901. St James, standing on a corbel, wearing the
cloak and broad-brimmed hat of a pilgrim, holding a
staff in his R hand, a wallet marked with scallop slung
from his R shoulder.
[+SIGI]LL' CONVENTVS ECCL[IE SC]I : IACOBI DE
WELLEB[EK] (Lom)
Pointed oval, c.50×30; red, tag. Deep clear impression,
upper part lost (figure headless). The Ns are reversed
in the legend. Also on DL 27/103 (1393); WARD
2/207/5 (1537). BM 4284–6.
E 322/256 Pl 24 1538

WELLOW (Lincs) Augustinian abbey
abbey seal
M902. St Augustine, standing, vested for mass,
blessing and holding a crozier.
SIGILLV ECC...SANCTI AVGVSTINI D...MESB (Lom)
Pointed oval, c.50×38; uncoloured, tag. Clear
impression, edge chipped. BM 3229.
DL 25/323 (1344–62)
abbey seal
M903. In adjoining canopied niches with tabernacle
work at the sides, standing figures: (L) St Augustine,
mitred, blessing and holding a pastoral cross; (R) King
Henry I (founder), crowned, holding a battle-axe. On
either side, a shield of arms: (L) *quarterly, Old France
and England*; (R)*England*. Below, a shield of arms: *on a
chevron between a crown and a lion in chief and a crozier in
base, three fleurs-de-lys* (the ABBEY).
[S': CO(MVN)]E: ABBT/ET:...VENT...AVGVSTINI DE/
GRIMESBY (Lom)
Pointed oval, c.65×42; red, tag. Fine impression,
points and part of edge lost. The matrix is in the
Fitzwilliam Museum, Cambridge. See *Journal of British
Archaeological Association*, Vol. XXV (1869), p. 384, and
plate. BM 3230 (describing the matrix as made by John
Utterby, abbot, 1369).
E 25/116 Pl 36 1534
abbot's seal
M904. In a canopied niche with tabernacle work at the
sides, St John the Baptist, standing, holding a book
before him in his R hand and the Holy Lamb on a disk
on his L side.
SIGILLVM : IO...GRIMESBY (BL)
Pointed oval, c.50×27; red-brown, tongue. Fine
impression, lower part lost, all edge damaged.
E 135/10/20, no. 12 (1400)

WELLS (Som) St John the Baptist's, hospital
common seal
M905. St John the Baptist, with nimbus, standing,
holding the Holy Lamb on a disk in his L hand,
pointing to it with his R hand; on either side, a crozier.
...GILL':HOSPITAL':S...IOHANNIS : D' : WELLES (Lom)
Pointed oval, c.55×35; red, tag. Deep clear impression,
points lost, slightly flattened. BM 4289.
E 322/257 Pl 19 1539

WENDLING (Norf) Premonstratensian abbey
abbot's seal; Robert
M906. A fesse with an indistinct inscription; above, a
star and a crescent; below, a head facing R.
No legend.
Pointed oval, c.25×c.15; uncoloured, tag. Indistinct
impression, part lost.
WARD 2/177/110 1292

WENLOCK see MUCH WENLOCK

WEST ACRE (Norf) Augustinian priory
priory seal
M907. In an upper canopied niche with church-like
super-structure, the Holy Trinity in a mandorla. In a
lower niche, under a rounded arch with cusping, the
Virgin, crowned, seated on a bench-type throne, her
feet on a wyvern, holding the Child, who stands and
holds a fleur-de-lys in his L hand, on her L knee, and a
globe in her R hand. In the tabernacle work on either
side, a niche containing a standing figure: (L) an
ecclesiastic; (R) a knight.
S' CAPITVL...ARIE...MNIV...   (Lom)
Pointed oval, 90×60; red, tongue. Very fine
impression, most of edge lost. Has counterseal, M908.
Also on E 25/117/2 (1534), E 322/258 (1538).
Pedrick, plate XXV, 50. BM 4296.
E 25/117/1   Pl 19   1534
   counterseal
M908. An oblong gem: a man's head in profile to R,
crowned, his hair tied with a fillet. Above, a star; below,
a crescent.
*MVNDVS ABIT MVNDVM CONTERE MVNDVS ERIS   (Lom)
Pointed oval, 45×28; red, on tongue, as counterseal to
M907. Complete, impression clear; the mark of a loop
for hanging the matrix shows at the top. Also on E
25/117/2 (1534). BM 4296.
E 25/117/1   Pl 54   1534

WEST DEREHAM (Norf) Premonstratensian abbey
   common seal
M909. The abbey church, with central tower topped
with a conical roof and ball, and cross finials on the
gables.
+SIGILL' ABBATIS ET CONVENT' DE DERH'   (Lom)
Pointed oval, 45×28; green, tag. Complete, deep clear
impression. Also on DL 25/53 (c.1232). BM 3050.
DL 25/52   Pl 18   1231–48
   abbot' seal: Anger
M910. The abbot, standing on a corbel, holding a
crozier and a book.
+SIGILLVM ABBA...DERHAM   (Lom)
Pointed oval, 37×20; green, tag. Clear impression,
lower edge lost. BM 3053.
E 30/14021   1237

WEST MALLING (Kent) Benedictine abbey (F)
   priory seal
M911. In a canopied and vaulted niche with tabernacle
work and cusping at the sides, the Virgin, crowned,
seated, holding a fleur-de-lys sceptre in her L hand and

the Child, with nimbus, standing on her L knee. Below,
under an arch, a figure, half-length, holding a crozier.
SIVILLV:COMMUNE:MON...TE:MARIE:DE...MALLING
                                              (BL)
Pointed oval, c.70×45; red, tag. Nearly complete, sharp
impression of an elaborate late gothic seal, edge
damaged, partly flattened. BM 3597.
E 322/147   Pl 24   1538

WESTMINSTER (Midd) St James's by Charing
Cross, hospital
   common seal
M912. St James (?), with nimbus, long-haired, wearing
a close-fitting robe and a cloak, standing, holding a tall
cross in his L hand, his R hand extended.
+SIGILL'.SANTI.IACOBI.INFIRMARVM   (Lom)
Pointed oval, 70×45; orange, tag. Complete, deep clear
impression. Also on E 42/475 (1268). BM 3524.
DL 27/66   Pl 1   (1228–44)
   seal ad causas and for receipt of revenues
M913. A pilgrim, wearing a hat with brim and
chin-strap, standing, a scrip hanging from his L
shoulder, holding a water-bottle in his L hand and a
staff in his R hand.
Legend lost.
Pointed oval, c.30×c.22; red, tag. Central fragment of a
deep clear impression, flattened.
E 212/118   1341
   master's seal: Henry de Purley
M914. Under a double canopy, on R, the master,
kneeling in prayer before the Virgin, who stands
holding the Child. Above the master's head, a scallop;
in front of him, two scallops.
...TER.VIRGO...V.M...   (Lom)
Oval, c.25×20; red, tag. Large fragment of a deep clear
impression.
E 212/118   1341

WESTMINSTER (Midd) St Mary's Rouncivall near
Charing Cross, hospital
   common seal
M915. The Assumption. The Virgin, irradiate and with
nimbus, frontal, standing on a crescent; on either side,
three demi-angels issuing from clouds bear her up;
below her feet, a demi-angel, with wings outspread,
rises from a cloud; above her, on clouds, the three
persons of the Trinity.
...IGIL.../MARIE.D'... (On a scroll)   (BL)
Oval, 60×c.55; red, tag. Deep clear impression,
flattened, most of edge lost. Dugdale gives the legend
from this impression as SIGILLVM.COE . HOSPITAL' .
BEATE . MARIE . DE . ROUNCIVALLE.
E 322/138   Pl 36   1544

WESTMINSTER (Midd) St Peter's, Benedictine abbey

abbey seal

M916a. *Obv.* St Peter as pope, with nimbus, mitred and vested for mass, seated on a decorated bench-type throne, holding a long-shafted cross in his R hand and two keys in his L hand. Under his feet, a prostrate figure, crowned and in armour.

+DIMIDIA:PARS:SIGILL':ECCLESIE:SANCTI:PETRI:WEST
MONASTERII   (Lom)

  Rev. King Edward the Confessor, seated on a decorated bench-type throne, holding a cruciform church with central tower in his L hand and a sceptre with flowered tip in his R hand. Under his feet, a prostrate figure. In the field on L and R, conventional flowers.

+dimidia:pars:sigill':ecclesie:sancti:petri:west
monasterii   (Lom)
Round, 70; yellow-brown, tag. Complete, deep clear impression. A number of impressions of this seal are attached to the Foundation Indentures (1504) of Henry VIII's chapel at Westminster, most of them clearly impressed and complete or nearly so, viz.
E 33/2; E 33/20; E 33/26, nos. 34–62. Further impressions are on E 40/1551 (1530); E 40/2076 (1283); E 41/213 (1531); E 41/455 and 456 (1399); E 322/260 (1539);
E 329/368 (1539); SC 13/F119 (n.d.). BM 4300.
E 329/389 Pl 52   1534

seal ad causas

M916b. Under a triple canopy seated figures of (L) St Peter, holding keys, and (R) St Paul, holding a sword; on either side a canopied niche containing (L) St Edward, standing, crowned, holding a long sceptre, (R) St John the Evangelist. Above, a shield of arms: *on a chief indented a crozier and a mitre.* Below, under an arch, St Edward, half-length, crowned, holding a church and a sceptre; on either side a shield of arms: (L) *St Edward impaling two keys in saltire,* (R) *quarterly France modern and England.*

SIGILLU.COMUNE.ECCLIE.BEATI PETRI WEST
MONASTERII AD CAUSAS   (BL)
Pointed oval, 75 × 50; red, tag. Complete, fine impression slightly flattened. BM 4305.
E 329/409   (1444)

abbot's seal: Richard of Ware

M917. The abbot, standing on a corbel carved with a bull's head, mitred and vested for mass, holding a crozier in his R hand and a book before him in his L hand.

+S:RICA...RII   (Lom)
Pointed oval, c.70×40; dark green, tongue. Fine impression of a fine seal, cracked, sides lost. BM 4306.
E 42/474 Pl 54   1281

abbot's seal: Walter

M918. Under a canopy with towers, the abbot, standing.
Legend lost.
Pointed oval, over 25; green, tongue. Fragment.
E 135/8/3   1286

abbot's seal ad causas: William

M919. Under two adjoining crocketed arches, standing figures: (L) a king (St Edward), crowned, holding a sceptre and a model church; (R) St Peter, wearing a tiara, blessing and holding a key. Above, in a compartment, the Virgin, seated, holding the Child on her L knee. Below, under an arch lettered along the moulding S'W AB' AD CAVSAS, the abbot, half-length, praying to R, holding a crozier.
HII.DVO.PATRONI.CVM.VIR(GIN)E.SINT.MICHI.PRONI
(Lom)
Pointed oval, 53×34; brown, tongue. Complete, deep sharp impression, points lost.
E 43/110 Pl 36   1331

abbot's seal: Richard

M920. Under a panelled canopy, St Peter, wearing a tiara, seated, blessing and holding a key, between standing figures: (L) St Katharine, crowned, holding her wheel; (R) St John the Evangelist, holding a chalice and serpent and a palm branch. Above, a shield of arms: *a fesse dancetty.* Below, under an arch, the abbot, praying.
Legend lost.
Pointed oval, c.60×c.45; red. Clear but not sharp impression, edge lost. BM 4308.
E 326/11731   1423

abbot's seal: John Islip

M921. Under a canopy, St Peter, as pope, wearing a tiara, enthroned, blessing and holding a patriarchal cross; above, a shield with two keys in saltire. On either side, under a smaller canopy surmounted by (R) the Virgin and (L) the angel of the Annunciation, standing figures: (L) St Edward the Confessor; (R) St John the Evangelist, holding a chalice and serpent and a palm-branch.
SIGILLU' IOHIS [ISSLEP ABBAT' WESTMONASTERII] (BL)
Pointed oval, c.60×c.50; red, tag. Deep clear impression, flattened, points and most of edge lost.
Also on SC 13/O64 (n.d.). BM 4309.
E 329/128 Pl 50   1526

sacristan's seal

M922. Under a canopy, St Peter as pope, wearing a tiara, enthroned, blessing and holding a key.
...RISTE /...MONASTERII   (BL)
Poined oval, c.38×c.23; red-brown, tongue. Deep impression, flattened, broken. Used by Ralph

Tonworth (1400). Also on E 213/37, used by Peter Combe (1412).
E 213/358 (15c)

sacristan's seal: Edmund Kyrton
M923. Under a double canopy, standing figures: (L) St Peter, holding keys; (R) St Edward the Confessor, crowned, holding a sceptre and ring. Below, under an arch, a figure, kneeling, between two shields of arms: (L) *two keys in saltire* (the ABBEY); (R) *a cross patonce between five martlets* (King EDWARD).
Legend lost.
Pointed oval, c.50×c.30; black, tongue. Deep but rather indistinct impression, flattened, edge lost. Also on E 213/78 (1435).
E 213/357 1435

WESTWOOD (Worcs) Fontevraldine priory (M and F)
priory seal
M924. The Annunciation.
Legend defaced.
Pointed oval, 42×22; red, tag. Complete, very indistinct impression. BM 4324.
E 40/12696 1532

WETHERALL (Cumb) Benedictine priory
prior's signet: Ralph Hartley
M925. Ornamental knot between initials RH (BL). No legend.
Shield-shaped, 16×14; light brown, tag. Complete, uneven impression. Used in place of the priory seal. BM 4325.
E 322/262 1538

WEYBOURNE (Norf) Augustinian priory
priory seal
M926. The Virgin, crowned, standing, holding a large fleur-de-lys. On L, a crescent.
S.GILL...BT...DE . WABVRN (Lom)
Pointed oval, 70×42; red, tongue. Deep uneven impression, L and R edges defaced. The legend is very crudely engraved. BM 4277.
E 25/112/1 Pl 50 1534

WEYBRIDGE (Norf) Augustinian priory
priory seal
M927. The Virgin, crowned, seated on a bench-type throne, holding a lily in her R hand and the Child, with nimbus, blessing and holding a book, on her L knee.
SIGILL' COMMVN... (Lom)
Pointed oval, c.60×c.30; red, tag. Deep but blurred impression, damaged at edges and foot.
E 42/263 1390

WHALLEY (Lancs) Cistercian abbey
abbey seal
M928. Under a canopy, the Virgin, crowned and veiled, seated on a throne, holding the Child on her L knee and an apple in her R hand; both throne and canopy are richly decorated. Below, under a triple arcade, a monk, kneeling in prayer to L. On either side of the throne, a shield of arms: (L, under a pierced star) *three sheaves* (see of CHESTER); (R, under a crescent and fleur-de-lys) *a lion rampant* (LACY, founder).
S' COMVNE ABB'IS ET CONVENTVS/LOCI BENEDICTI DE WHALLEY (Lom)
Round, 48; mottled green, on blue and green plaited silk laces. Complete, fine impression, slightly flattened. Also on E 40/12317 (1525). BM 4326.
DL 27/119 Pl 18 1360

abbot's seal: John Lindley
M929. Under a canopy, the Virgin, crowned, seated, holding the Child on her L knee; on L, a star above a shield of arms: *three whales with croziers issuing from their mouths* (the ABBEY). Below, under an arch, the abbot, half-length, praying to L.
...ABBATIS DE... (Lom)
Pointed oval, c.40×c.20; green, tag. Clear impression, most of edge lost.
E 41/458 1363

abbot's privy seal: John Lindley
M930. Under an elaborate double canopy, standing figures: (L) the Virgin, crowned, holding the Child on her L side; (R) St John the Baptist, holding the Holy Lamb on a disk. Below, under an arch between panels of tracery, the abbot, facing L, wearing a biretta and holding a crozier; the arch's moulding is inscribed IHC.TEP' (?).
S' FRIS...DE LINDELEY (Lom)
Oval, c.27×23; red, tongue. Fine impression, slightly flattened, R and lower edge lost.
DL 27/120 1362

WHISTONES (Worcs) Cistercian priory (F)
priory seal
M931. Under a canopy, St Mary Magdalene, standing, holding a covered cup. On R, (a kneeling nun; lost).
S...[DA] / LENE : W... (Lom)
Oval, 55×40; red, tongue. Clear impression, R half lost, edge damaged. Also on E 213/359 (two impressions, 1412 and 1444).
E 213/91 1431

WHITBY (Yorks) Benedictine abbey
seal ad causas
M932. St Peter, standing, mitred, blessing and holding a key.

SIGILL' SCI PETRI & SCE HILDE DE WY[TEBY : AD CAS]

(Lom)

Pointed oval, 55×40; bronze, detached, on tag inscribed Whitby Ebor no. 924 30 Hen. VIII. Nearly complete, deep impression, heavily flattened, legend defaced. Has counterseal, **M933**. Clay, p. 33, plate IX, 8. BM 4329.

SC 13/R59 (13c)

counterseal

M933. St Hilda, standing.

[+.YM]AGO . VIR[GI]NIS . [HY]LD[E] (Lom)

Pointed oval, 55×30; bronze, on tag, as counterseal to **M932**. Nearly complete, indistinct, heavily flattened. Clay, pp. 33–34.

SC 15/R59 (13c)

WHITLAND (Carm) Cistercian abbey
abbey seal

M934. Between tabernacle work, the Virgin(?), standing; above, another figure. Below, under an arch, the abbot.

...INI (Lom)

Pointed oval, c.60×c.30; red, tag. Central fragment, heavily flattened. Also on E 210/4308 (1538). Has counterseal, **M935**.

E 210/4307 1538

counterseal

M935. A hand issuing from R, holding a crozier; on L, a star.

No legend.

Round, 13; red, on tag, as counterseal to **M934**. Complete, deep uneven impression.

E 210/4307 1538

WIGMORE (Heref) Augustinian abbey
abbey seal

M936. Under a canopy, St George, wearing a helmet and surcoat, standing, holding a sword and shield. Under two smaller adjoining canopies, St James and St Victor, both standing. Below, under an arcade of three arches, the abbot, kneeling in prayer to L.

...ONASTERII.SANCTOR'.IACOBI.ET.VICTORIS.DE.WIG...

(Lom)

Pointed oval, c.75×43; light brown, tag. Deep uneven but clear impression, points lost. Pedrick, plate XXXVI, 72. BM 4332.

E 322/263   Pl 1 1538

abbot's seal: Richard

M937. The abbot, vested for mass, standing on a corbel, holding a crozier and a book. On either side, a pierced cinquefoil with a flower above and a star and a crescent below.

...ABB...E WYGE) [MOR.A...] (Lom)

Pointed oval, 35×25; dark green, tongue. Deep impression, most of edge lost. Also on E 329/212 (1346). BM 4334.

E 329/162 1345

WILTON (Wilts) Benedictine abbey (F)
abbey seal

M938. Fragment showing the head of St Edith and part of the legend +SIGILL'...HE, and at the top the imprint of a decorated loop or handle.

Red, on tag, clear impression. Also on SC 13/R60 (n.d.) fragment. BM 4335, from a nearly complete impression of this important early seal.

E 322/264 1539

WINCHCOMBE (Glos) Benedictine abbey
abbey seal

M939. In three adjoining vaulted and canopied niches, the Virgin, crowned, seated, holding the Child on her L knee, between two crowned standing figures. In a niche in the central canopy, the Holy Trinity. Below, under an arch, the abbot, half-length, holding a crozier, between two shields of arms: *a saltire* (the ABBEY). Below the shields, initials WW (for William of Winchcombe, abbot 1454–74).

S' ABBIS.T.CONVET/DE WYN... (BL)

Pointed oval, 65×45; red, tag. Deep impression showing much detail, cracked, edge chipped. BM 4340.

E 25/120/1   Pl 55 1534

abbot's seal: Richard Anselm or Munslow

M940. In three richly canopied niches, the Holy Trinity between standing figures: (L) the Virgin, crowned, holding the Child on her R side; (R) a king, crowned, holding a sceptre. Below, under an arch, between initials R and A (Lom), a shield of arms: *a saltire* (the ABBEY).

S' RICARDI.ANCILMVS / ABBIS : DE : WINCHECOMB

(BL and Lom)

Pointed oval, 60×40; light brown, detached, on laces, in metal skippet. Complete, centre deep and clear, legend uneven. The first words of the legend (s' RICARDI ANCILMVS) are in Roman lettering, the rest in black-letter, all crudely engraved in contrast to the rest of the fine matrix; the name ANCILMVS in particular is unclear.

SC 13/O37 (1525–39)

WINCHESTER (Hants) Benedictine cathedral priory
priory seal

M941. St Peter, with nimbus, vested for mass, seated on a church-like throne, holding a key and a book. Legend lost.

Pointed oval, c.85×60; green, tag. Deep indistinct impression, edge lost. Has counterseal, **M944**. Also on E 42/482 (1284) which has counterseal **M946**; E 135/3/32–35 (all 1279). BM 2262 identifies the figure as St Swithun and furnishes part of the legend +SIGILLVM . SAN... THVN [I.E.]PI, but the key indicates St Peter. The matrix is of very early pattern, possibly c.1100.

E 42/392　　Pl 18　　　　　　　　　　　　　1279

priory seal

M942. *Obv.* In three adjoining canopied niches, seated figures: (centre) St Swithun, mitred and vested for mass, blessing and holding a crozier; (R) St Paul holding a sword; (L) St Peter, holding a key. Above the canopy's roof, (R) a crescent moon and (L) a flaming sun.

...:COM...PET : ET : PAVLI ET : SCI : SWITHI WINT... (Lom)

Rev. In three adjoining canopied niches (the design resembles that of *Obv*), a king, crowned, seated, holding a fleur-de-lys sceptre, between two standing mitred bishops: (L) holding a crozier; (R) blessing and holding a book. Above the canopy, (L) a trefoil and (R) a lily. Below, under three arches, four monks, half-length, praying to L.

+FACTVM : ANNO : GRIE : M : CC : NONAGES'' : III° : ET : [REGIS : EDWARDI XX)II (Lom)
Round, 90; bronze, tongue. Fine impression, L side damaged, R side of legend blurred. Also on E 33/2 (1504); E 326/8904 and 9312 (both 1405); E 329/444 (1351). BM 2263. The combination of the year A.D. and regnal year places the making of the matrix between 25 March and 19 November 1294, when William de Basing was prior.

E 42/284　　Pl 23　　　　　　　　　　　　　1387

prior's seal: John de Dureville

M943. Under an arch, the prior, vested for mass, standing on a carved corbel, holding a book before him. On either side, an arcaded compartment with a roundel containing: (L) the head of St Peter with keys above; (R) the head of St Paul with a sword above.

S : FRIS : IOH'IS : PRIORIS : [W]INTONENSIS ECCL' [IE] (Lom)
Pointed oval, 52×33; green, tag. Nearly complete, deep clear impression. Also on E 42/483 (1278); E 135/3/32, 34 (1279) and 35 (1279, with counterseal **M944**).

E 42/392　　Pl 18　　　　　　　　　　　　　1278

prior's privy seal

M944. A lion passant, crowned.

+SECRETVM PRIOR' WINTON (Lom)
Oval, 17×15; green, tag. Complete, clear impression. Also on E 135/3/32, 33 and 34 (1279, as counterseal to **M941**), 35 (1279, as counterseal to **M943**).

E 42/392　　　　　　　　　　　　　　　　1278

sub-prior's seal

M945. St Swithun, half-length, blessing and holding a crozier. Below, under an arch, a monk, praying.

...GILLVM : SVPPRIORIS...ITHVNI . WINTO (Lom)
Pointed oval, 40×c.20; uncoloured, tag. Deep clear impression, points lost.

E 135/3/22　　　　　　　　　　　　　　(13c)

percentor's seal

M946. Under a canopy surmounted by St Swithun, half-length, the precentor, vested for mass, standing on a carved corbel, facing R, holding a tall staff in his L hand, his R hand touching a book open on a lectern before him; behind him, on L, a choir.

...PRECENTOR' : SCI : SWITHVNI : WI (Lom)
Pointed oval, c.40×25; uncoloured, on tongue, as counterseal to **M941**. Clear impression, upper point lost.

E 42/482　　　　　　　　　　　　　　　1284

WINCHESTER (Hants) Nunnaminster, Benedictine abbey (F)

abbess's seal: Lucy

M947. Under a canopy, the abbess, standing, holding a crozier and a book, between two nuns, standing, holding (L) a taper and (R) a reliquary(?). Above, the Coronation of the Virgin (figures half-length).

...E : SCE : MA...W...ON' (Lom)
Pointed oval, c.55×31; dark green, tongue. Clear impression, cracked across, most of edge lost.

E 42/481　　　　　　　　　　　　　　　1285

WINCHESTER (Hants) St Cross, hospital

master's seal: Thomas Forest

M948. On a mount, the Crucifixion, between kneeling figures of (L) Cardinal Beaufort and (R) Bishop Henry (benefactor and founder); over each, an inscribed scroll: (L) (illegible); (R) CRVCEM TENEBO. Below, two shields of arms: (L) ENGLAND; (R) *a lion*.

...SIGILLVM : ...ELEMOSINAR...CTE CRVIS... (BL)
Round, 50; brown, tongue. Clear impression, badly cracked and defaced.

E 213/60　　　　　　　　　　　　　　　1452

WINCHESTER (Hants) St John the Baptist's, hospital

common seal

M949. In a pointed oval with traceried ends, the Holy Lamb with banner; field diapered.

SIGILLVM : HOSPITAL...ON (BL)
Pointed oval, c.50×c.25; brown, tag. Deep clear impression, L side lost, legend crudely engraved.

C 146/2606　　　　　　　　　　　　　　1476

WINCHESTER (Hants) Hyde abbey, New Minister)
Benedictine abbey
abbey seal
M950. *Obv.* In a canopied niche, St Barnabas, with
nimbus, standing, holding a crozier and a book. On
either side, in a similar but smaller niche a standing
figure: (L) St Grimbald, holding a book with both
hands; (R) St Valentine, holding a head(?) with both
hands. In the field outside the niches, three
inscriptions: (L) s'GRIMB'; (R) s'VALENT'; (below)
s'BARNAB'+.
[HY]DA PATRONORVM:IVGI:PRECE:TVTA:SIT:
HORVM (Lom)
tiara, seated on a bench-type throne, holding keys and a
book. On either side, a flying buttress encloses a niche
containing a standing figure: (L) King Edward the
Elder, crowned, holding a small church with spire; (R)
King Alfred. In the field outside the niches, three
inscriptions: (L) REX...; (R) REX AL...; (below) s'PETRV.
Above the two outer pinnacles, two censing demi-
angels.
Legend defaced.
Round, 75; uncoloured, tag. *Obv* nearly complete, deep
firm impression. *Rev* complete, deep indistinct
impression, much worn at edge. Pedrick, plate XXIV,
48. BM 3310.
E 322/108 1538–9
abbot's seal: John Sulcot or Saltcot
M951. In a canopied niche with tabernacle work at the
sides, a bishop, standing, mitred and holding a crozier.
Below, a shield of arms (defaced, but showing a *lion
rampant* in base).
SIGILLVM:IOHIS:SAULC...DEI:G...ABBATIS DE HIDA (BL)
Pointed oval, 75×45; red, detached, on pink tapes, in
metal skippet. Nearly complete, deep clear impression,
parts flattened.
SC 13/O15 Pl 26 (1530)

WITHAM (Som) Carthusian priory
priory seal
M952. Under a canopy, Our Lord on the Cross,
between standing figures: (L) the Virgin Mary; (R) St
Mary Magdalene. Below, in a lozenge, a wheel(?).
Background cross-hatched.
s' DOMVS . BEATE . M[ARI]E . DE . WI]TH]EHAM (Lom)
Pointed oval, 45×29; dark green, tag. Nearly complete,
deep clear impression. Also on E 43/113 (1329);
E 326/9496 (1363). BM 4349.
E 329/169 Pl 54 1349
priory seal
M953. In a niche under a triple canopy, Our Lord on
the Cross, between standing figures of (L) the Virgin
Mary and (R) St John, each with nimbus. Below, under

an arch, a bishop, mitred and holding a crozier,
kneeling in prayer to L.
s'.COE.DOMVS.BE.MARIE.DE.WITHAM.ORDINIS.CARTHUS
(BL)
Pointed oval, 54×55; red, tag. Nearly complete, deep
clear impression, slightly flattened. BM 4351.
E 322/270 1539

WIX (Essex) Benedictine priory (F)
priory seal
M954. The Virgin, crowned, frontal, seated on a
bench-type throne with footstool, holding in her R
hand an orb from which rises a branch with a perching
bird and in her L hand a church with tower with conical
roof and cross. Before her, on her lap, the Child, with
nimbus, blessing.
+SIGILLVM ECCLESIE SANCTE MARIE DE WICHES (Lom)
Pointed oval, 70×50; green, on russet silk plaited laces.
Complete, deep clear impression. Has counterseal,
M955. Also on E 42/389 (n.d., temp. Idonea, prioress),
476 (n.d., temp. Constance, prioress, c.1235–47) and
478 (n.d., temp. Christina, prioress, early 13c); E
40/13673 (1251) and 14010 (1302). Of these examples
E 42/476 shows a fine impression of the L, central and
lower parts, and has the prioress's seal **M955** as
counterseal.
E 42/477 Pl 54 1246–7
prioress's seal
M955. The prioress, standing, extending her L hand
and holding a book in her R hand.
+AVE MARIA GRACIA PLENA DOMINVS TECVM (Lom)
Pointed oval, 45×27; dark green, on russet silk plaited
laces, as counterseal to **M954**. Deep clear impression,
legend partly flattened. Also on E 40/13749 (n.d. used
by Christina, prioress) and 13837 (n.d. used
Constance, prioress); E 42/477 (n.d., temp. Constance,
prioress), legend clear, as counterseal to **M954**.
BM 5378.
E 42/476 Pl 50 (c.1235–47)
prioress's seal: Maud de Whelnetham
M956. St Thomas Becket, blessing and holding a
cross. Below, under an arch, a figure, praying.
SANCTE THOMA ORA PRO MATILDA (BL)
Pointed oval, 25×20; green, tag. Complete, clear
impression. Also on E 40/13963 (1369).
E 40/13921 1366

WOBURN (Beds) Cistercian abbey
abbot's seal
M957. Under a rich canopy, the Virgin, enthroned,
holding the Child, between panels of tracery. Below,
under an arch, a figure, kneeling to R.
Legend lost.

Pointed oval, c.50×c.33; red, tongue. A badly damaged and blurred impression of a fine seal.

E 43/633 (14c)

abbot's privy seal: William

M958. On L, the Virgin, crowned, standing, holding the Child on her L side; before her, on R, a clerk, kneeling in prayer to L; between them, an inscription REXSHVL(?).

S'...LELMI . VOCATVR (Lom)

Oval, 28×23; red, tongue. Complete, deep impression, legend defaced.

E 43/111 1357

abbot's signet (?): William de Wardone

M959. In a traceried circle, initial W.

SIGILLVM : FRATRIS : WILLELMI : DE : WARDONE (Lom)

Round, 20; green, tag. Complete, clear impression. Used by John, abbot.

E 41/457 1363

WOODBRIDGE (Suff) Augustinian priory

priory seal

M960. In a vaulted and canopied niche with tabernacle work at the sides, the Annunciation: on L, the archangel, kneeling, holding a long scroll inscribed AVE GRATIA. Below, a shield of arms: *a cross*.

*SIGILLUM . COE . CAPLI . BTE . MARIE . DE .
WODEBREGGE (Lom)

Pointed oval, 60×38; light brown, tag. Complete, deep clear impression, slightly flattened. BM 4354.

E 25/122/2 Pl 54 1534

WOOTTON WAWEN (Warw) Benedictine priory

prior's seal: Ralph

M961. A pelican in her piety, the next with five young birds on top of a bush with prickly leaves.

*S' RADVLFI PRIORIS DE WOTHONA (Lom)

Pointed oval, 31×22; dark green, tag. Complete, clear impression.

E 329/371 1240

WOODSPRING (Som) Augustinian priory

priory seal

M962. The upper part of a church, with a tower having round-arched windows and spire with knobbed finial. Below, under an arch, a bust of St Thomas, facing R; behind him, on L, an altar with a chalice on it; from R issues a hand holding a sword, cleaving St Thomas's head.

SIGILL' SANCTI TH/OME DE...NG (Lom)

Pointed oval, 50×30; brown, tag. Deep uneven impression, upper point lost. BM 5371.

E 25/123 Pl 21 1534

WORCESTER (Worcs) Benedictine cathedral priory

priory seal

M963a. The Virgin, crowned, frontal, seated on a bench-type throne, her feet on a carved corbel, holding the Child before her on her lap, and a lily in her R hand.

SIGILLVM . S[CE.DEI.GENETRICIS] MARIE . WIGORNENSIS . ECLE (Lom)

Pointed oval, 80×55; dark green, on a skein of red and yellow silk. Deep even impression, rubbed, edge chipped. Has counterseal,

priory seal

M964. Also on E 326/3772 (1276) and 11566 (1297). BM 2295.

E 327/115 Pl 36 (13c)

M963b *Obv.* In a canopied niche the Virgin, crowned, seated on a bench-type throne, holding a fleur-de-lys sceptre in her L hand, the Child standing on the throne on her R side and holding a cross. Above, in a niche, the Trinity. On either side, in a canopied niche, an angel, standing, swinging a censer; at either edge a tree bearing a shield of arms: (L) *quarterly France modern and England*, (R) *ten roundels* (the SEE).

SIGILL':CONVENTVS:ECCLESIE:CATHEDRALIS:BEATE:DEI;
GENETRICIS:MARIE:WYGORNIE (Lom)

Rev. In adjoining canopied niches St Oswald (L, holding a pastoral cross) and St Wulstan (R, holding a crozier), standing, mitred and vested for mass, R hands raised in blessing. Above the canopies, the Coronation of the Virgin, between two angels standing and swinging censers; above and at either side, a kneeling monk.

OSWALDVS:PATRES:T:WULSTANVS:MONACHOR':SERVANT
HOS FRATRES:DELEANT:COMISSA:REORV' (Lom)

Round, 75; red, tag. Complete, fine impression slightly flattened. Also on E 326/9055 (1511). BM 2297.

E 25/122/3 1534

counterseal

M964. A gem: before a pillar on R, a woman, standing, facing L, pouring a libation (?)

HABVNDANS CAVTELA N NOCET (Lom)

Oval, 32×23; dark green, on skein of red and yellow silk, as counterseal to M963. Complete, deep impression. Also on E 326/11566 (1297). This impression shows the print of the seal's handle. BM 2295.

E 327/115 Pl 21 (13c)

sacrist's seal: Thomas Ledbury

M965. Under a canopy, the Coronation of the Virgin. Below, under an arch, a figure, praying.

...RIS... (BL)

Pointed oval, c.40×c.25; dark red, tongue. Clear impression, most of edge lost.

E 329/146 1437

WORCESTER (Worcs) Dominican house
common seal
M966. In a niche under an elaborate double canopy, the Coronation of the Virgin. Below, under an arch, a figure, praying.
S' COMV [NE...] WIGOR [...] (Lom)
Pointed oval, c.40×28; red, tag. Deep clear impression, most of edge lost.
E 212/36 1421

WORCESTER (Worcs) St Wulstan's, hospital
common seal
M967. In a vaulted and canopied niche with tabernacle work at the sides, St Wulstan, standing, mitred and vested for mass, blessing and holding a crozier. Below, under an arch, a clerk, half-length, frontal, praying.
SIGILLVM : COMUNE : HOSPITALIS : SANCTI : WLFSTANI : WIGORN (BL)
Pointed oval, 60×35; red, tag. Complete, fine impression. Also on E 322/271 (1540).
E 25/120/2 Pl 18 1534

WORMLEY (Heref) Augustinian priory
priory seal
M968. Under a double canopy, standing figures: (L) an archbishop, blessing and holding a pastoral cross; (R) an abbot, holding a crozier. Above, the Virgin, half-length, holding the Child on her L side. Below, under an arch, the prior, kneeling in prayer to R.
S' COMMVNE CAPITVLI ECCE SANCTI LEONARDI DE WORMELEYE (Lom)
Pointed oval, 50×32; bronze-green, tag. Complete, fine impression. Also on E 326/9489–9497 (all 1378–9). BM 4369.
E 326/9490 1378

WROXALL (Warw) Benedictine priory (F)
priory seal
M969. Under an arch with a panelled buttress on either side and a bell-cote on top, St Leonard, half-length, holding a staff and a book.
SIGI...ONARDI DE W...KESHALA (Lom)
Round, 50; red, tongue. Deep clear impression, centre flattened, edge chipped. BM 4373.
E 25/124/1 1534

WROXTON (Oxon) Augustinian priory
priory seal
M970. Under a flattened arch with cusping, the prior, frontal, seated holding a book before him; on either side, three canons, seated. Above, the Virgin, crowned, seated on a throne with fleur-de-lys arms, holding the

Child on her L knee. Below, under a similar arch, a half-length figure, frontal, holding up a helmet and shield (?).
SIGILL' PRIORIS ET CONVEN[TVS L]OCI SCE MARIE DE WROCSTAN (Lom)
Pointed oval, 70×40; light brown, tag. Complete except for lower point, deep clear impression. Pedrick, plate XXXVI, 71. BM 4374.
E 25/124/2 Pl 36 1534

WYKEHAM (Yorks) Cistercian priory (F)
priory seal
M971. The Virgin, crowned, seated on a bench-type throne, holding the Child on her L knee. Below, under an arch, a nun, kneeling in prayer to R.
+SIGILLVM PR/ORATVS DE WYKHAM (Lom)
Pointed oval, 40×20; red, tag. Complete, deep impression, flattened.
DL 25/335 1341
priory seal
M972. The Virgin, crowned, seated on a bench-type throne, holding the Child, with nimbus, on her L knee.
SIGILLUM... (BL)
Pointed oval, 60×35; red, detached, on tag. Nearly complete, indistinct impression, flattened. Clay, p. 34. BM 4377.
SC 13/R63 (n.d.)

WYMONDHAM (Norf) Benedictine abbey
abbey seal
M973. Under a church-like canopy, the Virgin, seated on a bench-type throne, holding the Child, with nimbus, on her L knee; below her feet, in a trefoil, the prior, half-length, praying to R. On either side, an angel, kneeling, holding a censer.
SIG...ET : CONVENTV...AM (Lom)
Round, 65; red, tongue. Fine impression, edge damaged. BM 4381.
E 25/126 Pl 55 1534

WYMONDLEY (Herts) Augustinian priory
priory seal
M974. In a canopied niche, the Virgin, crowned, standing on a masonry corbel, holding the Child on her L side; in the field, roses.
...CAPITVLI BEAT...IE . DE . WILMVNDL/ (Lom)
Pointed oval, c.50×30; red, tag. Deep clear impression, points lost. BM 4379.
E 25/127/1 1534

YARM (Yorks) Dominican house
common seal
M975. Under a double canopy, the Annunciation.

Below, under an arch, the head and shoulders of a friar, praying to L.
SIG/ILLVM . CONVENTVS . FRM . PREDICATORVM . D' . IAR'   (Lom)
Pointed oval, 49×30; red, tag. Complete, fine impression. Clay, p. 34, plate IX, 10. BM 4384.
E 322/273   1538

YEDINGHAM (Yorks) Benedictine priory (F)
   priory seal
M976. The Virgin, crowned, standing, holding a fleur-de-lys and an open book.
...SCE...   (Lom)
Round, c.40; uncoloured, detached, on tag. Large fragment of a deep impression. Clay, p. 34, plate IX, 11.
SC 13/R64   (n.d.)

YORK (Yorks) Austin Friars' house
   common seal
M977. In a canopied niche with tabernacle work at the sides, a king, crowned, standing, holding a sceptre. Below, under three arches, three friars, half-length, praying to R.
...FRM HE...AR' ORD...SCI AVGVSTINI EBOR   (Lom)
Pointed oval, 43×28; red, tag. Deep but uneven impression, much flattened, points lost. Also on E 327/599 (1511). BM 4413.
E 322/274   1538
   prior's seal
M978. In a canopied niche with tabernacle work at the sides, St Katharine, crowned, standing, holding her wheel in her R hand and a sword point downwards in her L hand. Below, under an arch, a half-length frontal figure.
S' PRIORIS CO...INIS / EREMITOR'...TINI   (BL)
Pointed oval, 60×35; red, tag. Deep impression, slightly blurred, part of R edge lost.
E 327/599   1511

YORK (Yorks) Carmelite house
   common seal
M979. A defaced fragment apparently as BM 4411.
E 322/277   1538

YORK (Yorks) Dominican house
   common seal
M980. The Noli Me Tangere scene. On R, Our Lord, standing, holding a tall cross in his L hand, extending his R hand over St Mary Magdalene who kneels on L at his feet. On L, in the field, NOLI ME TAGE.
S' C/O...IS . FRM . PREDICATO [...M EBOR]   (Lom)

Pointed oval, c.40×c.25; red, tag. Nearly complete, very blurred and uneven impression. Also on E 329/455 (1525).
E 322/275   1538
   prior's seal
M981. The Noli Me Tangere scene. On R, Our Lord, standing, extending his R hand in blessing over St Mary Magdalene who kneels on L at his feet; between them, a flowering plant.
...RIS . FRATRVM . PREDICATOR' . EB ...   (Lom)
Pointed oval, c.40×25; dark green, tongue. Very deep clear impression, upper point and R edge damaged.
E 43/123   1329

YORK (Yorks) Franciscan house
   common seal
M982. Under adjoining canopies with tabernacle work at the sides, two saints, each with nimbus, standing, holding indistinct objects. Below, under three arches, three friars, kneeling in prayer to R.
S' CO/MVNITATIS. FRATRVM . MINORVM . E/BOR   (Lom)
Pointed oval, 42×26; red, tag. Complete, deep clear impression, partly flattened. BM 4410.
E 322/276   1538
   warden's seal
M983. Under a canopy, St Peter, crowned, standing, holding keys and a church.
Legend lost.
Pointed oval, c.30×23; red, tongue. Deep impression, flattened, edge lost.
E 213/18   1319

YORK (Yorks) St Andrew's, Gilbertine priory
   priory seal
M984. The Virgin and Child, enthroned ?
...ATE(?)   (Lom)
Pointed oval, 60×35; red, tag. Complete, almost entirely defaced.
E 322/278   1538

YORK (Yorks) St Leonard's, hospital
   treasurer's seal
M985. Under a canopy, St Leonard, standing, holding a crozier and a book; background diapered. On L, a shield of arms: ENGLAND. Below, under an arch, a clerk, kneeling in prayer to L.
S' OFFICII SC...CAR' HOSP'/SCI LEONAR/D' EBOR   (Lom)
Pointed oval, 55×40; red, detached, on tag. Nearly complete, deep impression, heavily flattened. Pedrick, plate XXX, 60. BM 4406.
SC 13/R65   (n.d.)

YORK (Yorks) St Mary's, Benedictine abbey
abbey seal
M986. The Virgin, crowned, seated, frontal, holding the Child on her L knee, with her R hand plucking an apple from a tall curling tree. The Child, crowned, holds a book in his L hand and points with his R hand; above him, a star.

...IGILLVM SANCTE MARI... (Lom)

Oval, c.65×c.55; mottled green, tag. Very deep clear impression, edge damaged. The N in the legend is reversed, and the legend begins at the foot on L. Has counterseal, **M987**. Also on DL 25/60 (1257). BM 4385.

DL 25/59   Pl 36   1257
counterseal
M987. The Virgin, crowned, seated on a bench-type throne, holding the Child on her L knee. On either side of the Virgin's head, the word TE/CVM, completing the legend. The Child extends his R hand, holding an orb with a cross. On L, a monk, half-length.

+AVE MARIA GRACIA PLENA DOMINVS (Lom)

Pointed oval, 25×15; green, on tag, as counterseal to **M986**. Complete, deep clear impression which includes that of a handle at the top. Also on DL 25/60 (1257).

DL 25/59   1257
abbot's seal: Robert
M988. The abbot, standing on a corbel, vested for mass, holding a crozier and a book.

SIGILL' ROBERTI DEI GRACIA ABBTIS SCE MARIE EBOR...
                                            (Lom)

Pointed oval, 67×43; uncoloured, painted crimson, tag. Nearly complete, clear impression.

DL 25/215   (c.1215)
abbot's seal: Edmund Whalley
M989. Under a canopy, the abbot, mitred, standing on a pedestal, holding a book. On, and on either side of, the pedestal, three shields of arms (defaced).

S' DNI EDMONDI...ALLE ABB'/...BEATE MARIE IVXTA EBOR
                                            (BL)

Pointed oval, 80×50; red-brown, detached, on pink tapes, in metal skippet. Complete, deep indistinct impression.

SC 13/O66   (1521–30)
abbot's privy seal (?)
M990. The Virgin, crowned, seated, holding the Child on her L knee.

*FRANCE . & . LEGE...GEME (Lom)

Oval, 21×18; dark green, on tongue, as counterseal to **M991**. Two impressions, both incomplete.

E 43/112   1332, 1333
abbot's seal deputed for the collection of tenths
M991. A gem: a robed winged figure, wearing a hat with brim, standing, facing L, picking fruit from a tree.

[DEO]...FAC BONVM (Lom)

Oval, 30×22; dark green, tongue. Two clear impressions, cracked, damaged. Each has counterseal, **M990**. Also on E 43/760 (1333).

E 43/112   1332, 1333
privy seal
M992. Under a double canopy with arcading at the sides, the Annunciation.

SIGILLUM PRIVATU... (BL)

Round, c.35; red, tag. Deep impression, blurred and flattened, most of edge lost. BM 4389.

E 329/110   1426

YORK (Yorks) St Peter's, hospital
common seal
M993. St Peter, standing, blessing and holding keys.

+SI...EBORACI (Lom)

Pointed oval, c. 75×45; orange, tag. Fair impression, edge broken. Also on E 40/706 (n.d.); E 327/461 (n.d.). BM 4404.

E 326/1195   (13c)

YSTRAD MARCHELL see STRATA MARCELLA

Printed for HMSO by W. J. Linney Ltd
Dd 737380 C.6 12/86

PLATE 1

M339

M912

M936

M339

PLATE 2

M669

M331

M319

M747

M311

M753

M308

PLATE 3

M084

M841

M044

M552

M702

PLATE 4

M536

M534

M530

M891

M318

M513

M115

M673

M544

PLATE 5

M770

M426

M488

M096

M463

M459

M142

M322

M137

PLATE 6

M525

M674

M685

M787

M677

M395

M744

PLATE 7

M394

M394

M749

M433

M421

M786

M429

M791

PLATE 8

M709   M707    M711

M721    M708    M109

M640    M497    M030

PLATE 9

M416

M418

M009

M499

M086

M569

M457

M632

PLATE 10

M079 M087 M024

M443 M199

M090 M088 M588

PLATE 11

M392 M106 M437

M491 M144 M134

M490 M516 M767

PLATE 12

M641

M634

M869

M670

M419

M110

M831

M549

PLATE 13

M631

M826

M631

M587

PLATE 14

M599   M623   M611

M598

M602

M836

M464   M464

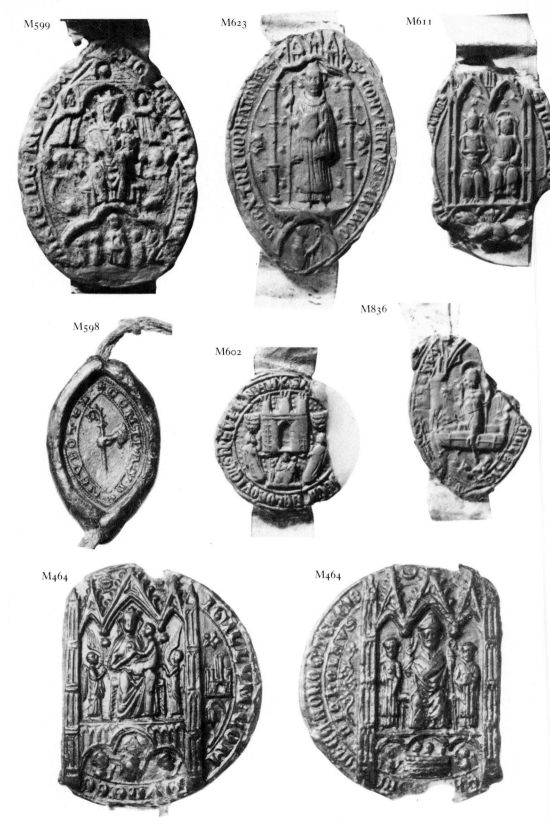

PLATE 15

M515

M845

M113

M849

M842

M572

M584

M068

M864

PLATE 16

M294 M409 M282

M296 M305 M290

M275 M735 M306

PLATE 17

M032

M025

M082

M166

M166

PLATE 18

M941

M293

M943

M737

M898

M909

M967

M928

PLATE 19

M342

M340

M151

M905

M907

M402

M397

M401

PLATE 20

M871

M102

M417

M608

M608

PLATE 21

M819

M804

M815

M162

M453

M962

M890

M964

PLATE 22

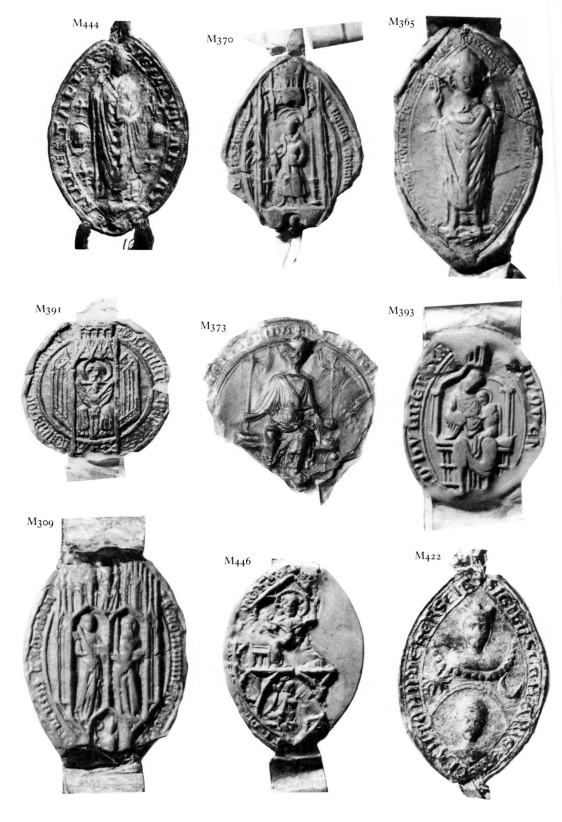

M444

M370

M365

M391

M373

M393

M309

M446

M422

PLATE 23

M508

M547

M942

M942

M403

PLATE 24

M911   M399   M386

M350   M160   M413

M901   M878   M277

PLATE 25

M664

M116

M683

M415

M698

M439

M384

M471

M500

PLATE 26

M498

M494

M661

M951

M119

M123

M430

PLATE 27

M742   M039   M739   M557

M101   M101

M263   M249   M266

PLATE 28

M532

M008

M085

M313

M313

M460

M470

M069

PLATE 29

M174

M727

M158

M307

M273

M300

M165

M155

M182

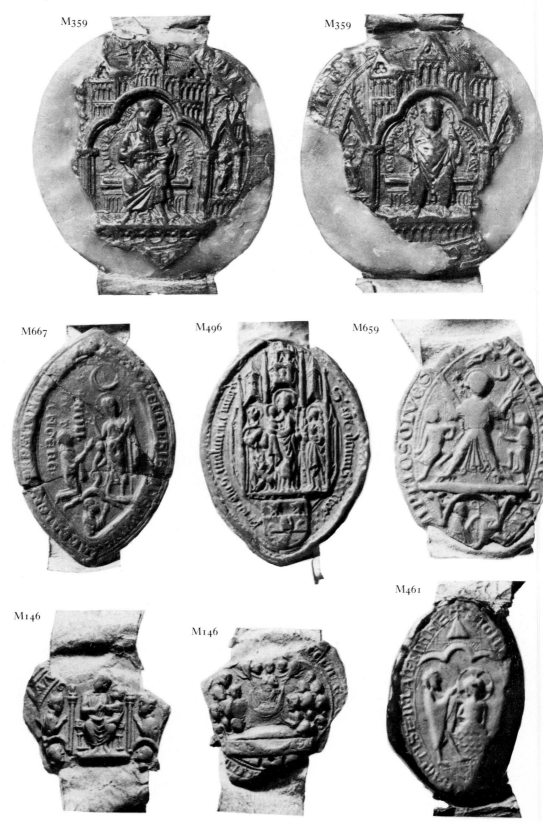

PLATE 30

M359   M359

M667   M496   M659

M146   M146   M461

PLATE 31

M346

M168

M341

M344

M338

M154

M355

M351

M348

PLATE 32

M208

M228

M568

M032

M435

M583

M238

M213

M193

PLATE 33

M194

M013

M772

M265

M657

M761

PLATE 34

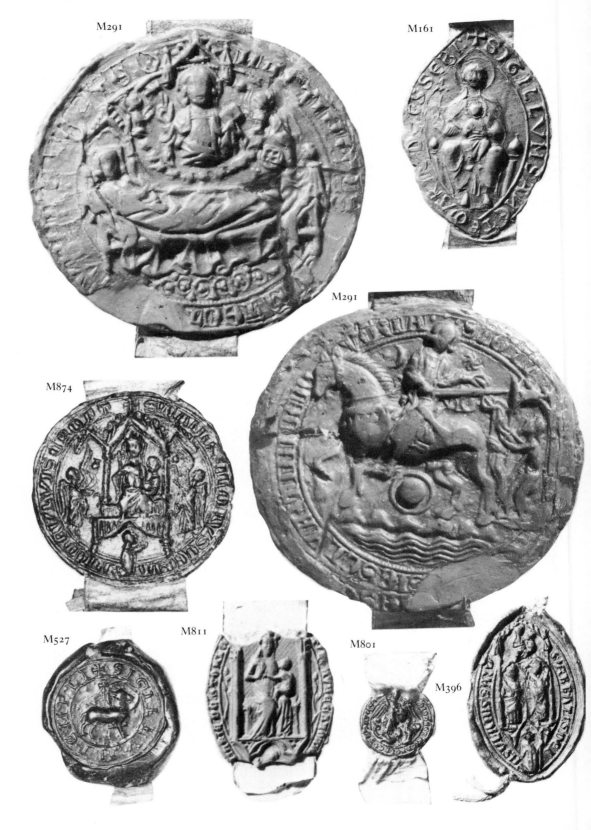

M291

M161

M291

M874

M527

M811

M801

M396

PLATE 35

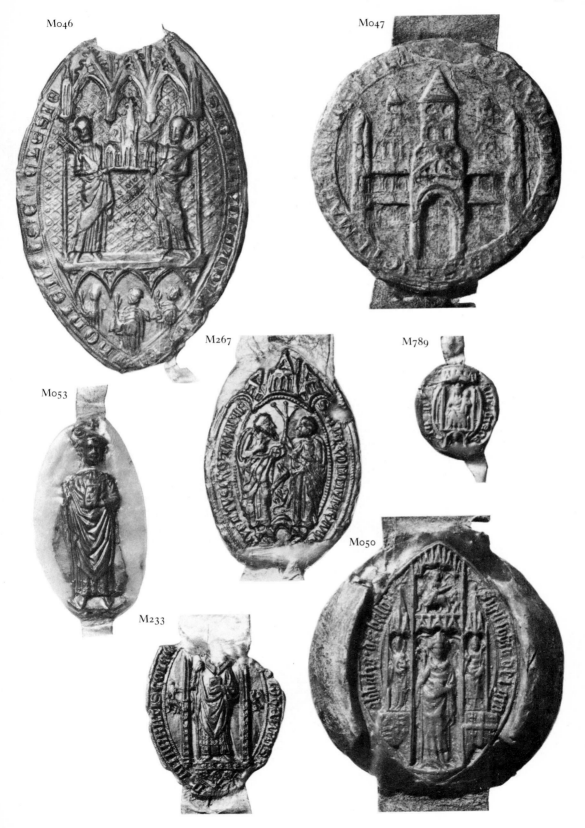

M046

M047

M267

M789

M053

M050

M233

PLATE 36

M986

M903

M970

M963b

M915

M503

M540

M501

M919

PLATE 37

M466

M465

M455

M693

M564

M774

M535

M762

M764

PLATE 38

M792

M227

M248

M231

M758

M766

M269

M209

PLATE 39

M607　M604　M559　M565

M621　M645　M615

M642　M140　M140

PLATE 40

M734

M644

M734

M837

M585

M824

PLATE 41

M169

M474

M077

M169

PLATE 42

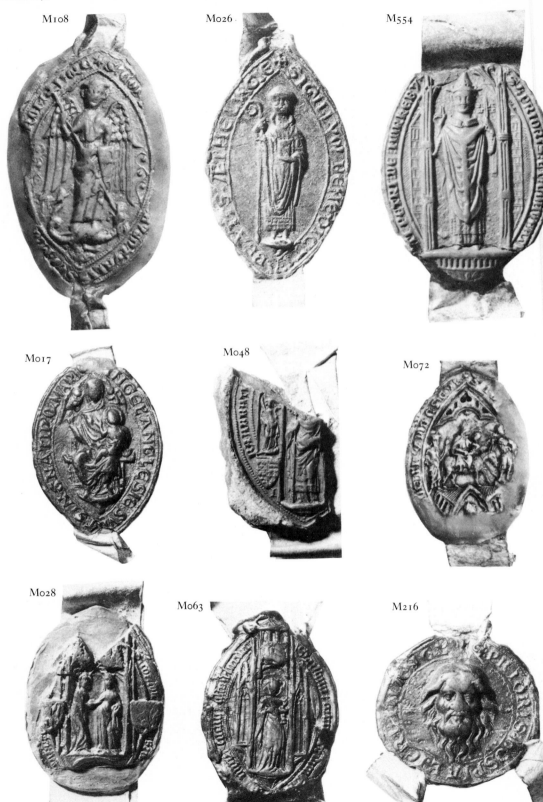

M108 M026 M554

M017 M048 M072

M028 M063 M216

PLATE 43

M788

M295

M627

M561

M027

M479

M654

PLATE 44

M073

M121

M067

M595

M614

M014

M145

M059

PLATE 45

M230

M018

M022

M230

M529

M529

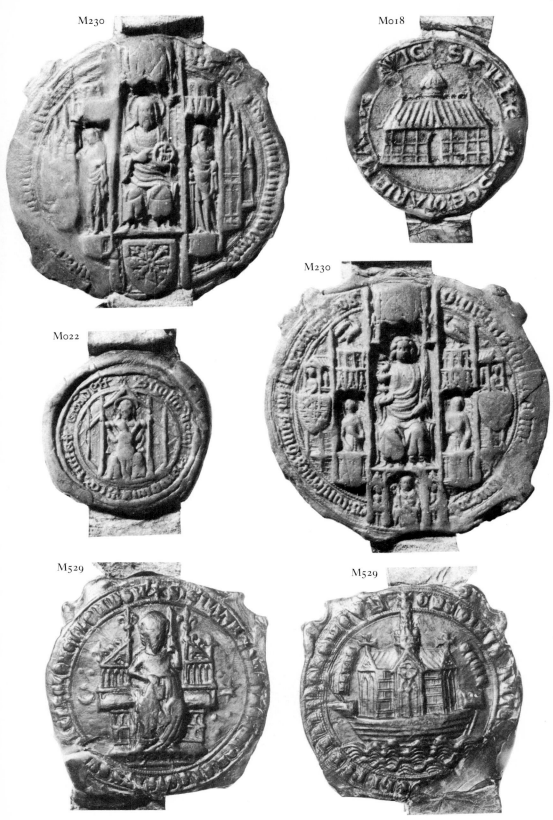

PLATE 46

M600

M699

M715

M715

M635

PLATE 47

M628

M380

M388

M825

M653

M065

M577

M107

M850

PLATE 48

PLATE 49

M548 M538 M324

M325 M546 M333

M334 M686 M691

PLATE 50

M921 M926 M821

M955 M510 M800

M523 M543 M507

PLATE 51

M170

M655

M170

M366

M052

M190

PLATE 52

M916a

M916a

M732

M244

M244

PLATE 53

M881

M731

M839

M840

M865

M679

M679

PLATE 54

M960

M877

M908

M406

M952

M954

M886

M917

PLATE 55

M410

M817

M884

M813

M808

M973

M887

M939

M389

PLATE 56

M245

M888

M187

M240

M272

M207

M007

M270